Bd. Heckman 8/29/74

FELIX MENDELSSOHN: LETTERS

FELIX MENDELSSOHN: LETTERS

Edited by G. Selden-Goth

With Illustrations

VIENNA HOUSE
New York

This Vienna House edition,
first published in 1973,
is reprinted by arrangement
with Random House, Inc.

International Standard Book Number: 0-8443-0108-6
Library of Congress Catalog Card Number: 73-86922

Printed in the United States of America

CONTENTS

1/15/74 Pub.

LIST OF ILLUSTRATIONS

INTRODUCTION

MENDELSSOHN has been more adored and fêted by English music lovers than any German composer before or since. On British soil he enjoyed a popularity verging on idolatry; there his works were still given full and unreserved appreciation at a time when, in his own country, he suffered a gradual eclipse with the rise of a more complex and passionate romanticism in music. Thus it is little short of astonishing that no sizeable collection of Mendelssohn's letters has been published in English since 1863. In that year, Lady Grace Wallace, of Edinburgh, began her assiduous translating activities which, in the course of a decade, flooded England with more or less exact English interpretations of the letters of distinguished German musicians. Her translation of Mendelssohn's letters, originally published by the composer's brother, Paul Mendelssohn-Bartholdy, remains the chief source of later English selections. Several minor volumes of "Recollections" and "Memoirs" of the composer's German friends and contemporaries, (Moscheles, Hiller, Devrient, and others), all of which also contain Mendelssohn letters, have been wholly or in part translated. A number of the composer's original English letters, most of them addressed to his London publishers, can be picked out from the last century's music periodicals or can be found in books dealing with the musical and cultural life in England during the eighteen-thirties and forties. But a complete presentation of his letters, which would constitute the best possible monument to what is human in a great artist's soul, is still lacking in England as well as in Germany.

The Germans have honoured several of their outstanding musicians as they have honoured their greatest poets by publishing editions of their letters, complete to the most casual line of the least important note. The exhaustive and authentic collections of Mozart's and Beethoven's letters, edited by Ludwig Schiedemayer and Alfred Kalischer respectively, give evidence of the loving zeal and the conscientious research of German musicologists when dealing with tasks like these. In spite of many arid and insignificant pages, these voluminous publications give the genuine image of the letter-writers' real selves. They permit the reader to peer into the intimate recesses of their characters, to observe their greatness and their frailties, their creative ecstasies and their human failures. The homage of such a compilation has not yet been rendered to Mendelssohn. For considerable periods his exact position among the great masters had been contended in his own country. Then, following the law of change in the evaluation of art, appreciation of his work was again in the ascendant in Germany when the Nazi bias removed the figure of this Jewish-born composer from the spiritual horizon of the German people. It is doubtful whether even a future of inevitable reaction will afford an opportunity for further Mendelssohn research.

At a time when Mendelssohn's name is outlawed in his own country it seems appropriate to publish a new selection of his letters in English. In assembling and editing this volume, I have been guided by the wish to recall to the memory of the English reading public, through the medium of his own thoughts expressed in his own words, one of the sincerest, most attractive figures of musical history.

Mendelssohn's original English letters are reproduced here exactly, to the last comma.[1] As for the translations from the German—the older ones, as well as those made for this volume [2]—all have been revised by Mrs. Marion Saerchinger. An attempt has been made throughout to find an English idiom in harmony with the quaint flavour of the English used by Mendelssohn himself. This has not been easy. As Sir George Grove, Mendelssohn's unexcelled biographer, observes: "To convey Mendelssohn's happy expressions, true and gay, but never tinted with slang, into equivalent English, is a very difficult task". By checking the material against the German originals, as far as they were available, a number of errors have been corrected.

Most of the letters have been given in their complete text as far as the sources have permitted. However, certain abridgements and excisions have proved necessary in view of the too frequently repeated introductory and closing phrases as well as words of thanks of the indefatigably polite writer. I had no scruples about suppressing a number of idiomatic expressions which have become faded and outworn through ceaseless usage, or are unpalatably sentimental today. In these instances the omissions are indicated by the symbol . . .

Passing events, which at the time had an interest for intimate friends and relatives, may prove rather insipid reading now; many of the per-

1. To be found on pages 204, 208(I), 331, 332, 333, 336, 346, 349, 350.
2. To be found on pages 25, 29, 37, 94, 104, 187, 220, 233, 329, 357.

sonal allusions to men and women whose names have been swept into oblivion in the course of a century mean nothing to the average musical reader. There are letters which are but loosely linked to the important events in the composer's life and to the psychological development of his personality and his art. It is often impossible to pick up the threads of chatty remarks and time-bound small talk in which Mendelssohn frequently liked to indulge. Thus I have tried to limit this selection to such parts of his correspondence as might still captivate and fascinate the music lovers of our day.

All the above mentioned sources have been studied and drawn upon for this publication. The letters are arranged chronologically. The series opens with the first and closes with the last letter by Mendelssohn which have been found in the hitherto available documents.

Samuel Johnson enumerates different states of mind predominating in those who sit down to write to their friends. "Some are all affection" —thus he begins. It is this state of mind which characterises Mendelssohn, the letter-writer. The affection, the devotion, the gratitude for the slightest sign of fondness, the untiring sympathy with which he addresses friends and relatives, are hardly paralleled in the literature of letters—except in love-letters. And here we face a most curious fact: we know of no love-letter written by Mendelssohn. None has so far been published. With the exception of a few excited utterances, announcing his prospective betrothal to his family, there is not a single line in the whole epistolarium that discloses how this handsome, brilliant, eminently impulsive young man, so fond of life and its beauties and pleasures, thought and felt about love. ". . . We flirt awfully with Fraeulein Schauroth, but there is no danger for I am in love already with a young Scotch girl whose name I do not know . . ." is about one of the most daring passages the young Adonis risks in reference to sex. Concerning this temperamental quirk of Felix, an interesting observation is found in the "Memories of a German Physician", published in 1875 by Dr. Strohmeyer, Surgeon General of the German Army, who frequently visited the Berlin home of the Mendelssohns, and who later followed Felix's life and development with deep interest. Dr. Strohmeyer, who formerly had deplored the too exclusive atmosphere in which the highly sensitive child was brought up in the paternal home, writes in the year of Felix's marriage: "Felix's devotion for his parents left no room in his heart for another great passion. After a long period of deliberation he became a happy husband—a Romeo does not usually undertake a trip to the Rhine before deciding to offer heart and hand to his beloved . . ."

Without doubt, all the selections published shortly after Mendelssohn's death under the close supervision of his relatives, were governed by a desire to observe the proprieties in making public the emotional life of one who belonged to a distinguished and wealthy bourgeois Berlin family of that period. The preface to the second volume of the letters (covering the mature years 1833-1847) edited by the composer's brother, even says that "the minute details of the pure and elevated happiness which Mendelssohn enjoyed in his most intimate domestic relations are expressly withheld, as being the peculiar treasure of his family". Apparently the letters to his adored fiancée and wife, Cécile Jeanrenaud, were counted strictly among those treasures, as no publication includes a single one addressed to her. Yet it is improbable that Cécile was left without a daily letter at a time when the young husband wrote to his English translator, the music critic Henry Fothergill Chorley: "I know how fidgety I feel without my wife, even among my best friends"; and when reports on daily adventures and triumphs in England came in a flood to parents, sisters and friends in Germany.

It is doubtful whether this regrettable gap in Mendelssohn's correspondence will ever be filled. Miss Eleonore Mendelssohn, one of the last descendants of the family's ancestor, Moses Mendelssohn, who is now a resident of New York, tells us that a whole archive, containing intimate correspondence, documents and records of the family, was donated a long time ago by Geheimrat Ernst von Mendelssohn, a nephew of Felix, to the Berliner Staatsbibliothek. Only at the end of the war will it be known whether the Mendelssohn inheritance has been tucked away in some basement, or has shared the fate of other spiritual products of Jewish origin—destruction. If the latter is the case, Felix's letters to his wife, as well as other documents that might ultimately have thrown some light on hidden aspects of this peculiarly and universally gifted human being, will have vanished forever. In that case, no complete edition of his letters can ever be published.

There is still another element that may be found wanting: readers interested in how a prominent artist takes up and defends his attitude towards the spiritual problems of his era may note with some disappointment how Felix Mendelssohn passed over important topics in his letters or altogether ignored them. Since the day when Hitler's

Germany disavowed its love for Mendelssohn's *Lieder*—more German than any German songs—burned his scores and set out to find "Aryan" music for the "Midsummer Night's Dream", world's Jewry has proclaimed the Jewish-born composer as one of its greatest glories. Yet the artist had nothing to say about Jews, much less about being one of their race himself, though it was in his lifetime that German Jews achieved their most important step towards emancipation. In the year of his birth, Wilhelm von Humboldt prepared the "Draft of a New Constitution for the Jews". And three years later the German chancellor, Count Hardenberg, declared that he could not approve of any legislative decree concerning the Jewish question that contained more than the four words: "Same rights, same duties". The widespread bickering over the granting of full civil rights to the Jewish minority during those decades, the pogrom in Heidelberg in the year that Mendelssohn reaped his first spectacular successes in England, the reactionary activities of his staunchest protector at the Prussian court, Minister von Eichhorn, none of this engrossed Mendelssohn's attention. He was far too absorbed in the shaping of his own life and career to bother about the fate of his fellow-Jews.

The truth is that it was not the racial issue, merely the religious one, that had been raised in the Germany of that time. Conversion was intensely urged upon the Jews. Even in the periods of recurrent anti-semitism, moral and social bait was held out by every denomination. Heine had his good reasons for proclaiming baptism "the ticket of admission to European culture". The famed conversion of Abraham Mendelssohn and his family had lifted the talented child far above the complex and problematic intellectual world of his forefathers. He did not think, he did not feel, he did not dream like a Jew. Neither did he compose like a Jewish musician cognisant of the musical heritage of his people. There is not a single bar in his compositions inspired by motives of Jewish folksong or synagogue music, nor did he profess any interest in such material. All in all, Mendelssohn—even if this may not agree with the Nazi concept of race—was no longer a Jew. He was a religious man, strictly brought up in the Protestant faith, and, above all, he was a German, nothing but a German, and as such, eminently conscious of his nationality, and completely, though not uncritically, devoted to his fatherland.

It might not prove without interest to quote here a tribute to Mendelssohn given by Heinrich von Treitschke, the standard historian of

Nazi Germany. In his "Deutsche Geschichte", published in the years 1879-1894, Treitschke writes:

"A German from top to toe, Felix Mendelssohn-Bartholdy never was able to feel perfectly at ease for any length of time even in the most enchanting southern landscape. Among foreigners he was never fully understood by Frenchmen, only by Britons of Germanic kin-race. With his 'Paulus' he wakened the oratorio of the Protestant Church to new life, and it is he who has given to the German *Lied* its deepest and most solemn expression. Almost as much as his compositions, which raised his reputation high above that of any living composer, his activities in the concert halls proved successful. At the youthful age of twenty he ventured to perform for the first time in Berlin Johann Sebastian Bach's forgotten 'St. Matthew's Passion'. And since, he always endeavoured to bring nearer to the educated public the noble, truly German art forms of the symphony, the oratorio, and the sonata. He made accessible to the comprehension of the nation the works of Bach and Haendel, and also the last symphonies of Beethoven which for a long time had not been relished. Since this musician, known and beloved throughout the whole of Germany, commenced wielding his baton in Berlin, Duesseldorf, Frankfort and Leipzig, music, which had degenerated into sheer entertainment, regained esteem as the highest of arts. It is to him that Germans have to be grateful if their audiences have retained a nucleus of pure taste, particularly at a time when anarchy started in the opera. Thus a German of Jewish origin has led back our distinguished society to the old traditions of their national art."

Proudly, and yet devotedly, Mendelssohn carried the banner of German national art; racial or religious issues never burdened his halcyon soul. Nor was his life seriously disturbed by other emotional conflicts. He never knew want, family quarrels, thwarted affections, or a bitter battle for artistic recognition, of the kind that undermined the strength of Mozart and Schubert—two musicians who, with him, form an extraordinary trio of miraculous musical creative precocity. His vitality was not rapidly sapped, as is so often the case with prodigies. He deeply mourned the loss of his beloved ones, he was not completely spared professional vexation, inevitable in a life lived from childhood in the glare of publicity, and sometimes signs of failing health depressed him as forebodings of an early death. But his letters give the impression of an exceptionally happy human being, centered in, and satisfied with himself; never wavering in his aims, never doubting his special vocation, never torn by inner conflicts. Only towards the end, his letters show signs of overstrain and fatigue. Of this time, the above mentioned recollections of Dr. Strohmeyer say: "When I met him (Felix) in 1845, I found he had aged prematurely. He had grown little taller than he was as a youth, his face bore the traces of severe mental strain, his habit to keep his eyelids half-closed had got so much worse that he hardly noticed his closest acquaintances when they passed him in the street. His head was tilted forward and his carriage had lost all vigour and elasticity." The final balance of Mendelssohn's thirty-nine years, however, is an unusually favourable one. Much was given to him, and he was asked to pay but little for it.

It has been said more than once that, had the balance sheet of his life ledger been more heavily weighted on the debit side, the work of the composer Mendelssohn might have benefited. His music has been blamed for too much placid symmetry, for too equable moods of sweet beauty. The lack of an occasional stirring unrest, which rouses a struggling artist's soul through torment and travail to the climax of inspiration, has been deplored. But the fact that a considerable part of that work has been assigned an uncontested place among the most perfect and beloved masterpieces of our musical heritage may be evidence that woe and want are not necessarily the cradles of the highest achievements in music. On the other hand, Mendelssohn's production bears the imprint of too facile and flawless a technique, which tempted him to make light of the responsible task of creation, and inebriated him with the ability to produce much in a short space of time. The reader of his letters cannot but marvel how little time, comparatively, must have been needed to bring forth Mendelssohn's musical œuvre. Although he did not develop the amazing productivity of Mozart or Schubert, the number of his compositions is remarkably large. In connection with his lifelong activities as piano and organ virtuoso, as conductor, organiser and director of important musical institutions, it indicates an imposing capacity for work. When one also considers his ceaseless travelling, his talent for sketching which he so often indulged and the time he whole-heartedly devoted to the interests of his family and his friends, the steady flow of his correspondence is quite astonishing. "This is my thirty-fifth letter since yesterday" he once writes to his mother. Oversize quantities of outgoing mail are mentioned on various other occasions.

—"If God spare him, his letters will in long, long years to come create the deepest interest. Take care of them as of a holy relic; indeed, they are already sacred as the effusion of so pure and childlike a mind. You are a happy mother and you must thank providence for giving you such a son. He is an artist in the highest sense, rare talents combined with the noblest, tenderest heart . . ." wrote Henrietta Mendelssohn, the erudite spinster aunt, to her sister-in-law, Leah Mendelssohn, who had forwarded to her a letter by Felix, aged twelve. The boy reported on a visit to old Goethe in his Weimar home. Our selection begins with this letter. Whatever Felix wrote, at any age, at any time, has been preserved with care. It is fortunate for a posterity that gladly slips for a refreshing breath into the less burdened atmosphere of former days that a certain utterance of Goethe does not hold true for Mendelssohn's letters. The poet writes in his "Wahlverwandtschaften": "We lay aside letters never to read them again, and at last we destroy them out of discretion, and so the most beautiful, the most immediate breath of life disappears irrecoverably for ourselves and others." Some of the beautiful and immediate breath of Felix Mendelssohn's life is preserved in the following pages.

To provide the reader with a more comprehensive view of the short earthly career illuminated by these letters, the selection has been divided into three parts, presenting letters of the boy, the youth, and the man. For the information of those not familiar with the outline of his life, a few biographical notes introduce each period. They try to give a brief summary of the events and conditions which determined the letters. The division into sections is somewhat arbitrary, because the changes from year to year in the course of Mendelssohn's life were accomplished smoothly and without shocks, and it is difficult to determine points of transition from one period to another. Moreover, one cannot say of a particular moment that Mendelssohn as an artist had attained maturity. The music he wrote as an adolescent between sixteen and eighteen years is not only mature and exquisitely equilibrated, but also the most masterly he was ever able to produce. It never was surpassed by works of later years. One can hardly imagine that, had it been granted him to live to a fourth life-chapter, that of old age, he could have created anything more perfect than the "Midsummer Night's Dream" overture, or the octet for strings. Graphologists may find another proof for this singular precocity—which was in fact a genuine maturity—in the phenomenon that Mendelssohn's handwriting scarcely changed or developed as he passed from boyhood to manhood. He wrote the same beautiful, meticulously clear letters and notes at fifteen as at thirty-nine.

The events which really influenced Mendelssohn's emotional life and can be said to be its turning points, were changes in his unusually close and intense relations to the members of his family. It is known that the sudden loss of his favourite sister Fanny prostrated him physically and spiritually, and hastened his own premature death. More closely than to anyone else in his life, however, Mendelssohn was attached to his father. The intimacy of this mutual paternal-filial affection bears a strong likeness to the one that had existed between Mozart and his father. There is a marked intellectual relationship between the methods which Abraham Mendelssohn and Leopold Mozart adopted when writing to their sons, advising and guiding them through the intricacies of their professional careers. Abraham Mendelssohn was not enough of a musician, not even of an artist, to steer the vocational education of his son with the absolute authority that Leopold Mozart rightly claimed and from the beginning assumed. Nevertheless, he shrewdly recognised the genius of Felix, knew how to select teachers and tutors for him, minutely supervised his studies, and succeeded in creating a home atmosphere in which, despite the strain of continuous public appearances, a sensitive and unusually advanced child could achieve natural growth. Felix adored and worshipped his father for good reasons. Abraham Mendelssohn was a remarkable man and represented much more than the "son of his father and the father of his son", as he modestly used to call himself. He was also more than just the efficient business man whose healthy common sense and quick power of discrimination played such an important part in the rise of the internationally known banking firm of the Mendelssohns. Felix's letters give full evidence of his father's natural insight into musical matters—one that was enhanced by a more than average general culture. One cannot marvel that the youth preferred discussing all his personal and professional problems more thoroughly with the understanding elder man than with anybody else. But Abraham's stern patriarchal régime sometimes heavily overshadowed the adolescence of his children who had to refer every move to his self-confident, superior knowledge. His boundless ambition for the most gifted offspring frequently made him forget that there could be more than one way—his own, personal way—for the young musician to solve his problems and achieve his goals, and Felix had to submit unconditionally to his judgment.

Thus it was an event when, in 1829, the boy was sent abroad for the first time without the company of a mentor, to stand on his own feet, and to try, independently and unassisted, to captivate his fellow-musicians, the public, and the world. From this first trip to England dates Mendelssohn's assurance in every kind of social intercourse, and his extraordinarily circumspect supervision of his own career. From a gay, careless, well-shielded boy he had grown into a not less gay, but judicious and ambitious youth who knew well how to watch over himself and his music. This year stands as the borderline between the first two periods of his life. The second line may be drawn on November 19, 1835, the date of Abraham Mendelssohn's death. It is said that a man only attains full maturity on the day he loses his father. Then the link that ties him to past generations is severed, a gap opens in the lineage of his ancestors; it is he, himself, who must now become the head of the family, its patriarch, its ancestor. Something of the security which the young child senses when he slips his small hand into his father's big one has remained latent in the man; now the subconscious feeling that an older and wiser one stands behind him to make decisions and to carry responsibilities evaporates. On the day when the news of Abraham Mendelssohn's having quietly passed away was broken to the youth by his brother-in-law, Felix Mendelssohn entered the third and final phase of his life.

G. Selden-Goth

LETTERS OF THE BOY

1821–1829

Felix Mendelssohn-Bartholdy, born on February 3rd, 1809, at Hamburg, displayed exceptional musical talent from his earliest childhood. He began studying the piano at four and composition at eight. He made his first public appearance at nine and started systematic composition at eleven.

At twelve he was taken by his music teacher, Carl Friedrich Zelter, to Weimar for a visit to Goethe.[1] The report of this trip which Felix sent to his family is remarkable not only because of the descriptive eloquence and shrewdness of observation far beyond his age, but also because few better and more life-like portraits of Goethe have been sketched even by the most distinguished friends and contemporaries of the poet, and certainly few such sympathetic ones.

---

1. *Previously—on October 26th—Zelter had announced from Berlin the forthcoming visit to his poet-friend with the following lines:*

". . . Tomorrow early I start for Wittenberg with a pupil of mine, Herr Mendelssohn's son, a lively boy of twelve, to attend the fête there . . . I should like to show your face to my best pupil before I leave this world—in which, however, it is my desire to remain as long as possible. The pupil is a good and pretty boy, lively and obedient. To be sure, he is the son of a Jew, but no Jew himself. The father, with remarkable self-denial, has seen to it that his children learn something and educates them properly. It would really be eppes rores *(something rare) if the son of a Jew turned out to be an artist . . ."*

This last phrase may sound strange today. But we must remember that up to Zelter's time no outstanding musician of Jewish descent was known in Germany either as a composer, or a performer, except one Salomone Rossi, musician at the court of Mantova in the seventeenth century. Zelter himself probably had never heard of him.

In 1822 Felix writes to Professor Zelter an amusing narrative of a holiday trip to Switzerland, which Abraham Mendelssohn took with his wife, four children, their tutor Dr. Heyse, his physician and several friends.

In the following years Felix continued his studies in composition and was already considered an authority by other youthful musicians. At the age of sixteen he spent two months in Paris with his father, meeting many outstanding musicians and scoring his first great successes as a pianist and composer. On the return journey he again visited Goethe and delighted him with the dedication of his piano quartet op. 3. The composer remained under the spell of the poet's influence all his life.

Only a few letters exist from the following years. Felix composed assiduously, produced a number of piano and chamber music works, and in 1826, the overture to the "Midsummer Night's Dream". He also attended lectures on law, literature and classical languages at Berlin University. In 1827 he made a holiday excursion to Bavaria, Baden and the Rhine, visiting, in Heidelberg, Antoine-Charles-Just Thibaut, professor of law and owner of a famous collection of old Italian church music.

At the age of twenty Felix revived Bach's "St. Matthew Passion" with an impressive performance in the Berlin Singakademie. This event had a lasting influence on the subsequent development of musical life and culture in Germany. 1829 is the year marked by the first of ten visits to England. Inebriated with joy he announces his plans to the devoted friend of the Mendelssohn children, Karl Klingemann, a young diplomat who had recently been transferred as secretary to the Hanoverian Legation in London. Felix is now his own master, free to do as he pleases. He is not a boy any more.

FROM LETTERS TO HIS FAMILY

Weimar, November 6-10, 1821.

. . . Now all of you listen, everyone. Today is Tuesday. On Sunday the Sun of Weimar—Goethe—arrived. In the morning we went to church where they gave half of Haendel's 100th Psalm. The organ is large but weak; the Marien-organ, small as it is, is much more powerful. This one has fifty stops, forty-four notes and one thirty-two-foot pipe.

Afterward I wrote you the note dated the 4th, and went to the Elephant Hotel where I sketched the house of Lucas Cranach. Two hours later Professor Zelter came and said: "Goethe is here—the old gentleman is here!" and at once we were down the steps and in Goethe's house. He was in the garden and just coming around a hedge. Isn't it strange, dear father? That was exactly how you met him. He is very friendly, but I find all his pictures unlike him. Then he looked at his interesting collection of fossils which his son has arranged for him and kept saying: "H'm, h'm! I am very much pleased". After that I walked in the garden with him and Professor Zelter for half an hour. Then came dinner. One would never take him for seventy-three, but for fifty. After dinner Fraeulein Ulrike, the sister of Frau von Goethe,[1] asked for

1. *Frau von Goethe, later referred to as Ottilie, was the wife of Goethe's son, August, and shared Goethe's house. Fraeulein Ulrike (von Pogwisch), her sister.*

a kiss and I did the same. Every morning I get a kiss from the author of "Faust" and "Werther" and every afternoon two kisses from Father and Friend Goethe. Think of that!!

In the afternoon I played to Goethe for over two hours, partly Bach fugues, and partly I followed my own fancies. In the evening they played whist and Professor Zelter, who at first played with them, said: "Whist means that you are to hold your tongue!" How very expressive! That evening we all ate together, even Goethe, though usually he never eats in the evening. Now, my dear croaking Fanny! Yesterday I took your songs to Frau von Goethe, who has a pretty voice. She is going to sing them to the old gentleman. I told him you had written some and asked him whether he would like to hear them. He said: "Yes, yes, with pleasure". Frau von Goethe liked them especially, which is a good omen. He is to hear them today or tomorrow . . .

. . . On Monday I went to see Frau von Henkel, and also His Royal Highness, the hereditary Grand Duke, who was very much pleased with my sonata in G minor. On Wednesday evening a very pretty opera, "Oberon", by Wranitzky, was given. On Thursday morning the Grand Duke, the Duchess and the hereditary Grand Duke came to visit us and I had to play for them. I played from eleven until ten in the evening with two hours' interruption, finishing with the fantasy by Hummel. When I was with him the other day I played the sonata in G minor which he liked very much, also the piece for Begas, and the one for you, dear Fanny. I play much more here than at home, seldom less than four hours, and sometimes six and even eight. Every afternoon Goethe opens his piano (a Streicher) with the words: "I have not yet heard you today—now make a little noise for me". And then he generally sits down beside me, and when I have finished (I usually extemporise) I ask for a kiss or I take one. You have no idea how good and kind he is to me, any more than you can imagine all the treasures in minerals, busts, prints, small statues and large original drawings, etc., etc., which the polar star of poets possesses. His figure does not strike me as imposing; actually he is not much taller than father; but his bearing, his speech, and his name—these are imposing. The sound of his voice is tremendous, and he can shout like ten thousand warriors. His hair is not yet white, his step is firm, his way of speaking is mild.

On Tuesday Professor Zelter wanted to take us to Jena and from there straight to Leipzig. (We are often at Schopenhauer's, on Friday I heard Molke and Stromein there. There is a girl singer aged fourteen in the theatre here—think of that, Fanny!—a singer who in Oberon the other day freely attacked a high D, pure and strong, and whose range goes to F.) On Saturday evening Adele Schopenhauer (the daughter) was with us, and Goethe, too, contrary to custom, spent the whole evening in our company. Our departure was spoken of, and Adele decided that we should all throw ourselves at Professor Zelter's feet and beg for a few extra days. We dragged him into the room and then Goethe began, in his voice of thunder, to abuse Zelter for wanting to take us along to "that old hole". He ordered him to be silent and to obey without contradiction; to leave us here, go to Jena alone and come back again, and so completely took the wind out of his sails that he will do everything as Goethe wished. And then Goethe was properly mobbed; everyone kissed him on his mouth and hands, and whoever could not get close enough patted and kissed his shoulders. If he had not already been at home, I believe we should have taken him home in triumph, as the people of Rome did with Cicero after the first Catilinarian speech. Fraeulein Ulrike also embraced him; and as he pays court to her (she is very pretty), it all helped the general effect.

On Monday at eleven there was a concert at Frau von Henkel's. Of course, when Goethe says: "There is company tomorrow at eleven, little one, and you too must play us something", I cannot say no . . .

Wenn über die ernste Partitur
Queer Steckenpferdlein reiten;
Nur zu! auf weiter Töne-Flur
Wirst manche Lust bereiten,
Wie Du's gethan mit Lieb und Glück,
Wir wünschen dich allesamt zurück.

Weimar
d. 20. Januar
1822.

Goethe

Silhouette cut by Adele Schopenhauer and poem written by Goethe for Mendelssohn's album in 1882.

When up the score and down again
Small hobby-horses ride,
Away o'er music's wide domain
Fresh pleasure you'll provide,
As you have done with loving gain—
We all here wish you back again.

TO CARL FRIEDRICH ZELTER

Secheron, September 13, 1822.

As I did not write to you again from Interlaken, dear Professor Zelter, I will continue the description of my journey from here at Secheron (an inn near Geneva). But I will make it briefer than in my last letter because I want to tell you something about the organs which, so far, I have had the chance to see, hear, and play on.

I closed my letter as we were about to start for our trip to the famous valleys of Lauterbrunnen and Grindelwald. Between Interlaken and the village of Lauterbrunnen we counted forty waterfalls which mostly roared down on the right side of the road and all headed for the White Lutschine, a wild mountain torrent coming from the smaller Grindelwald Glacier, halving the Lauterbrunnen valley and emptying itself into the Black Lutschine. Its icy waters spread a cool, almost cold temperature in the valley. Behind Lauterbrunnen the famous Staubbach cascade pours from a rock 800 feet high. But it is less imposing to look at than some other, smaller cascades; at least so it seemed to me, but maybe I was disappointed because I expected too much. We thought the Jungfrau was glorious as she peered down on us from behind another mountain, but we were to see her in still greater glory.

The next day we made the ascent of the Wengernalp and, accompanied by a fine rain, arrived at the cowherds' huts, which are built on the spot that gives the best view of the Jungfrau. From the highest crest to below the Wengernalp, thick snow covers the slopes. We saw several glaciers sparkling with a greenish light and we also saw avalanches fall; the Jungfrau towers more than 7000 feet above the huts. By the way, such a hut is not as picturesque as one is likely to imagine. It is built of sturdy grey pinelogs, cleverly fitted together. The thatched roof is protected from the blasts of wind by heavy rocks. It projects far beyond the house to give cover from the rain to a small area where the shepherds milk their cattle in bad weather. The floor of the cottage is bare earth, on which the hearth stands. It is difficult to get inside because the excavations, in which each of these huts is built, are so befouled by the cows that one can reach the door only by means of the stones and planks which the shepherds throw over the mire. A wooden partition divides this beautiful building into two parts. The part in front has one window and two doors. Here we sat down, one on a protruding board, another on one of those tiny stools which the shepherds use for milking, the third on a wooden block on which, behind him, the fourth stood, yelling to make himself heard: "I want some bread too, I want some cream too!" The guides and porters retired into the back room, made a fire and gathered around it; now and then one of us joined them, in order to get warm, because it was very cold. One had cold feet, another cold ears, a third noticed that his nose was turning purple, and all of us were desperately hungry. Sometimes our lively conversation was interrupted by the thunder of the avalanches; then we all rushed to the window—those who were not pushed through the door—and a herd of reddish-brown pigs accompanied with sweet sounds the frightful noise of the avalanche.

As the room in the rear has no opening at all, it was pitch-dark, like a bag; and only the fire gave some light. On one side a ladder leads to the space where the shepherds sleep. This is under the roof, and its ceiling is so low that I could not stand upright in it. When at nightfall the cows have been milked, everybody crawls into the hay and vies in snoring with the oxen and the pigs which, I believe, also sleep in the huts. We cut a rather funny figure in such surroundings, and the food was funny too. To see in such huts shawls, lace-bordered neckerchiefs, and goodness knows what all these modish things may be called, was just as extraordinary as to eat the chocolate and candy which the ladies had brought, together with the shepherds' sour cream and cheese. And all that in sight of the glorious Jungfrau!

Now I apologise for having described so minutely the poetic chalets; but I had promised you such a description, and with this I have kept my word. Fanny has probably told you about the rest of our journey and, besides, I want to save a few things for when we come home. But I do want to tell you something about the singing of the Swiss.

First of all, the yodeling. I say "first of all" because it is familiar throughout Switzerland and every Swiss knows how to yodel. It consists of notes which are produced from the throat and generally they are ascending sixths, for instance:

Certainly this kind of singing sounds harsh and unpleasant when it is heard near-by or in a room. But it sounds beautiful when you hear it with mingling or answering echoes, in the valleys or on the mountains or in the woods, and there, such shouting and yelling seems truly to express the enthusiasm of the Swiss people for their country. And when one stands on a crest early in the morning, with a clear sky overhead, and hears the singing accompanied, now loudly, now softly, by the jingling of cowbells from the pastures below, then it sounds lovely; indeed, it fits perfectly into the picture of a Swiss landscape as I had imagined it.

Secondly there is the highly praised singing of the Swiss girls, which is especially indigenous in the Bernese Overland. Unfortunately I cannot say much about it that is good. True, they mostly sing in four parts, but everything is spoiled by one voice which they use like a flauto piccolo. For this girl never sings a melody;

she produces certain high notes—I believe just at her discretion—and thus, at times, horrible fifths turn up. For instance, I heard:

this evidently should be:

without the top voice.

Otherwise they could be good singers, because they completely prove the saying: "Cantores amant humores". Four of them once put away twenty-four bottles of wine!

And thirdly something about the Swiss organs, as far as I got to know them. I was greatly pleased to find in the pastoral canton of Appenzell, one of the smallest in Switzerland, a tiny organ. I found one too in Zug, but in the worst possible condition. But it was delightful to make the acquaintance of Professor Kaiser in this same country-town. Our landlord introduced me to him. He has a good piano, the Haendel Suites and many of his fugues, and the Wohltemperiertes Clavier of Bach, and he loves both enthusiastically. In Bern I played on the organ in the Cathedral, a truly grand instrument with fifty-three stops, several sixteen-foot stops in the manual, a thirty-two in the pedal and eight bellows, which, however, leak, and often make the old organ sigh. Also two pipes of the 16 F Principal rattle together murderously. In Bulle, a small town in the canton of Fribourg, I found an excellent organ in very good condition. It has about twenty-eight stops, two manuals, and I found only one fault with it, that the pedal reaches only to high A; B and C are missing, so that nothing of Bach's can be played on it. All the stops worked, the instrument is in good condition, because Aloys Moser, who built it, is in Bulle. The man, who has recently completed his sixty-fourth work in Geneva, dresses like a peasant with his plain grey coat and his large shoes. The soft voices and the full organ are particularly fine.

We are proceeding today to Ferney where Voltaire lived, and thus I close, without forgetting Mr. Heyse's greetings which he asked me to send to you.

F. M.

TO WILHELM VON BOGUSLAVSKI

Berlin, September 30, 1823.

Your letter has given me very great pleasure because I see that you have not yet forgotten me. Do not be cross with me because of my tardy answer. You wish to have my conscientious judgment on your symphony. But the score came into my hands six weeks later than the letter; the post office did not deliver it in time. That is why I could not write earlier. As you really want me to give a verdict, I must do it. Well:

In general I must first say that I very much like all the themes of the first movement, that I thoroughly like the adagio with the exception of the forte theme in the middle, and that to me the minuet seems pretty and gay, all but a protraction at the end that delays it. The theme of the last piece with the first forte and the development up to the piano are not bad either, but from there on it seems to me just a little weak, and I do not at all care for the end with its trumpeting.

Secondly, in detail and more precisely: you find fault with the introduction with its single violin, which, I presume, must be played as a solo. I like it quite well, and also the successive entrances of the four instruments. But the adagio as a whole is much too long. It is meant to be an introduction, but you have made an independent movement of it, with modulations and development, so that the listener is tired before he gets to the allegro. But I have not cut out anything and await your order to do it. The theme and the way you draw it out in the allegro is very pretty; but later, when you ought to conclude in A major (the dominant of D major) you close, instead, in D major and start again in G major. As a result the modulation becomes very monotonous. Then again you modulate quite cleverly into D major and begin a good, new theme and develop it regularly, but just as one expects this part to draw to a close, you move again into F-sharp major and through several successive sevenths into A major, and only from there back to D major. This is quite unnecessary. The introduction of the return to the theme at the end of the first part is pleasant, clear, brief and very well distributed among the instruments. The beginning of the development is good and appropriate. But I do not at all like the end because of the modulations into A-flat major and A-flat minor in a piece in G major. The coda is pretty and not too long.

In the adagio the part for two violins and viola is too long. The entry of the violoncelli relieves it. You must cut out something in the middle part.

I have already given you my opinion about the minuet and the last movement.

As a whole, the symphony has given me great pleasure, and I know how to appreciate the fact that you are abandoning your Pandects and the Corpus Juris in order to devote your time to counterpoint. Farewell, thanks again for letter and music.

F. M. B.

LETTERS OF THE BOY

FROM LETTERS TO HIS FAMILY

Paris, April 1, 1825.

. . . Early Monday morning I called on Hummel; . . . at first he did not recognise me, but when he heard my name he behaved as if he had gone mad, hugged me a hundred times, ran about the room, shouted and wept, made me a foolishly exaggerated speech of praise before Onslow, and then tore away with me to see his father. When we found that his father had gone out, he made such an uproar in the hotel that all the people came running to see what was the matter. He then took leave, ran back after me on the stairs, hugged me, etc. Yesterday morning he came rumbling in with four porters and brought up his wife's grand piano, taking our bad instrument instead.

Paris, April 20, 1825.

. . . To appease your wrath I will tell you that last night we were in the Feydeau Theatre where we saw the third act of an opera by Catel, "L'Aubergiste", and "Léocadie" by Auber. The theatre is spacious, cheerful and pretty, the orchestra very good. . . . I will not speak of the first opera, for I only heard half of it and that was dull and very weak, although not without some light, pretty melody. But the famous Auber's famous "Léocadie"! You cannot imagine anything more pitiable. The subject, taken from a bad novel of Cervantes, has been made into a bad libretto, and I would not have believed that such a common, vulgar piece could have remained in the repertoire, let alone had any success with a French public who have so much fine feeling and tact. To this novel from Cervantes' crude, wild period, Auber has set music so tame that it is deplorable. I will not even mention that there is no fire, no substance, no life, no originality to be found in the opera; nor that it is pasted together out of reminiscences, alternately of Cherubini and Rossini; nor will I say that there is not the slightest seriousness nor a single spark of passion in it; nor even that at the most critical moments the singers have to perform gurgles, trills, and florid passages. But a grey-haired man, a pupil of Cherubini and the darling of the public, ought at least to be able to orchestrate, in our times especially, when the publication of the scores of Haydn, Mozart and Beethoven has made it so easy. But not even that. In the entire opera, full as it is of set pieces, just fancy that there are perhaps three in which the piccolo does not play the principal part! This little instrument serves to illustrate the fury of the brother, the pain of the lover, the joy of the peasant girl; in short, the whole opera might be excellently transcribed for two flutes and a Jew's harp ad libitum. Alas!

You say, Fanny, that I should become a missionary and convert Onslow and Reicha to a love for Beethoven and Sebastian Bach. That is just what I am endeavouring to do. But remember, my dear child, that these people do not know a single note of "Fidelio", and believe Bach to be nothing but a wig stuffed with learning. I played Onslow the overture to "Fidelio" on a very bad piano, and he became quite distracted, scratched his head, added the orchestration in his mind, at last sang with me; in short went quite mad with delight. The other day, at the request of Kalkbrenner, I played the organ preludes in E minor and B minor. My audience pronounced them both "wonderfully pretty", and one of them remarked that the beginning of the prelude in A minor was very much like a favourite duet in an opera by Monsigny. Everything went green and blue before my eyes.

Your last letter, dear Fanny, made me somewhat furious and I resolved to scold you a bit; nor will I let you off, although time, that kind divinity, has softened my temper and will pour balm into the wounds inflicted on you by my flaming wrath. You talk of prejudice and bias, about grumbling and scoffing, and about the "land flowing with milk and honey", as you call this city. Do think a little, I beg of you! Are you in Paris, or am I? So I really ought to know better than you. Is it my way to let my judgment of music be influenced by prejudice? But supposing it were, is Rode prejudiced when he says to me: "C'est ici une dégringolade musicale"? Is it prejudice that makes Neukomm say: "Ce n'est pas ici le pays des orchestres"? Is Herz biased when he says: "Here the public can only understand and enjoy variations"? And are ten thousand others prejudiced who abuse Paris? It is you, you who are so biased that you believe less in my entirely impartial accounts than in the lovely image of Paris as an Eldorado that you have created in your own mind. Look at the Constitutionnel: what else is performed in the Italian Opera besides Rossini? Look at the music catalogue: what is published, what is sold, but romances and potpourris? Come and hear "Alceste", come and hear "Robin des Bois",[1] hear the soirées (which, by the way, you have confused with salons; soirées being concerts for money and salons private parties), hear the music in the Chapelle Royale, and then judge, then scold me, but not now when you are filled with prejudices and completely blinded!!! But forgive me for this Allegro feroce!

GOETHE TO MENDELSSOHN

Weimar, June 18, 1825.

You have given me very great pleasure, my dear Felix, with your valuable present which, though previously announced, took me by surprise. The print, the title-page and the splendid binding, all vie with one another to make it a magnificent gift. I regard it as the

1. *French version of "Der Freischutz".*

graceful embodiment of that beautiful, rich, energetic soul which so astonished me when you first let me become acquainted with it. Pray accept my very best thanks, and let me hope that you will soon give me another opportunity to admire in person the fruits of your astonishing activity. Remember me to your good parents, your equally gifted sister and your excellent master. May a lively remembrance of me always be maintained in such a circle.

Yours faithfully

J. W. Goethe

FROM A LETTER TO HIS MOTHER

Heidelberg, September 20, 1827.

. . . "O Heidelberg, beautiful town, where it rains all day"—is what the cads say; but what does a jolly chap, a convivial fellow like me, care about rain? There are still grapes left, instrument-makers, journals, inns, Thibauts—no that is wrong; there is only one Thibaut, but he is worth six. What a man!

I indulge in a truly wicked gladness that I did not make his acquaintance out of obedience to your letter, dear mother, but that I had already spent a few hours with him yesterday, twenty-four hours before the receipt of your letter. It is strange; the man does not know much about music, even his historical knowledge of it is limited, his judgments are mostly purely instinctive, I know more about it than he does, and yet I have learned a great deal from him and owe him many thanks. For he has shown me how to appreciate old Italian music, and warmed me with his passion. There is a glow and an enthusiasm in his speech that I call flowery language! I have just taken leave of him, and as I had told him much about Sebastian Bach and said that the fountainhead and most important things were still unknown to him—because everything was comprised in Sebastian—he said at parting: "Farewell, and we will build our friendship on Luis de Vittoria and Sebastian Bach, like two lovers who promise each other to look at the moon, and then fancy they are not far apart".

But first I must tell you how I came to pay him a visit. Yesterday afternoon, when the weather was very bad and we all three felt very dull, it occurred to me that Thibaut in his book had mentioned a composition of "Tu es Petrus", and as I am now composing that very text, I plucked up my courage and my good coat and walked straight to the Kaltethal and into his house. He could not give me the piece in question, but had others, better ones, and showed me at once his large library of music of all nationalities and periods. He played and sang to me, explained the pieces, and several hours passed thus, till a visitor came and I took my leave, not without being asked to come again this morning. What I liked best was that he never asked my name. I loved music and that was enough. As they had taken me for a student, I had been ushered into his study unannounced. This morning again we spent two hours together before he thought of asking my name, and, kind as he had been before, he was now even more so. We made music together and talked, and he lent me a magnificent piece of Lotti's to copy. I promised to bring it back to him this evening; but immediately after dinner, while I was taking advantage of some tolerable weather to go for a walk to the Riesensteine, he himself, Thibaut in person, came to the hotel to return my visit, so unfortunately I missed him. But then I found him at his own home afterwards, and so, except for eating, writing and walking time, I have spent pretty much my whole day with him.

As it was half-past six when I left him yesterday, I spent the time by going to the instrument-maker's and improvising on his piano. When I took my leave, the man, seizing his hat and stick, protested that I must see better specimens of his work, and that Herr Schroeder had an excellent grand piano. Good. We are off, through the rain, to Herr Schroeder, a student. We arrive; the instrument-maker introduces me without knowing my name; no matter, a human being has come! Then he runs off because he has to return to his work, but I must be sure to come back to him. Now I am alone with the student on his sofa. He begs me to make myself comfortable, I should please smoke a pipe while I extemporise, and he sends an immense dog (growling at my music) under the sofa. "Hanne, a bottle of Hochheimer! We must have a drink together, little friend!" And so we did. And I played to my heart's content, until I had enough of it, and was tired. Now today the student will be our guest at dinner, and this evening again we are invited to the student's. After this, who will deny that I am a convivial fellow?

TO KARL KLINGEMANN

Berlin, March 26, 1829.

Dear Klingemann,

Not another word. In four weeks I may already be flinging myself into your arms because I intend to leave here on April 10th, to be in Hamburg on the 12th, to take the boat there on the 18th and to nestle down in your home on the 20th. Forward the enclosed letter with the utmost speed to Moscheles. I am asking him to find living quarters for me, and also to let me know which of my compositions he thinks I ought to take along. He will give you the necessary information about a number of things which I beg you to write to me, stante penna; then everything will be all right. If you want to be remembered to any people in Hamburg let me *have your instructions and provide me with letters of introduction. I am looking forward to the oysters!*

The "Passion" has been performed for the second time, by general request. There was a crowd and a noise the like of which I have never experienced at a concert of sacred music. Fanny will surely write you more about it, also about Paganini and H. Franck, who paid a visit and sends his regards.

NEXT AUGUST I AM GOING TO SCOTLAND,
with a rake for folksongs, an ear for the lovely, fragrant countryside, and a heart for the bare legs of the natives.

Klingemann, you must join me; we may lead a royal life! Demolish the obstacles and fly to Scotland. We want to take a look at the Highlanders.

Your distracted, hurried and really weeping

F. M. B.

LETTERS OF THE YOUTH

1829–1835

This period includes three years of Mendelssohn's extensive travelling for professional and educational purposes in England, Austria, Italy and Switzerland, a phase which has been vividly described in many of his long letters to his family. The correspondence of 1830-1832, dealing mainly with impressions of the two last named countries, was published in a separate volume, "Reisebriefe", as early as 1861, and has remained the most popular source of information on young Mendelssohn. From a musician's point of view the recurringly interpolated, strictly professional accounts of Italian music to Zelter—genuine shop-talks of many pages—are of special interest. Other letters tell about festive events in the family life, events that affected him greatly, such as the marriage of his favourite sister Fanny to the painter Wilhelm Hensel, and the silver wedding of his parents which inspired the composition of the charming operetta "Son and Stranger".[1] In 1830 the foundation of a lifelong friendship with the famous pianist and composer, Ignaz Moscheles and his wife Charlotte was laid.

The bulk of Mendelssohn's main orchestral works was produced in these years, and at the same time, the first plans for his oratorio "St. Paul" occupied him intensely. At the age of twenty-four he was appointed General Music Director in Duesseldorf, at twenty-six he took up residence in Leipzig as conductor of the Gewandhaus Orchestra. In the meantime he visited England repeatedly with enormous success, conducted the Lower Rhine Music Festival at Duesseldorf, and hunted

1. *See facsimile on pages 66-67.*

in vain for an adequate libretto for the opera he had always longed to write. The correspondence with his father on the subject throws much light on this permanent frustration of his career, and at the same time, discloses again the unaltered link of affection between father and son, never severed in spite of occasional divergence of judgment. One letter of Abraham, written shortly before his death and selected from a large collection of letters of similar tendency, is reproduced in this series and will certainly not be read without interest. The letters that close this period are full of deep grief and the feeling of absolute loss which Mendelssohn experienced after the fatal 19th of November.

TO HIS FATHER AND SISTER

London, April 25, 1829.

Dearest Father and dearest Becky,

Having just reached London, the first thing I want to do is to send you word of my safe arrival. Our passage was not good and was very long, for it wasn't until today at twelve o'clock that we landed at the Custom House. From Saturday evening to Monday afternoon we had contrary winds and such a storm that all on board were ill. Once we had to stop for a while on account of a dense fog, and then again in order to repair the engine; even last night at the mouth of the Thames we were obliged to cast anchor to avoid colliding with other ships. Fancy, moreover, that from Sunday morning till Monday evening I dragged myself from one fainting fit to another, out of disgust with myself and everybody on the boat, cursing England and particularly my own "Meeresstille", and scolding the steward with all my might. When on Monday at noon I asked him if we finally could see London, he calmly replied that there was no chance of it before Tuesday midday. But let me turn to the bright side and tell you of the moonlight last night on the sea and the many hundreds of vessels gliding round about us, of our sail up the Thames early this morning between green meadows and smoky towns, of our running a race with twenty steamers, soon getting ahead of all the others, and finally beholding the awful mass of London.

My ideas are still as incoherent as my last sentence, and I only write this letter to tell you of my safe passage; do not therefore expect anything further. I will write at once to Berlin, as a post by Rotterdam gets there in four days. I must also go to my lodgings (for here I am still sitting in Klingemann's room, who is prevented by business from sending his respects first hand). I must find Moscheles, who expects me; I must eat some dinner, something I have not done for three days (oh, I was very wretched!); I must get shaved; in short, I must be made to look human again. Farewell! . . .

It is fearful! It is mad! I am quite giddy and confused. London is the grandest and most complicated monster on the face of the earth. How can I compress into one letter what I have experienced in the last three days! I hardly remember the chief events, and yet I dare not keep a diary, for then I should have to see less of life, and that I do not wish. On the contrary, I wish to take everything that offers itself. Things toss and whirl about me as if I were in a vortex, and I am whirled along with them. Not in the last six months in Berlin have I seen so many contrasts and such variety as in these three days. Just turn to the right from my lodging, walk down Regent Street and see the wide, bright thoroughfare with its arcades (alas! it is again enveloped in a thick fog today) and the shops with signs as big as a man, and the stage-coaches piled up with people, and a row of vehicles left behind by the pedestrians because in one place the smart carriages have crowded the way! See how a horse rears before a house because his rider has acquaintances there, and how men are used for carrying advertisements on which the graceful achievements of accomplished cats are promised, and the beggars, and the negroes, and those fat John Bulls with their slender, beautiful daughters hanging on their arms. Ah, those daughters! However, do not be alarmed, there is no danger in that quarter, neither in Hyde Park, so rich in ladies, where I drove about yesterday in a fashionable manner with Mme. Moscheles, nor at the concerts, nor at the Opera, (for I have already been to all these places); only at the corners and crossings is there any danger, and there I sometimes say softly to myself, in a well-known voice: "Take care lest you get run over". Such confusion, such a whirl! But I will become historical, and quietly relate my doings, else you will learn nothing about me.

If you could but see me beside the heavenly grand piano—which Clementis have sent me for the whole of my stay here—by the cheerful fireside within my own four walls, with shoes and grey filigree stockings and olive-coloured gloves (for I am going out to pay a visit), and could you see the immense four-poster bed in the next room, in which at night I can walk to sleep, and the gay curtains and quaint furniture, my breakfast tea with dry toast still before me, the servant-girl in curl-papers who has just brought me my newly hemmed black necktie, and asks for further orders, whereupon I attempt a polite English backward nod; and could you but see the highly respectable, fog-enveloped street and hear the deplorable voice with which a beggar down there pours forth his ditty (he will soon be drowned out by the street-vendors) and could you suspect that from here to the City is a three-quarters-of-an-hour drive, and that along the whole way, at every cross street of which one catches a glimpse, the uproar is the same, if not far greater, and that one has then traversed only about a quarter of residential London, then you might understand how it is that I am half distracted. But I must be historical!

After I had sent off my last invalid letter to you, Klingemann took me first of all to an English coffee-house (for here everything is English) where, of course, I read the Times. As, like a true Berliner, I looked first for the theatrical news, I saw that "Otello" and the first appearance of Mme. Malibran were announced for that very night. In spite of weariness and sea-sickness, I resolved to go. Klingemann lent me the necessary grey stockings, as I could not find mine in the hurry, and yet had to appear in full dress, with a black cravat, like all the rest of the genteel world. Then I went to my lodgings, and from there to the Italian Opera at King's Theatre, where I got a seat in the pit (half a guinea). A large house, entirely decorated with crimson stuff, six tiers of boxes, out of which peep the ladies bedecked with great white feathers, chains and jewels of all kinds; an odour of pomade and perfume assails one on entering, and gave me a headache; in the pit all the gentlemen, with fresh-trimmed whiskers; the house crowded; the orchestra very good, conducted by a Signor Spagnoletti (in December I will give you an imitation of him; he is enough to make you die of laughter). Donzelli (Otello), full of bravura and flourishes fraught with meaning, shouts and forces his voice dreadfully, almost constantly singing a little too high, but with no end of haut goût (for instance, in the last passionate scene where Malibran screams and raves almost disagreeably, instead of shouting the recitatives, as he usually does, he drops his voice, so that the last bars are scarcely audible—and similar things). Mme. Malibran is a young woman, beautiful and splendidly made, bewigged, full of fire and power, and at the same time coquettish; setting off her performance partly with very clever embellishments of her own invention, partly with imitations of Pasta (it seemed very strange to see her take the harp and sing the whole scene exactly like Pasta and finally even in that very rambling passage at the end which I am sure you, dear father, must remember). She acts beautifully, her attitudes are good, only it is unfortunate that she should so often exaggerate and so often border on the ridiculous and disagreeable. However, I shall go to hear her every time—only not tomorrow when "Otello" is to be repeated. This I only wish to hear again when Sontag appears in it; she is expected daily. Levasseur, by the way, is something of a "beer-bass", and Curioni a "semi-beer tenor", and yet they were furiously applauded with hands and feet. After the second act came a long divertissement with gymnastics and absurdities, just as with us, that went on till half-past eleven. I was half dead with weariness, but held out till a quarter to one, when Malibran was dispatched, gasping and screaming disgustingly.

That was enough and I went home. But it must have been long before the theatre was over, for afterward came the celebrated ballet, "La Sonnambula". In between I constantly had to keep a firm hold on my seat because I still felt as if the whole house were swaying to and fro; nor did this giddy sensation leave me until yesterday, and last night for the first time did not disturb my sleep. On the day after "Otello", when I was still fast asleep, a soft hand touched me very gently, and that could be nobody but Moscheles, who sat by my bed for a good hour, and immediately gave me all kinds of instructions.

I can find no expression for the way Moscheles and his wife behave toward me. Whatever could possibly be agreeable, useful, or advantageous to me, they have procured for me. Yesterday morning, in spite of his piled-up work, he drove about with me to Latour's, Cramer's, Clementi's, Neukomm's; and when last night I was obliged to play my violoncello variations at his house, and had not quite finished copying the parts, he copied the remaining half whilst I was out at dinner. Mme. Moscheles took me yesterday in her elegant cabriolet to Hyde Park; today she will show me Regent's Park in the same way. Think of me in a carriage, taking a drive with a lady! Me! (In my new suit, of course.) Then she drove me to Buelow's, and when I ended my long visit and came down, she was waiting for me in the carriage, saying that I could not find my way alone. In short, they are both of them kindness itself . . .

TO HIS FATHER AND SISTER

London, May 1, 1829.

. . . I am in very good health: London life suits me excellently. I think the town and the streets are beautiful. Again I was struck with awe when I drove in an open cabriolet yesterday to the City, along a different road, and everywhere found the same flow of life, everywhere green, yellow, red bills stuck on the houses from top to bottom, or gigantic letters painted on them, everywhere noise and smoke, everywhere the ends of the streets lost in fog. Every few moments I passed a church, or a market-place, or a green square, or a theatre, or caught a glimpse of the Thames, on which the steamers can now go right through the town under all the bridges, because a mechanism has been invented for lowering the large funnels like masts. To see, besides, the masts from the West India Docks looking across, and to see a harbour as large as Hamburg's treated like a pond, with sluices, and the ships arranged not singly but in rows, like regiments—all that makes one's heart rejoice over the great world.

The other day I went to see Dr. Spurzheim's phrenological cabinet, shown by a young physician. A group of murderers placed in contrast to a group of musicians interested me greatly, and my belief in physiognomy received strong confirmation; indeed, the difference between Gluck's forehead and that of a parricide is very striking, and removes all doubt. But when people want to enter into minute details and show me where Gluck had his bump of music and where his inventive power, or exactly where the philosophy is lodged in Socrates' skull, that is very precarious ground and, it seems to me, unscientific, although it may lead to most interesting results, such as the following. A beautiful young Eng-

lish lady who was there, desired to know whether she had a propensity for stealing, or any other crime, and it ended in a phrenological examination of the whole party present. One was pronounced good-natured, another fond of children, this lady courageous, that lady avaricious; and as the aforesaid young creature had to undo her long fair hair to allow the doctor to feel her bumps, and looked very beautiful with her hair loose and when doing it up again before the glass, I gave three cheers for phrenology, and warmly praised everything concerning it. That I possessed a taste for music and some imagination was obvious; the doctor found afterwards that I was rather covetous, loved order and little children, and liked flirting; music, however, he declared to be predominant. On Tuesday I am to have a plaster mask taken of my whole head, skull, face and all, and then I will check up on Hensel's likeness . . .[1]

TO THE SECRETARY OF THE PHILHARMONIC SOCIETY OF LONDON

Berlin, May 26, 1829.

Dear Sir,

I deeply feel the honour of which the Philharmonic Society has deemed me worthy in performing a Symphony of my own composition at the last concert, an honour which I can never forget. I know that my success, obtained through the brilliant performance of the orchestra, is due much less to my talent than to the

1. *Wilhelm Hensel, Felix's brother-in-law, had frequently made sketches of his head.*

indulgence shown to my youth; but encouraged by a reception so flattering I shall labour to justify the hopes entertained of me, to which I undoubtedly owe the kind feeling shown me . . .

FROM LETTERS TO HIS FAMILY

London, June 7, 1829.

. . . On Saturday I was to play at a concert, and I had never played on the brand new Clementi grand piano which the firm had sent. I went into the empty concert-room, where my symphony had been performed and which now echoed with every footstep, and I felt a little moved. The piano was locked; the key had to be sent for but did not come. Meanwhile I sat down at the old grey instrument, over which the fingers of several generations may have wandered, meaning to practice my piece thoroughly. But I lost myself unaware in strange fancies and dwelt in them until people began to come in and remind me by their presence that I ought to have been practicing; but the large hall had distracted me. In short, the concert hour (two o'clock) approached, and I had not once touched the instrument. However, I remained in good spirits and changed into my dress clothes (for Becky's journal of fashions: very long white trousers, brown silk waistcoat, black necktie and blue dress coat). But when I mounted the orchestra platform and found it completely filled with ladies who had not been able to find a place in the hall, and when I saw the hall fuller than it has ever been since I arrived (nothing but ladies' gay bonnets and fearful heat) as well as the unknown instrument, I was overcome with panic; and up to the moment I began I had terrible stage-fright; I think I was actually feverish. But as the gay bonnets gave me a nice reception and applauded when I came in,

as they were very attentive and quiet (which with this talkative concert public is a rare thing), and as I found the instrument was excellent and had a light touch, I lost all my above-mentioned tremors, calmed down completely, and was highly amused to see the bonnets become agitated at every little flourish—which reminded me and many critics of wind in a tulip-bed. I was also able to notice that some ladies on the platform were very lovely and that Sir George, on whom I cast a feeling glance, took a pinch of snuff. It went pretty well and they made a great noise when it was over; also the Times, which I study over my tea in the morning, has bestowed high praise on me. I was devilishly pleased to find that the public here is good to me and likes me, and that I owe a great many more acquaintances to my music than to my letters of introduction—which were really influential and numerous enough—in short, I was very happy on Saturday; and at the dinner, to which I went afterwards, I became intoxicated, but only from the effect of two very wonderful brown eyes, such as the world has never seen—or only rarely. To describe or praise them is unnecessary, for if they please you I shall be jealous par distance, and if they do not please you I shall be vexed—that, however, is impossible. The lady next to me had the said brown eyes, and they are wondrously beautiful, and their name is Louise, and they spoke English and retired at the cheese course, whereupon I immediately drank claret as I had nothing more to see. I had to be off into the country, found no carriage, and was obliged to walk in the cool of the evening; a number of musical ideas came to me, and I sang them out loud, for I was walking along a meadow path and met no one; the whole sky was grey with a purple streak on the horizon, and the thick cloud of smoke lay behind me. As soon as I find some peace and quiet, whether here or in Scotland, I shall write various things, and the Scottish bagpipe does not exist in vain . . .

I have been entrusted with a commission, and you will die laughing when you hear what it is. It gives me great pleasure, because it is unique, and possible only in London. I am to compose a festival song for a celebration which takes place in—Ceylon! The natives some time ago were emancipated, and intend to keep the anniversary of the event; they are to sing a song on the occasion; and Sir Alexander Johnston, the governor of Ceylon, has given me the order. It is really very mad and droll; and for two days I have been laughing to myself . . .

June 25, 1829.

. . . In the evening I went to Covent Garden: "Hamlet". I believe, my dears, that he was right who said that the English sometimes do not understand Shakespeare. At least this performance was mad; and yet Kemble played Hamlet, and in his way played him well. But alas! that way is crazy and ruins the whole piece. His appearing, for instance, with one yellow and one black leg, to indicate madness, his falling on his knee before the ghost in order to strike an attitude, his ejaculation at the end of every little phrase in that well-known applause-exacting, high tone of his, his behaving altogether like a John Bull Oxford student and not like a Danish Crown Prince, all that might pass. But that he should completely ignore poor Shakespeare's meaning regarding the proposed death of the king, and therefore coolly skip that scene where the king prays and Hamlet comes in and goes out again without having made up his mind to the deed (to me one of the finest passages in the piece), and that he constantly behaves like a bravado, treating the king in such a manner that he deserves to be shot down at once—for instance during the play on the stage, constantly threatening him with his fist and shouting into his ear the words that should have been quietly dropped—these things are unpardonable. Of course, Laertes and Hamlet do not jump into Ophelia's grave and wrestle there, for they never suspect why they should. And at the end, when Hamlet falls down and says "the rest is silence", and I expected a flourish of the trumpets and Fortinbras, Horatio actually leaves the prince, hurries down to the footlights and says: "Ladies and gentlemen, tomorrow evening 'The Devil's Elixir'." Thus ended Hamlet in England . . .

July 10, 1829.

. . . What has occupied me almost exclusively of late is the concert for the Silesians; as regards the choice of the pieces it will no doubt be the most brilliant of the season. Everyone who has attracted the slightest attention during the season will take part, most of them gratuitously; many offers of good performers have had to be declined, as the concert, even so, will last till the next day. Klingemann will send you the interminable program; it is really interesting. The opening work will be my "Midsummer Night's Dream" overture by request, and then I shall play the double concerto in E with Moscheles. Yesterday we had the first rehearsal at Clementi's piano factory. Mrs. Moscheles and Mr. Collard listened. I had no end of fun; for you cannot imagine how we coquetted; how the one constantly imitated the other and how sweet we were. Moscheles plays the last movement with remarkable brilliance; he shook the runs out of his sleeve. When it was over, they all said it was a pity that we had made no cadenza, so I immediately dug out a passage from the last tutti of the first part, where the orchestra has a pause, and Moscheles had to comply nolens volens and compose a big cadenza. We now discussed, constantly joking the while, whether the last little solo could remain where it was, since of course the people would applaud the cadenza. "We must have a bit of tutti between the cadenza and the solo," said I. "How long are they to applaud?" asked Moscheles. "Ten minutes, I dare say," said I. Moscheles beat me down to five. I promised to supply a tutti, and so we took the measurements, embroidered, turned and padded, set in sleeves à la Mameluke, and at last, with our mutual tailoring, produced a brilliant concerto. We shall have another rehearsal today: it will be a musical picnic, for Moscheles will bring the cadenza and I the tutti . . . Tomorrow at two the big instrumental rehearsal is to come off; after that I have a treat in prospect. I am invited to dinner by a Mr. Richmond with many daughters . . .

. . . The other day we walked home from a highly diplomatic dinner-party at Buelow's, and were satiated with fashionable dishes, sayings and doings. We passed a very enticing sausage shop, in which "German sausages, twopence each" were laid out for show. Patriotism overcame us, we each bought a long sausage, turned into Portland Street where it was quieter, and there consumed our purchases . . .

TO THE EDITOR OF "BRITANNIA"[1]

London, July 8, 1829.

Sir,

Having read in your last number an article under the head of "Music and Musicians", I beg to offer you some remarks, for the purpose of preventing any misconception which may arise from the article alluded to.

M. Fétis has, it appears, thought fit to drag my name before the public by referring to some expressions which may have fallen from me in private conversation with him, and also to draw conclusions therefrom in corroboration of his censure on a celebrated

1. *Fétis had quoted in the "Revue Musicale" some expressions of Mendelssohn judging very harshly and unfavourably a performance of Purcell's "Te Deum".*

English composer. You, sir, have further deemed it incumbent on you, while commenting on his strictures, to identify my alleged observations with the published censure of M. Fétis. While denying the right of M. Fétis thus to quote any private and detached expressions of mine in order to support his own opinions, I must, at the same time, question the justice of your holding me up to the British public as a co-censor with that gentleman. Whatever were the words used by me on the occasion referred to, they were uttered merely to give expression to a momentary feeling, caused by a performance, which, to use your own language, was "timid and unsatisfactory". Generally speaking, a single performance will, in no case, enable anyone to give a public judgment on the merits of an eminent composer; and whilst admitting this, I must, for myself, resist that criticism which, from a detached and single expression, uttered in private, draws a general conclusion as to the opinions of the individual so uttering it.

Feeling myself deeply indebted to English "music and musicians" for enjoyments which have made my short residence in this country a bright period of my life, I must say that the allusions in your paper of Sunday last were most painful for my feelings, by their appearing calculated to create misconceptions to my prejudice among those from whom I have received so much kindness, and for whom I feel the liveliest regard.

I am, Sir, your most obedient servant,

F. M. B.

FELIX MENDELSSOHN

FROM LETTERS TO HIS FAMILY

Hebrides, August 7, 1829.

. . . in order to make you understand how extraordinarily the Hebrides affected me, the following came into my mind there:

Glasgow, August 11, 1829.

. . . How much lies between my last letter and this! The most fearful sickness, Staffa, scenery, travel, people—Klingemann has described it all, and you will excuse a short note, the more so as the best that I have to tell you is described exactly in the above music . . .

Glasgow, August 15, 1829.

. . . This then is the end of our Highland journey and the last of our joint letters. We have been happy together, we have led a merry life, and roved about the country as gaily as if the storm and rain which all newspapers reported (by this time perhaps even those in Berlin) had not existed. But they did exist. We had weather that made the trees and rocks crash. The day before yesterday on Loch Lomond we were sitting in deep twilight in a small rowboat and were going to cross to the opposite shore, invited by a gleaming light, when there came a sudden tremendous gust of wind from the mountains; the boat began to rock so fearfully that I caught up my cloak and got ready to swim. All our things were thrown topsy-turvy and Klingemann anxiously called to me, "Look sharp, look sharp!" But with our usual good luck we got through it safely. When on shore, we had to live in a room with a cursing young Englishman, who was half sportsman, half peasant, half gentleman, and altogether insufferable, and with three other individuals of the same caliber. We were obliged to sleep in the next house close to the roof, so that from sitting-room to bedroom we walked with umbrellas, cloak, and cap. To describe the wretchedness and comfortless, inhospitable solitude of the country, time and space do not allow; we wandered ten days without meeting a single traveller; what are marked on the map as towns, or at least villages, are just a few sheds huddled together, with one and the same hole for door, window and chimney, for the entrance and the exit of men, animals, light and smoke. To all questions you get a dry "No"; brandy is the only beverage known, there is no church, no street, no garden, the rooms are pitch-dark in broad daylight, children and fowls lie in the same straw, many huts are without roofs altogether, many are unfinished, with crumbling walls, or just ruins of burnt houses, and even such inhabited spots are but sparingly scattered over the country. Long before you arrive at a place you hear it talked of; the rest is heath with red or brown heather, withered fir branches and white stones between, or black moors where they shoot grouse. Now and then you find beautiful but empty parks, broad lakes, but without boats, and the roads are deserted. And over all this the brilliance of the rich sunshine which changes the heath into a thousand colors, all so divinely gay and warmly lighted; and the cloud shadows chasing hither and thither! It is no wonder that the Highlands have been called melancholy. But two fellows have wandered gaily through them, laughed at every opportunity, rhymed and sketched together, growled at one another and at the world when they happened to be vexed or found nothing to eat, devoured everything edible when they did find it, and slept twelve hours every night; those two were we, and we will not forget it as long as we live! . . .

FROM A LETTER TO HIS SISTERS

London, September 10, 1829.

. . . My stay at the Taylors' was one of those times which will never vanish from my mind; it will put me in a flowery mood, and I shall always recollect the meadows and woods, and the pebbly brook with its babbling. We have become friends, I think, and I am so deeply fond of the girls, and believe they like me too, for we are happy together. Moreover, I owe them three of my best piano compositions.[1] When the two younger sisters saw that I took the carnations and rose in earnest and began to compose, the youngest once came with little, yellow, open bells in her hair, assuring me they were trumpets, and asking me whether I could not introduce them into the orchestra, as I had talked the other day of wanting new instruments; and when in the evening we danced to the miners' music and the trumpets were rather shrill, she gave it as her opinion that her trumpets would do better to dance to, so I wrote a dance for her—to which the yellow flower-bells played. For the middle one I composed "The Rivulet", which had pleased us so much during our ride that we dismounted

1. *Three Fantasies (or Caprices), op. 16.*

and sat down beside it. This last piece, I believe, is the best of its kind that I have done; it is so slow-moving and quiet, and a little boringly simple, that I have played it to myself every day, and have got quite sentimental over it. I would send you the pieces, but as I hope to have finished my quartet by next postday, and intend sending it to you, and as I must bring home something new in December, I shall keep back my five pieces—not "lions" as Rebecca calls them, but "darlings" of mine. One of them I have not even got in manuscript.

Yes children, you may be scandalised; I do nothing but flirt, and that in English! But seriously, it was a happy time, and passed very quickly. I drove away in the evening; the lights in the house sparkled through the bushes in the distance; in my open carriage I passed by several favourite places, the gentle brook already mentioned, the last hedge of the property, and then off I went at furious English speed. I was grumpy to all my unpleasant travelling companions, spoke not a word, but kept quiet, half dreaming, half thinking, half gloomy, just as I think one always does, when one dashes along one's two hundred miles in a mailcoach. It appeared almost like a magic-lantern of chance when, on the second evening of my journey (I travelled right through in order to reach London in the morning), the mail stopped because it met the mail from London to Chester, and putting my head out of the window in the deep twilight, whilst the two coachmen were talking, I saw peeping out of the other mail Fr. Cramer and his daughter (you remember Miss Marian?). Exchange a few words, then drive asunder, and part for years or longer—such is the world, moving onwards, meeting, coming near, going far away.

On my arrival in London I resumed my quiet life, which consists of composing and reading English. My quartet[1] is now in the middle of the last movement, and I think it will be completed in a few days; as will the organ piece for the wedding.[2] Then I shall

1. *Quartet in E-flat for Strings, op. 12.*
2. *Written for Fanny's wedding on October 3rd.*

begin my Reformation Symphony, the Scotch Symphony and the Hebrides affair as well, which are also shaping themselves gradually. Besides this, I have a great deal of vocal music projected and in my head, but I shall take good care not to say what kind or how, as yet. On the day of my arrival the Clementis sent me back the same beautiful piano I had during my former stay; and as I asked Mr. Collard to let me have it on hire this time, he sent me a few English verses and begged me to set them to music. This will be hard for me because I "must" . . .

TO HIS SISTER FANNY

London, September 25, 1829.

My dear Fanny,

This then is the last letter that will reach you before the wedding [1] and for the last time I address you as Miss Fanny Mendelssohn-Bartholdy, and I would have a good deal to say, but it still won't quite go. Although I began yesterday to sit up a little, and can therefore write better and smaller, my head is still quite dizzy from this long lying in bed and thinking of nothing, and the more I wish to compress into this moment, the more quickly it slips away past recall. You know that it is all the same to me, whether I express it well or badly, or not at all; but I feel as if I had lost all control over what I once mastered, and my various thoughts

1. *Fanny Mendelssohn-Bartholdy was married on October 3, 1829, to Wilhelm Hensel. Felix, to his great sorrow, could not be present at the wedding of his favourite sister because of an accident in London, the consequences of which kept him ill in bed for two months.*

Mendelssohn at the age of eleven.
Sketch by an unknown artist.

Mendelssohn at the age of twelve.
Painted by Begas, engraved by Weger.

about the coming change and new order of things, which at other times would have merged into one single flow as soon as I began to write to you, are now straying hither and thither in wild confusion. But so it is; and when we see daily how all trifling occurrences, which one pictures to oneself, are delayed, augmented or annihilated by reality, we stand with awe and humility before a real event in life. "With awe", but with that I mean with fresh, joyful confidence. Live and prosper, get married and be happy, shape your life so that I shall find it beautiful and homelike when I come to you (that will not be long), and remain yourselves, you two, whatever storms may rage outside. However, I know you both, and that is enough. Whether I address my sister henceforward as Mademoiselle or Madame means little. The name means little.

Indeed, I have learnt now that we ought to approach the slightest project shyly and rejoice at the smallest success; for even that depends on fortunate coincidence. I wrote to you from Llangollen, how my first two days without Klingemann turned out happy ones, and they were days which I had anticipated with dread from the very beginning of our journey. People, scenery, hours to which I had long joyfully looked forward, turned out to be cold, unenjoyable, often disagreeable; the smallest pleasures went wrong through mere chance, and great pleasures came to pass for the same reason; and all and everything turned out differently from what I expected, desired, feared. This always has been my experience and always will be. But instead of making me apprehensive or anxious, it inspires me with courage; and far from being fearful for small projects, I take up great ones with confidence. And so au revoir, this winter.

I ought to have written much better things, but it cannot be done. Say what you like, body and mind are too closely connected. I saw it the other day with real vexation when they bled me, and all those free and fresh ideas which I had had before, trickled drop by drop into the basin, and I became dull and bored . . . This letter shows it. I wager that every line reveals that I may not bend my leg. But when once I am well again, then I will fly away from here, for now I have had enough of the smoky hole, and will again set out, to the south and later to the west.[1] I no longer have a clear idea how our dinner-table looks at home, nor of Sunday evenings, and among all the dear faces. I never feel more homesick than when I dwell upon home trifles: the round tea-table, father's Turkish boots, the green lamps; or when I look at my travelling-cap, which hangs over my bed, and which I shall take off at home. Well, the days are already getting short and cold, coals are again an item on my weekly bill, as they were when I first came; everybody talks of next season, and that means spring; things that are usually calculated by quarters are now counted by weeks, and soon will be by days; soon I shall be free, soon we shall meet. May I be justified in anticipating a joyful time to come; and whatever blessed and happy thing God can send to His children, may He grant to you, and give you beautiful and never-to-be-forgotten days!

FROM A LETTER TO HIS FAMILY

London, November 6, 1829.

. . . I have just come home from my first drive which I took with Klingemann.[2] Air and sun are good things. I feel tired and exhausted, and yet so refreshed; healthier than ever. When I came slowly downstairs and the street-door opened once more before me, and the landlord's family stepped out of their rooms and congratulated me, and the driver offered me his arm to get into the

1. *Felix planned another long trip to Italy and France.*
2. *Felix had just recovered from a two-months' illness, due to an accident which had seriously injured his knee.*

carriage, an agreeable sensation came over me; but when we turned round the corner and the sun shone on me and the sky did me the favour of being a deep blue, I had for the first time in my life, a feeling of health, because I had never before done without it so long. London was indescribably beautiful. The red and brown chimney-pots contrasted so sharply with the blue sky, and all the colours glowed, the gay shops gleamed and the blue air poured out of every cross street and enveloped the background. Instead of the green, fluttering leaves I last saw from my gig I now saw red sticks, standing up stiffly, and only the lawns were still green. How beautifully the roses in Piccadilly gleamed in the sunshine, and how full of vitality everything seemed. It gave me a strange but very comforting sensation and I felt the power of returning health. I shall bring away very dear memories of this town, and when I drive off on the stage-coach (or rather inside, for I am a "burnt child"), I shall look back many a time and think of the pleasure I have had here. For indeed it does one's heart good when people are friendly and loyal, and it gives me the deepest pleasure to be able to say honestly that they are so here. My stay has therefore not been in vain, and the time will ever be dear to me when I think back upon it.

Your letters have reached me, my dear parents, in which you appear so anxious about me, and you, my dear father, even talk of making the terribly long journey here. What can I say to that? But as matters stand between you and me (alas! or rather thank God!) once for all let me leave unexpressed my thanks and affection, otherwise I should always be speaking of them and of nothing else; for I owe you all and everything, and so let my present feelings also be buried in silence. If only words were not so cold! especially written words!

In her letter of October 27, which I received only today by way of Hamburg, Fanny scolds me for my impatience. That is missing the mark, for since the third week of my illness a lazy apathy has taken hold of me, which goes beyond all limits. I could now sit all day long on the sofa and do nothing. The other day I did sit for half an hour alone in the twilight looking at the kindling flames, and thought of nothing at all, an enterprise over which I should at other times infallibly have fallen asleep; this time, however, I carried it out wide awake and comfortable . . . In short, if I just smoked a long pipe and had a nightcap on my head, what with my crutches in the background, I might well pass for a hearty old uncle taken with the gout . . .

FROM LETTERS TO HIS FAMILY

Weimar, May 21, 1830.

Never, in the whole course of my travels, do I remember a more glorious and inspiriting day for a journey than yesterday. Early in the morning the sky was grey and overcast; it was not until later that the sun came through; the air was cool and it was Ascension Day; the people were all dressed in their best. In one village I saw them going to church, in another I saw them coming out again, and in still another I saw them playing bowls. Gay tulips were growing everywhere in the gardens and I drove fast and looked at everything. At Weissenfels they gave me a little basket carriage, and at Naumburg actually an open carriage. My effects, including my hat and cloak, were piled up behind. I bought a few bunches of lilies-of-the-valley, and so went through the country as if I were on a pleasure trip.

Some undergraduates came past, beyond Naumburg, and envied me. Then we drove past President G., seated in a small carriage which had difficulty in containing him and his daughters or wives; in short, the two ladies with him, who appeared equally envious of my position. We actually trotted up Kosen Hill, for the *horses scarcely had to pull, and we overtook a great many heavily-laden carriages, the drivers of which no doubt also envied me, for I really was to be envied. The scene was so springlike and gleaming, colourful and gay. Then the sun sank so solemnly behind the hills, and the Russian ambassador was travelling in such a sullen and business-like manner in two large coaches, drawn by four horses apiece while I, in my open carriage, darted past him like a hare.*

In the evening I was given a pair of restive horses, so that I also had a little annoyance—which, according to my theory is a part of pleasure—and not a single bar did I compose all day, but enjoyed complete idleness. It was a wonderful day, that is certain, and will not be forgotten. I close this description with the remark that the children in Eckartsberge dance Ring-around-a-rosy, just as ours do at home, and that the appearance of a stranger did not disturb them in the least, although he observed them with a distinguished air; I should have liked to join in their game!

May 24.

I wrote this before going to see Goethe, early in the forenoon, after a walk in the park; I am still here and have found it impossible to get on with my letter. I shall probably remain here for a couple of days, which is no sacrifice, for I never saw the old gentleman so cheerful and amiable as on this occasion, nor so talkative and communicative. My reason, however, for staying two days longer is not at all a disagreeable one, and makes me almost vain, or I ought rather to say proud, and I do not intend to keep it secret from you. Namely, Goethe sent me a letter yesterday addressed to an artist here, a painter, which I am to deliver myself; and Ottilie confided to me that it contains a commission to make my portrait, as Goethe wishes to include it in a collection of likenesses of his friends, which he started some time ago. This circumstance gratified me exceedingly; as however I have not yet met the com-

Overture to the operetta "Son and Stranger" (Heimkehr aus der Fremde).

Composed in 1829 for the silver wedding of Mendelssohn's parents.
(Original manuscript, private collection.)

plaisant artist—nor, for the same reason, has he seen me—I shall have to remain here until the day after tomorrow. As I said before, I don't at all regret this, for, I live luxuriously here, and thoroughly enjoy the society of the old gentleman. Up to now I have had every midday meal with him, and am invited again today. This evening there is to be a party at his house, and I am to play. It is delightful to hear him conversing on every subject, and asking questions about everything.

But I must tell you everything properly, and in order, so that you may know all the details.

Early in the day I went to see Ottilie, who, though still delicate, and sometimes complaining, I found to be more cheerful than formerly, and quite as kind and amiable as ever towards myself. We have been almost constantly together since then, and this has given me great pleasure, and I am delighted to have become more closely acquainted with her. Ulrike is much pleasanter and more lovable than ever before. She has developed an innate earnestness and has a sureness and depth of feeling that make her one of the most attractive creatures I have ever met. The two boys, Walter and Wolf, are lively, industrious, obliging lads, and to hear them talking about "Grandpapa's Faust" is too sweet for words.

But to return to my narrative. I sent Zelter's letter to Goethe at once, who immediately had me invited to dinner. I found him outwardly unchanged, but at first rather silent and withdrawn; I think he wished to see how I demeaned myself. I was grieved, and thought he was now always in this mood. Happily the conversation turned on the Frauen-Vereine in Weimar, and on the "Chaos", a mad paper circulated by the ladies here among themselves. I have soared so high as to be a contributor. All at once the old man became quite gay, laughing at the two ladies about their charities and intellectualism, and their subscriptions and hospital work, which he seems especially to detest. He called on me to aid him in his onslaught, and as I did not require to be asked twice, he speedily became just what he used to be, and at last friendlier and more confidential than I have even known him. The assault soon became general. The "Robber Bride" by Ries, he said, contained all that an artist in these days required to live happily—a robber and a bride; then he attacked the universal yearning of the young people who are so melancholy. He then related the story of a young lady to whom he had once paid court, and who also felt some interest in him; then came a discussion on the exhibitions, and a bazaar for cripples, where the ladies of Weimar sold handwork, and where he declared it was impossible to purchase anything because the young people made a private agreement among themselves, and hid the different articles till the proper purchasers appeared.

After dinner he all at once began—"Gute Kinder—huebsche Kinder—muss immer lustig sein—tolles Volk", etc., his eyes looking like those of a drowsy old lion. Then he begged me to play to him, and said it seemed strange that he had heard no music for so long; that he supposed we had made progress, but he knew nothing of it. He wished me to tell him a great deal on the subject, saying "Do let us have a little rational conversation together"; and turning to Ottilie, he said "No doubt you have already made your own wise arrangements, but they must yield to my express orders, which are, that you must make tea here this evening, that we may be all together again". When she asked if it would not be too late, as Riemer was coming to work with him, he replied, "As you gave your children a holiday from their Latin today, that they might hear Felix play, I think you might also give me one day of relaxation from my work". Then he invited me to eat with them again today, and I played a great deal to him in the evening.

My three Welshmen, or three Welshwomen, have great success here; [1] and I am trying to rub up my English.

As I had begged Goethe to address me as Du, he desired Ottilie

1. *Three pieces for the piano, composed in 1829 for the album of three young English ladies; subsequently published as Opus 16.*

to say to me on the following day, in that case I must remain longer than the two days I had fixed, otherwise he could not again become accustomed to it. He repeated this to me himself, saying that he did not think I should lose much by staying a little longer, and invited me always to dine with him when I had no other engagement. I have consequently been with him every day, and yesterday I told him a great deal about Scotland and Hengstenberg, and Spontini, and Hegel's "Aesthetics." [1] He sent me to Tiefurth with the ladies, but prohibited my driving to Berka, because a very pretty girl lived there, and he did not wish to plunge me into misery.

I thought to myself, this is indeed the Goethe of whom people will one day say that he was not one single individual, but consisted of several little Goetheries. Today I am to play to him pieces by Bach, Haydn, and Mozart, and thus lead him on, as he said, to the present day. Incidentally, I am a conscientious traveller, and have seen the Library, and "Iphigenia in Aulis".

Felix.

May 25.

I have just received your sweet letter, written on Ascension Day. I cannot help myself, but must write you again from here. I will soon send you, dear Fanny, the copy of my symphony; I am having it written out here, and mean to forward it to Leipzig (where perhaps it will be performed), with strict orders to deliver it to you as soon as possible. Try to collect opinions as to the title I ought to select; Reformation Symphony, Confession Symphony, Symphony for a Church Festival, Juvenile Symphony, or whatever you like. Write to me about it, and instead of all the stupid suggestions,

1. Felix Mendelssohn attended the Berlin University as a matriculated student for more than a year; a vast number of sheets written by him at this period, during the lectures, are still extant.

send me one clever one; but I also want to hear the nonsensical ones sure to be produced on the occasion.

Yesterday evening I was at a party at Goethe's, and played alone the whole evening—the Concert-Stück, the Invitation to the Waltz, and Weber's Polonaise in C, my three Welsh pieces, and my Scotch sonata. It was over by ten o'clock, but I of course stayed on and we had all sorts of nonsensical games, and dancing and singing, until twelve o'clock; really I lead a heathenish existence. The old gentleman goes to his room regularly at nine o'clock, and as soon as he is gone, we begin our frolics, and never separate before midnight.

Tomorrow my portrait is to be finished; a large black-crayon sketch, and a very good likeness; but I look quite sulky. Goethe is so friendly and kind to me, that I don't know how to thank him sufficiently, or what to do to deserve it. Mornings I play to him for about an hour. He likes to hear the works of all the different great piano composers in chronological order and have me tell him how they have progressed. All this time he sits in a dark corner and his old eyes flash. He wanted to have nothing to do with Beethoven, but I told him I could not let him escape, and played the first part of the symphony in C minor. It had a singular effect on him; at first he said, "This arouses no emotion; nothing but astonishment; it is grandiose". He continued grumbling in this way, and after a long pause he began again, "It is very great; quite wild; it makes one fear that the house might fall down; what must it be like when all those men play together!" During dinner, in the midst of another subject, he alluded to it again. You already know that I dine with him every day; at these times he questions me very minutely, and is always so gay and communicative after dinner that we generally remain in the room by ourselves for an hour or more, while he talks on uninterruptedly.

I experience unique pleasure when he brings out engravings and explains them to me, as he once did, or gives his opinion of Ernani, or Lamartine's Elegies, or the theatre, or pretty girls. He has *several times lately invited people, which is an extremely rare thing now, so that most of the guests had not seen him for a long time. I then play a great deal, and he compliments me before all these people, and "stupendous" (ganz stupend) is his favourite expression. Today he has invited a number of Weimar beauties on my account, because he thinks that I ought also to enjoy the society of young people. If I go up to him on such occasions, he says, "My young friend, you must join the ladies, and make yourself agreeable to them". Incidentally, I have considerable tact, so I contrived to have him asked yesterday whether I was perhaps not coming too often; but he growled out to Ottilie, who put the question to him, that "he must now begin to speak to me in good earnest, for I had such clear ideas about my affairs that he hoped to learn much from me". I became twice as tall in my own estimation when Ottilie repeated this to me. He said so to me himself yesterday; and when he declared that there were many subjects he had at heart that I must explain to him, I said, "Oh, certainly!" but I thought, "This is an honour I can never forget"—often it is the very reverse.*

Felix.

TO HIS FAMILY

Munich, June 6, 1830.

It is a long time since I have written to you, and I fear you may have been anxious on my account. You must not be angry with me, for it was really no fault of mine, and I have been not a little worried about it. I expedited my journey as well as I could, inquiring everywhere about diligences, and invariably receiving false information. I travelled through one night on purpose to enable me to write to you by this day's post, of which I was told in Nuernberg; and when at last I arrive, I find that no post leaves here today; it is enough to drive one wild. I feel out of all patience with Germany and her petty principalities, her different kinds of money, her diligences, which require an hour and a quarter for a German mile, and her Thuringian forests, where there is incessant rain and wind—yes, even with her "Fidelio" this evening, for, though dead tired, I must do my duty by going to hear it, when I would far rather go to bed. Pray do not be angry with me, nor scold me for my long delay; I can tell you that last night while I was travelling, I constantly saw, peeping through the clouds, the shadow of your threatening finger; but now I shall explain why I could not write sooner.

Some days after my last letter from Weimar, I wished, as I told you, to set off for this place, and said so during dinner to Goethe, who remained quite silent. After dinner however he withdrew with Ottilie into the recess of a window, and said, "See to it that he remains here". She endeavoured to prevail on me to do so, and walked up and down in the garden with me. I wished however to be a man of determination, so I stuck to my resolve. Then came the old gentleman himself, and said there was no need of my being in such a hurry; that he had still a great deal to tell me, and I had still a great deal to play to him; and that as to what I had told him was the object of my journey, there was nothing in it; Weimar was at present the real objective of my travels, and he could not see what I was likely to find in tables-d'hôte elsewhere, that I could not get here: I would see plenty of hotels in my travels. So it went on, and as I was touched, especially as Ottilie and Ulrike added their persuasions, assuring me that the old gentleman never urged people to stay but more often insisted on their going away; and as no one can be so certain of the number of happy days in store for him that he can afford to throw away a few that are bound to be pleasant, and as they promised to go with me to Jena, I no longer wished to be a man of determination, and remained.

Seldom in the course of my life have I so little regretted any resolution as this, for the following day was by far the most delight-

ful that I ever passed in Goethe's house. After an early drive, I found old Goethe very cheerful; he began to discourse on various subjects, passing from the "Muette de Portici" to Walter Scott, and thence to the pretty girls in Weimar; to the students, and the "Robbers", and so on to Schiller; then he talked on uninterruptedly and with animation for more than an hour, about Schiller's life and writings, and his position in Weimar. He proceeded to speak of the late Grand Duke, and of the year 1775, which he called the intellectual spring of Germany, declaring that no man living could describe it so well as he; indeed, it had been his intention to devote the second volume of his life to this subject; but what with botany, and meteorology, and other stupid stuff of the same kind, for which no one cared a straw, he had not yet been able to fulfil his purpose. Then he told stories of the time when he was director of the theatre, and when I wished to thank him, he said, "It is mere chance, it all comes to light incidentally, called forth by your welcome presence". These words sounded marvellously pleasant to me; in short, it was one of those conversations that a man can never forget so long as he lives. Next day he made me a present of a sheet of the manuscript of "Faust", and at the bottom of the page he wrote, "To my dear young friend F.M.B., powerfully tender master of the piano—a friendly souvenir of happy May days in 1830. J. W. von Goethe". He also gave me three letters of introduction for here.

If that fatal "Fidelio" did not begin so soon, I could tell you much more, but as it is, I have only time for my farewell from the old gentleman. At the very beginning of my visit to Weimar, I spoke of a "Praying Peasant Family" by Adrian von Ostade, which nine years ago made a deep impression on me. When I went at an early hour to take leave of Goethe, I found him seated beside a large portfolio, and he said, "Yes, yes, you are really leaving; we'll have to see to it that we keep in good trim until you return; but we won't part now without some moments of devotion, and so we must have several looks at the Prayer together". He told me that

I must sometimes write to him—(courage! courage! I mean to do so from this very place), and then he kissed me, and we drove off to Jena, where the Frommanns received me with great kindness, and where the same evening I also took leave of Ottilie and Ulrike, and came on here.

Nine o'clock—"*Fidelio*" is over; and while waiting for supper I add a few words . . . My Germany is certainly a mad country; it can produce great people and then ignore them; it has plenty of fine singers, and many intelligent artists, but none sufficiently modest and subordinate to render their parts faithfully and without false pretension. Marzelline introduces all sorts of flourishes into her part; Jaquino is a blockhead; the minister a simpleton; and when a German like Beethoven writes an opera, then comes a German like Stuntz or Poissl (or whoever it may have been) and strikes out the ritournelle, and similar unnecessary passages; another German adds a trombone part to his symphonies; a third declares that Beethoven is overloaded; and then a great man is done for!

Farewell! be happy and merry; and may all my heartfelt wishes for you be fulfilled.

Felix.

FROM A LETTER TO HIS SISTER FANNY

Munich, June 11, 1830.

My darling little Sister,

Are you quite well again? and no longer angry with your wicked brother, who has not written for such a long time? He is sitting here in a nice little room, the green-velvet-book with your portraits before him, and writing by the open window. Listen a moment: I wish you were very happy and merry indeed, this moment, because I am just thinking of you; and if you were so every moment that I think of you, you would never be ailing or downcast. One thing is sure enough: that you are a capital creature and know something about music. I felt the truth of that last night whilst flirting very considerably. For your brother was trying last night to be as sweet as you are wise. There was a great soirée at the P. Kerstorf's, and Excellencies and Counts went about as thick as fowls in a poultry yard. Also artists and other cultivated minds. Delphine Schauroth, who is adored here (and deservedly), was something of all this together, her mother being a Freifrau von, and she herself an artist and very cultivated. I followed her around like a little lamb, to such purpose that we played the four-hand sonata of Hummel together, beautifully, and were applauded. I followed her lead and smiled, and held the A-flat in the beginning of the last piece for her "because her little hand could not reach it" And the lady of the house placed us next to one another at supper, healths were proposed, and so forth. But all I really wanted to say is that the girl plays very well, and the day before yesterday, when we played the piece together for the first time (we have now given it three times), she genuinely impressed me. But yesterday morning, when I heard her alone and again admired her very much, it suddenly came to my mind that we have a young lady in our garden-house who has a certain different conception of music in her head from that of many ladies put together, and I thought I would write to her and send her my best love. It is clear that you are this young lady and I tell you, Fanny, that I have only to think of some of your pieces to become quite tender and sincere, in spite of the fact that one has to lie a great deal in South Germany. But you really know what God was thinking when He invented music, so it is no wonder that it makes one happy. You can play piano, too, and if you need a greater

Mendelssohn at the age of twelve.
Painting by Begas.

Mendelssohn at the age of thirteen.
Drawing by P. Leo.

admirer than I, you can paint him, or have him paint you.[1]

While I am alluding to Hensel, I must tell him that Goethe asked after him a great deal and repeatedly inquired about what he was doing. I had to leave the green book with him for several days, and he bestowed much praise upon it. He looked at the lamb-group in my album, muttering: "They are well off—and look so dainty and pretty—so comfortable, and yet so lovely and graceful". And so he went on—in short, O Hensel, I must tell you that he is very much prepossessed in your favour.

Yesterday a noble countess graciously praised my songs, and remarked, interrogatively, wasn't the one by Grillparzer altogether delightful. Yes, I said, and she thought I was conceited until I gave her a full explanation by telling her that you were the composer,[2] and promised to play immediately, before company, the compositions you are about to send me . . .

They have just brought me a light and my neighbour opposite is tormenting his piano in the twilight, in the process of massacring Paganini's "Clochette" . . .

TO GOETHE

Munich, June 16, 1830.

Your Excellency

has been kind enough to allow me to write to you now and then, and to give an account of whatever important or pleasurable experiences I have had on my journey. This permission gives me courage once more to try to express in writing what I never succeeded in saying on a subject about which I therefore had to remain

1. *The painter Wilhelm Hensel whom Fanny had married the year before.*
2. *Fanny had often published her own songs under the name of her brother.*

silent; and that is my gratitude for the unforgettable days you gave me in Weimar. I wish I could tell you how happy you made me. Of course, you must be accustomed to such thanks, and you may find it immodest on my part to speak of it; but what one feels so intensely, one desires to put into words, and so I beg you to pardon me for what I have said.

Also I can only now properly appreciate the letters of introduction that you gave me, for, to my delight and instruction, I have become acquainted with the people to whom they were addressed.

Stieler in particular was wonderfully kind and amiable to me. The way in which he spoke of you and yours, the beaming delight which permeated his whole being when he recalled the time he had spent with you, made me at once feel specially drawn towards him. He is painting your "Fisher", and told me that the picture originated partly in his dislike of one which had made a great sensation at the Berlin exhibition, and in which the subject was treated in far too sensuous a manner. It may be true, but I don't know how he can succeed in avoiding the difficulty entirely, for if you are to have the figure of a woman rising fresh from the water, and at the same time singing and speaking in a lovable manner, she must be charming; and the Fisherman to whom she beckons must be a graceful youth; whereas his picture seems to be based on quite another conception. But as yet it is only sketched in, and at any rate the head of the nymph is already so exquisite and pretty that she is sure to please anyone. Stieler [1] has also just finished a portrait for the King's private collection of beauties and is perpetually looking about amongst the Munich girls for new models. He is delighted with this commission, and no wonder, for the ladies pay him no end of attention, and would give anything to please him so that he will give them the prize, and pick them out as the most beautiful.

---

1. *King Ludwig I of Bavaria, a lover of the arts and of pretty women, had commissioned the painter Heinrich Stieler to make portraits of the prettiest women of the city of Munich, which formed the King's "Schoenheitsgalerie".*

Music is very much run after here, and there is plenty of it, but it seems to me that almost everything makes an impression in this place, and that the impression does not last. It is most amusing to see the difference between a Munich and a Berlin musical party. In Berlin, when a piece of music comes to an end, the whole company sits in solemn silence, each one considering what his opinion is to be, nobody giving a sign of applause or pleasure, and all the while the performer is in the most painful embarrassment, not knowing whether, and in what spirit, he has been listened to. And yet, afterwards, he often finds that people have given all their attention and have been very deeply moved, though to all appearance they are so cold and indifferent. Here, on the contrary, it is great fun playing at a party, because the people can't help talking every minute about what they like; sometimes they even begin clapping and applauding in the middle of a piece; and it is not at all uncommon, when one gets up from playing, to find that everybody has moved, because sometimes, all of a sudden, they want to come and look at one's fingers, and stand all round the piano, or someone wishes to make an observation to someone else, and goes and sits down by him and talks. Afterwards they overwhelm you with compliments and kindness; but I don't know whether I should not be afraid that, after a day or two, much of the vividness of the impression will fade.

The Opera is supplied in the amplest manner, and yet does not produce anything out of the ordinary, because there is no leading spirit to direct the whole thing. Schechner, for example, is one of the most remarkable singers we have; but because they praise her good points up to the skies and pass over her failings, she is accustoming herself by degrees to all sorts of mannerisms. It seems moreover to be thought bon ton to abuse the opera and the theatre, and to pay a great deal of attention to the critics, who try to earn their scanty daily bread by scoffing and sneering; this again discourages the actors, the bitterness increases on both sides, and thus it happens that there is seldom much pleasure or real enjoy-

ment to be found at the theatre. The stage is tired and commonplace instead of being stimulating, fresh and gay. Nevertheless I am greatly enjoying my stay here, time passes quickly because life is so easy and comfortable with these jolly Southerners.

Once more I beg Your Excellency to pardon my long letter; but you yourself allowed me to report on how the new city and the new surroundings appear to me. And so I hope you will excuse my copiousness.

With the expression of my deepest respect
Your Excellency's most devoted
F.M.B.

TO CARL FRIEDRICH ZELTER

Munich, June 22, 1830.

Dear Professor,

I have wished to write to you for a long time and once more express my gratitude. But it is difficult for me to say "thanks" in writing; the words seem so cold and formal while what I enjoyed so greatly and want to thank you for, still appears so vividly to me. When you introduced me nine years ago into Goethe's house you were perfectly aware of how great a happiness your kindness had in store for me. But I could not know that myself at the time, nor could I fully appreciate a gift whose value was not yet clear to me. But now, that I have experienced greater delight and comfort with Goethe and his family than ever before, now that I have lived through a number of unforgettable days, when every hour brought nothing but elation, joy and pride—now at last I know how to appreciate it. Nevertheless, I cannot thank you as I ought. You did not do it in order to be thanked, and so you will excuse my speaking about it, even though my words have not the tone I would like to give them, and are not adequate for their purpose. Well, I am sure you know how I feel.

I have often played to Goethe in the morning hours. He wanted to get an idea of how music has developed and wished to hear the music of different composers in chronological order. He seemed rather wary of Beethoven; but I could not spare him this acquaintance because he had to hear "where sounds had turned to", and so I played for him the first movement of the C minor symphony which he liked very much. He was delighted with the overture by Johann Sebastian Bach, the one in D major with the trumpets, which I played on the piano as well as I could; "in the beginning it sounds so distinguished and pompous, one really sees the crowd of smartly attired people walking down the steps of a broad staircase." And I also played the Inventions and quite a few pieces of the Wohltemperiertes Clavier. One day he asked me if I would not care to pay a compliment to craftsmanship and call on the organist who might let me see and hear the organ in the cathedral. I said, yes, of course I would, and the instrument gave me great pleasure. I was told that you, too, had given your expert opinion on the repair work, and that therefore it had been done better than on any repaired organ I know of. Owing to the long narrow space in which it is housed, the pedal-pipe is fitted deep in the rear; nonetheless the full organ sounds ample and strong, the tone does not tremble in the least, and this shows that there must be plenty of wind. The pedal is in perfect proportion to the manual and there is no lack of beautiful, soft voices of various kinds. The organist offered me the choice of hearing something scholarly, or something for "people" (because he said that for people one had to compose only easy and bad music), so I asked for something scholarly. But it was not much to be proud of; he modulated around enough to make one giddy, but nothing unusual came of it; he made a number of entries, but no fugue was forthcoming. When my turn came to play to him, I started with the D minor toccata of Sebastian and remarked that this was at the same time scholarly and something for "people" too, at least for some of them; but mind, hardly had I begun to play when the superintendent dispatched his valet upstairs with the message that this playing had to be stopped right away because it was a weekday and he could not study with that much noise going on. Goethe was very much amused by this story.

Here, in Munich, the musicians behave exactly like that organist; they believe that good music may be considered a heaven-sent gift, but just in abstracte, and as soon as they sit down to play they produce the stupidest, silliest stuff imaginable, and when people do not like it they pretend that it was still too highbrow. Even the best pianists had no idea that Mozart and Haydn had also composed for the piano; they had just the faintest notion of Beethoven and consider the music of Kalkbrenner, Field and Hummel classical and scholarly. On the other hand, having played myself several times, I found the audience so receptive and open-minded that I felt doubly vexed by those frivolities. Recently, at a soirée given by a Countess, who is supposed to lead in fashion, I had an outbreak. The young ladies, quite able to perform adequate pieces very nicely, tried to break their fingers with juggler's tricks and ropedancer's feats of Herz's; when I was asked to play, I thought: well, if you get bored it serves you right, and started right out with the C-sharp minor sonata of Beethoven. When I finished, I noticed that the impression had been enormous; the ladies were weeping, the gentlemen hotly discussing the importance of the work. I had to write down a number of Beethoven sonatas for the female pianists who wanted to study them. Next morning the Countess summoned her piano-teacher and desired from him an edition of good, really good music, by Mozart, Beethoven and Weber. This story went around in Munich, and the good-natured musicians were very pleased that I had set myself up as the preacher in the desert. Subsequently I gave a long sermon to the leading pianist and reproached her for having contributed nothing towards the knowledge and appreciation of the works of the great masters here and for having just followed the popular trend instead of guiding the taste of the public—and she vowed to improve. Since that time I play only what I really like, however serious, and everybody listens to me with attention.

I am delighted to make so much music here, and though I have little time left to compose and to think, this gay life inspires me with many new ideas and proves to be cheering and refreshing. I have a sacred piece in mind; as soon as I find time to write it down, I shall mail it to you. Goodbye for today, dear Professor Zelter. With the most cordial greetings for you and yours and the best wishes for your health and happiness.

Always your faithful

F. M. B.

TO HIS BROTHER

Pressburg, September 27, 1830.

Dear Brother,

Peals of bells, drums and music, carriages on carriages, people hurrying in all directions, everywhere gay crowds, that is the general aspect around me, for tomorrow is to be the coronation of the King, which the whole city has been expecting since yesterday. Everyone is now imploring that the sky may clear up, and waken bright and cheerful, for the grand ceremony which ought to have taken place yesterday, had to be deferred on account of the torrents of rain. Now the sky has been blue and beautiful since this afternoon, and the moon is shining down tranquilly on the tumult of the city. Tomorrow at a very early hour the Crown Prince will take his oath (as King of Hungary) in the large market-place; he will then go to church in grand procession, attended by a whole *array of bishops and nobles of the realm, and then finally will ride to the Koenigsberg, which lies opposite my window, and there on the bank of the Danube he will wave his sword towards the four quarters of the globe, and thus take possession of his new realm.*

Thanks to this little journey, I have become acquainted with a new country; for Hungary with her magnates, her high dignitaries, her oriental luxury, side by side with her barbarism, can be seen here, and the streets offer a spectacle which to me is both unexpected and new. One finds oneself really closer to the east here; the frightfully stupid peasants or serfs; the troops of gipsies; the equipages and retainers of the nobles overloaded with gold and gems, (for the grandees themselves are only visible through the closed windows of their carriages); then the singularly bold national physiognomy, the yellow hue, the long mustaches, the soft foreign idiom—all this makes the most motley impression in the world.

Early yesterday I went alone through the streets. First came a long array of jovial officers, on spirited little horses; behind them a crew of gipsies, making music; between them Viennese fashionables, with eyeglasses and kid gloves, conversing with a Capuchin monk; then a couple of those short, barbaric peasants in long white coats, their hats pressed down on their foreheads, and their straight black hair cut even all round; they have reddish-brown complexions, a languid gait, and an indescribable expression of savage stupidity and indifference. Then came a couple of sharp, acute-looking students of theology, in their long blue coats, walking arm-in-arm; Hungarian proprietors in their dark blue national costume; court servants; and numbers of carriages arriving every moment, covered with mud. I followed the crowd as they slowly moved on up the hill, and so at last I arrived at the dilapidated castle, which commmands an extensive view of the whole city and the Danube. People were looking down on all sides from the ancient white walls, and from the towers and balconies; in every corner boys were scribbling their names on the walls for the benefit of posterity; in a small chamber (perhaps it was otherwise a chapel, or some sleeping-apartment or other) an ox was being roasted whole, and as it turned on the spit, the people shouted with delight; a great row of cannons stood before the castle, ready to thunder forth at the coronation.

Below, on the Danube—which rages wildly here, and pours through the pontoon bridge with the speed of an arrow—lay the new steamer, which had just arrived, laden with strangers; then the extensive view of the flat but wooded country, and meadows overflowed by the Danube; of the embankments and streets swarming with human beings, and mountains clothed with Hungarian vines—all this was not a little foreign and strange. Then the pleasant contrast of living in the same house with the best and most friendly people in the world, and finding novelty doubly surprising in their society. These were really among the happy days, dear brother, that a kind Providence so often and so richly bestows on me.

September 28, one o'clock.

The King is crowned—the ceremony was wonderfully beautiful. What point is there in a lot of description? An hour hence we will all drive back to Vienna, and thence I pursue my journey. There was a tremendous uproar under my windows, and the militia collected, but only for the purpose of shouting "Vivat!" I pushed my way through the crowd, while our ladies saw everything from the windows, and I shall never forget the effect of all this unbelievably brilliant magnificence.

The people crowded like mad into the great square of the Hospitallers, for that is where he had to take his oath, on a platform hung with cloth; and afterwards the people were allowed to tear down the cloth for their own garments; close by there was also a fountain spouting red and white Hungarian wine. The grenadiers could not keep the crowds back; one unlucky hackney coach that stopped for a moment was instantly covered with people, who clambered on the spokes of the wheels, and on the roof, and on the box, swarming over it like ants, so that the coachman, unable to drive on without becoming a murderer, was forced to wait quietly where he was. When the procession arrived, which was received bare-headed, it was only with the utmost difficulty that I could take my hat off and hold it above my head; an old Hungarian, however, behind me, with whose view it interfered, quickly found a way out, for without ceremony he snatched my poor hat, and in an instant flattened it to the size of a cap; then they yelled as if they had all been spitted, and fought for the cloth; in short they were a mob. But these Hungarians! The fellows looked as if they were born into the nobility and a life of idleness, and as if the fact made them very melancholy; and they ride like the devil.

When the procession descended the hill, first came the embroidered court servants, the trumpeters and drummers, the heralds and all that class, and then suddenly, galloping along the street, came a mad Count, en pleine carrière, his horse plunging and capering, and the caparisons edged with gold, the Count himself a mass of diamonds, real aigrettes, and velvet embroidery (he had not yet assumed his state uniform, because he had to ride so madly—Count Sándor is the name of this ferocious cavalier). He had an ivory sceptre in his hand with which he prodded his horse; each time it would rear and make a tremendous bound forward.

When his wild career was over, a procession of about sixty more magnates arrived, all in the same fantastic splendour, with handsome coloured turbans, amusing mustaches, and dark eyes. One rode a white horse covered with a gold net; another a dark grey, the bridle and housings studded with diamonds; then came a black charger with purple cloth caparisons. One wore sky-blue from head to foot, thickly embroidered with gold, a white turban, and a long white dolman; another was dressed entirely in cloth of gold, with a purple dolman; each one was richer and more colourful than the other, and all riding so boldly and fearlessly, and with such defiant gallantry, that it was a pleasure.

At length came the Hungarian Guards, with Esterházy at their head, dazzling in gems and pearl embroidery. How can I describe it? You ought to have seen the procession deploy and halt in the spacious square, and all the jewels and bright colours, and the high golden mitres of the bishops, and the crucifixes glittering in the brilliant sunshine like a thousand stars!

Well, tomorrow, God willing, I proceed on my journey. Now, brother, you have a letter; write soon, and let me hear how you are getting on. So you have had an insurrection in Berlin? And by tailors' apprentices, at that. What did it all mean?

I will send you my farewell once more from Germany, my dear parents, and brother and sisters. I am leaving Hungary for Italy, and from there I hope to write to you more frequently and more at leisure. Be of good cheer, dear Paul, and go forward in a confident spirit; enjoy everything enjoyable, and think of your brother who is wandering about the world. Farewell.

Yours,

Felix.

TO CARL FRIEDRICH ZELTER

Venice, October 16, 1830.

Dear Professor,

I have entered Italy at last, and this letter is the beginning of regular reports which I intend to send you about everything that seems to me to be particularly worthy of notice. The fact that up to now I have written you only one proper letter is to be blamed on the state of constant excitement in which I lived, both in Munich and in Vienna. It was impossible for me to tell you about the parties in Munich, which I attended every evening and where

I played the piano more unremittingly than I ever did before in my life, because one crowded so closely on the heels of another that I really never had a moment to collect my thoughts. Moreover, it would not have particularly interested you, for after all, "good society which does not offer material for the smallest epigram", is equally vapid in a letter. I hope that you have not taken my long silence amiss, and that I may expect a few lines from you, even if they contain nothing save that you are well and cheerful.

The aspect of the world at this moment is very bleak and stormy, and much that was once thought unchangeable and permanent has been swept away in the course of a couple of days. It is then doubly welcome to hear well-known voices, to convince us that there are certain things which cannot be annihilated or demolished, but remain firm and steadfast. As I am very uneasy now at not having received any news from home for four weeks, and as I found no letters from my family, either at Trieste or here, so a few words from you, written in your old fashion, would both cheer and gratify me, especially as it would convince me that you still regard me with the same kindness you have always done since my childhood.

My family will probably have told you of the exhilarating impression made on me by the first sight of the plains of Italy. I hurry from one enjoyment to another hour by hour, and constantly see something novel and fresh; but during the very first days of my arrival I discovered a few masterpieces which mean so much to me that I study them a couple of hours every day. These are three pictures by Titian. The "Presentation of Mary as a Child in the Temple"; the "Assumption of the Virgin"; and the "Entombment of Christ". There is also a portrait by Giorgione, representing a girl with a zither in her hand, lost in thought, and gazing out of the picture in serious meditation (she is apparently about to begin a song, and you feel as if you must do the same); besides many others.

To see these alone would be worth a journey to Venice; for the opulence, power, and devotion of the great men who painted these pictures, seem to emanate from them afresh as often as you gaze at their works, and I do not much regret that I have heard scarcely any music here as yet; for I suppose I must not include the music of the angels in the "Assumption", encircling Mary with joyous shouts of welcome, one gaily beating the tambourine, a couple of others blowing away on strange crooked flutes, whilst another charming group is singing—or the music floating in the thoughts of the player. I have only once heard anything on the organ, and that was doleful. I was gazing at Titian's "Martyrdom of St. Peter" in the Franciscan Church. Divine service was going on, and nothing inspires me with more solemn awe than when on the very spot for which they were originally designed and painted, those old pictures with their mighty figures, gradually steal forth out of the darkness in which the long lapse of time has veiled them.

As I was gazing at the enchanting evening landscape with the trees, and the angels among the branches, the organ commenced. The first sound was enjoyable; but the second, third, and in fact all the rest, quickly roused me from my reveries, and sent me straight home, for the man was playing in church, during divine service, and in the presence of respectable people, thus:

et cetera animalia.

with the "Martyrdom of St. Peter" close beside him! I was therefore in no great hurry to make the acquaintance of the organist. There is no regular Opera here at this moment, and the gondoliers no longer sing Tasso's stanzas; moreover, what I have seen of modern Venetian art, consists of poems, framed and glazed, on the subject of Titian's pictures, or Rinaldo and Armida, by a new Venetian painter, or a St. Cecilia by a ditto, besides various specimens of architecture in no style at all. As all these are fairly insignificant, I cling to the ancient masters, and study how they worked. Often, after doing so, I feel musically inspired, and since I came here I have been busily engaged in composition.

Before I left Vienna, a friend of mine made me a present of Luther's Hymns, and on reading them over I was again so much struck by their power that I intend to compose music for several next winter. Since I have been here, I have nearly completed the chorale "Aus tiefer Noth", for four voices a capella; and the Christmas hymn, "Von Himmel hoch", is already in my head. I wish also to set the following hymns to music: "Ach Gott, vom Himmel sieh darein", "Wir glauben all' an einen Gott", "Verleih uns Frieden", "Mitten wir im Leben sind", and finally "Ein' feste Burg". I am thinking of composing all the latter, however, for a choir and orchestra. Pray write to me about this project of mine, and say whether you approve of my retaining the ancient melodies in them, but not adhering to them too strictly: and, for instance, if I were to take the first verse of "Vom Himmel hoch" quite freely as a grand chorus. Besides this, I am working on an orchestral overture, and if an opportunity for an opera offered, it would be most welcome.

I finished two little pieces of sacred music in Vienna—a chorale in three movements for chorus and orchestra ("O Haupt voll Blut und Wunden") and an Ave Maria for a choir of eight voices, a capella. The people I associated with there were so dissipated and frivolous, that I became quite spiritual-minded, and conducted myself like a divine among them. Moreover, not one of the best pianists there, male or female, ever played a note of Beethoven, and when I hinted that he and Mozart were not to be despised, they said, "So you are an admirer of classical music?"— "Yes", said I.

Tomorrow I intend to go to Bologna to have a glance at the St. Cecilia, and then proceed by way of Florence to Rome, where I hope, God willing, to arrive eight or ten days hence. From there I will write you more fully and satisfactorily. I only wished to make a beginning today, and to beg you not to forget me, and kindly to accept my heartfelt wishes for your health and happiness.

Your faithful

Felix.

TO HIS PARENTS

Rome, November 8-9, 1830.

Today I must write to you about my first eight days in Rome; how I have arranged my time, how I look forward to the winter, and what effect my heavenly surroundings have had on me; but this is no easy task. I feel as if I were entirely changed since I came here. Formerly I either tried to check my impatience and eagerness to press forward and hasten my journey, or merely attributed it to force of habit; but I am now fully convinced that it arose entirely from my anxiety to reach this goal. Since I have at last attained it, my mood is so tranquil and joyous, and yet so earnest, that it is impossible to describe it to you. What it is that thus works on me I cannot exactly define; for the awe-inspiring Coliseum, and the serene Vatican, and the genial air of spring, all contribute; and so do the kindly people, my comfortable apartments, and everything else. But besides that, I am different. I am healthier and happier than I have been for a long time, and take such delight in my work, and feel such an urge for it, that I expect to accomplish much more than I anticipated; indeed, I have already done a good deal. If it pleases Providence to grant me a continuation of this happy mood, I look forward to the most delightful and productive winter.

Picture to yourself a small house, with two windows in front, in the Piazza di Spagna, No. 5, which has warm sun the whole day long, and rooms one flight up, where there is a good Viennese grand piano; on the table some portraits of Palestrina, Allegri, etc., along with the scores of their works, and a Latin psalm-book, from which I am going to compose the Non Nobis; that is where I now reside. The Capitol was too far away, and above all I dreaded the cold air, from which I certainly have nothing to fear here; when I look out of my window in the morning across the square, and see every object sharply defined in the sunshine against the blue sky. My landlord was formerly a captain in the French army, and his daughter has the most splendid contralto voice I ever heard. Above me lives a Prussian captain, with whom I talk politics—in short, the situation is excellent.

When I come into the room early in the morning, and see the sun shining so brightly on my breakfast (you see a poet has been lost in me), I immediately feel thoroughly comfortable; for it is now far on in the autumn, and who, in our country, can still expect warmth, or a bright sky, or grapes and flowers? After breakfast I begin my work, and play, and sing, and compose till about noon. Then Rome in all her vastness lies before me like a problem in enjoyment; but I go deliberately to work, selecting a different historical object every day. Sometimes I visit the ruins of the ancient city; another time I go to the Borghese Gallery, or to the Capitoline Hill, or St. Peter's, or the Vatican. That makes every day memorable, and as I take my time, each impression becomes more firmly and indelibly fixed. When I am at my morning work

I dislike leaving off, and wish to continue my writing, but I say to myself: you must also see the Vatican; and when I once get there, it is just as hard to leave again; thus each of my occupations gives me the purest pleasure, and one enjoyment follows on the heels of the last.

If Venice, with its past, seemed to me like a mausoleum, where the crumbling, modern palaces and the perpetual reminders of former grandeur made me feel somewhat out of sorts, and sad, Rome's past seems to me like the embodiment of history. Her monuments are exhilarating, they make one feel at once serious and stimulated, and it is a joyful thought that man can erect something which, after a thousand years, can still give enjoyment and strength to others . . .

One of my home pleasures is the reading—for the first time—of Goethe's "Journey to Italy"; and I must admit that it is a source of enormous pleasure to me to find that he arrived in Rome the very same day that I did; that he also went first of all to the Quirinal, and heard a Requiem there; that he was seized with the same fit of impatience in Florence and Bologna; and that he also felt so tranquil, or, as he calls it, solid, here: everything that he describes happened to me precisely the same way, so I am pleased.

November 9, morning.

And so every morning brings me fresh anticipations, and every day fulfils them. The sun has again just shone on my breakfast, and I will get to work. I will send you, dear Fanny, at the first opportunity, what I composed in Vienna, and anything else that may be finished; and to you, Rebecca, my sketchbook; but I am far from being pleased with it this time, so I intend to study the sketches of the landscape painters here, in order to acquire if possible a new manner. I tried to produce one of my own, but no!

Felix M. B.

TO CARL FRIEDRICH ZELTER

Rome, December 1, 1830.

Dear Professor Zelter,

I have just come down from the Quirinal where the Pope died last night, and as I will probably have little or no leisure to write in the next days, I do not want to omit thanking you today for your last kind letter, nor to beg that as soon as your leisure allows you will again let me have a few lines. You know how greatly I enjoy hearing from you, and therefore I hope again to see something from your hand in the near future.

It is a little difficult to start sending from here the report that you requested because there is so endlessly much to say and such a variety of wonderful impressions to describe that I do not know where to begin. The impression of Rome as a whole is so solemn and at the same time so inspiring, it fills one's inner being so intensely, that it is in fact precisely as one would like to picture life in ancient times. Other ruins are depressing and melancholy, but these are solid monuments of a glorious past. Whilst in other places everything reminds me of destruction and decay, here I delight in their eternal magnitude and might. Thus the Colosseum and the Basilica of Constantine stand there for men to see what man has created, and feel exalted.

Also I have to be grateful for so much that is not actually music: to the monuments, the paintings, the serenity of nature, which itself is mostly music. But I have also had a number of interesting experiences with "musical music"—if I might use such an expression!—and I will try to tell you something about it. I have heard the Capella del sommo pontifice (Papal Choir) four times, twice in the Quirinal (the summer residence of the Pope), once in the San Carlo and once in the Sistine Chapel. It is a chorus of ecclesiastics who sing only in the presence of the Pope or of his representative. Their full complement is thirty-two, but they are said to be rarely complete. The conductor sings with them, and conducts with his voice by helping out in each part, when necessary jumping from a deep bass to a discant entrance in falsetto voice. There are no boys' voices and so far have never been any, and Baini, who complained that every year fewer sopranos become available, was almost offended when I asked if he could not substitute boys. As to the special style of performing Palestrina's music, which people say has been preserved by tradition in the Papal Chapel, I have been able to detect very little of it. It seemed to me that the only peculiarity in their way of singing consisted of forcing their voices almost throughout and holding the long notes in uniform and undiminished volume, which with us I think would be considered incorrect. But it sounds very good coming from the large, beautiful voices of the basses and sometimes from the tenors, too; only the top voices sometimes sound repulsively shrill. It might also be reckoned among their oddities that they retain the little ornaments and trills such as were popular at the beginning of the last century, although that could really be called practically a mistake, because all the inner voices, without exception, participate in these embellishments and thus occasionally produce very strange sound effects.

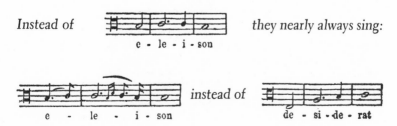

Instead of 

they nearly always sing:

instead of 

always 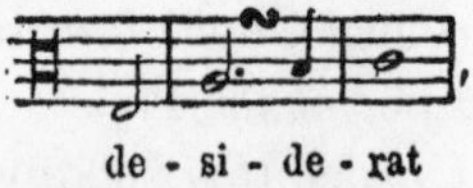

and in the Dies Irae,

instead of  and other similar passages, they

sang throughout, .

You can imagine what a singular effect it has when it is sung consistently by all the inner voices through a whole Mass. Incidentally this style of singing: 

instead of: 

and of carrying over each note into the next, is at times completely justified, and gives the whole thing a beautiful, smooth tone; and if now and then very peculiar dissonances result, the effect in the music they sing is not at all bad; but they had better not do it with Johann Sebastian Bach. The music as well as the solemn service are very cleverly and successfully calculated to produce a great effect. Many people wonder why Palestrina makes so much more profound an impression here than in Germany, and yet it is quite natural. Before starting a piece the whole chorus sings the responses in the following manner: the tenor and bass always in thirds, and soprano and contralto in unison, an octave above the basses. Like this, for example: 

That often goes

on for a long time, and it is sung with full voice and as loudly as possible. So when they finally begin one of those pieces, the mere sound of the first chord produces a lovely effect. Even in the responses themselves, they sometimes—though very rarely—sing perfect cadenzas, and they sound wonderful, though it is nothing but:

They also sing the responses in unison, as for instance this one, which they often repeat and which I wrote down at the Quirinal:

(The words are different, but their enunciation is so vague that it is hard to tell what words they are singing or whether they are singing any at all.) After this, the precentors follow one another, each starting in a different key. For instance, I heard the chorus end in D major; a brief pause followed, and then the next precentor started in B-flat minor:

It makes a very strange impression; one entirely loses a sense of key and follows the notes without any guide, up and down, to the point where the first chord of a piece broadens again, completely resolves the sense of uncertainty and gives back the feeling of the music. Besides this, the service takes place in the Sistine Chapel, where Michelangelo's "Prophets", and "Sibyls", and the "Last Judgement" are; the Pope sits on his throne, surrounded by all the Cardinals, each of whom has his own abbot, clad in a violet cloak, sitting at his feet. Crowds of monks and young priests kneel outside and the whole effect is extraordinarily solemn and impressive. The first time, they sang a Dies Irae by Baini, then one by

Pittoni; in the San Carlo they performed a Mass by Palestrina and in the Sistine Chapel a motet by Allegri. Incidentally, I had an opportunity to sing something by Palestrina with one of the papal choristers—actually the leading tenor—from his notes, and I may say I read it better than he; his attacks were very uncertain. Now we are going to have a Requiem every day for the deceased Pope, and I am not going to miss one of them.

The enclosed letter is from Abbot Santini [1] who owns a remarkable music library. He has had several of his scores copied and daintily bound for you and is just waiting for an opportunity to send them. It is he who translated the "Death of Jesus",[2] and he is preparing the performance of the work in Naples. He had a letter from there telling him: "Tutti i nostri dilettanti non vogliono udire adesso che musica di Graun e di Haendel; tanto è vero, che il vero bello non si puo perder mai." [3] He intends to introduce more German music, and to this end he is translating into Latin your motet "Man Liveth", and Johann Sebastian Bach's "Sing a New Song unto the Lord", and Haendel's "Judas Maccabeus" into Italian. He is graciousness itself, and a most lovable old gentleman. If you could occasionally see that he gets some German music, you would make him very happy; all his thoughts and wishes are concentrated on introducing German church music to Italy, but at present he owns only Sebastian Bach's "Magnificat" and such motets as are printed; and Graun's "Te Deum" and "Passion". I believe he is in touch with Trautwein, at least he has sent him a number of things, and he is awaiting daily, and with impatience, the arrival of Sebastian Bach's "Passion".

Next time I will tell you about my personal acquaintance with Baini and others from the Papal Chapel, as well as about their compositions; also about the singing of the nuns, the organs, other

---

1. *Abbot Fortunato Santini (1778-1862), Italian ecclesiastic composer.*
2. *Famous oratorio of the German composer Karl Heinrich Graun (1703-1759).*
3. *"All our amateurs now wish to hear only music of Graun and Haendel; truly, the genuinely beautiful cannot be lost".*

church music, etc. And there is much that is amusing to tell you about the theatres, the orchestra and the musical parties. But now I am called away by the ringing of bells and the subdued beat of drums outside. The air is balmy, the sun is shining and I am writing at the open window. Farewell, and remember in friendship your devoted

F. M. B

TO HIS FATHER

Rome, December 10, 1830.

Dear Father,

It is a year this very day since we kept your birthday at Hensel's, and so now let me give you some account of Rome, as I did at that time of London. I intend to finish my overture to the "Einsame Insel" [1] as a present to you, and if I write under it December 11th, I shall feel, when I take up the sheets, as if I were about to place them in your hands. You would probably say that you could not read them, but still I should have offered you the best it was in my power to give; and though I desire to do this every day, still there is a peculiar feeling connected with a birthday. Would I were with you! I need not offer you my good wishes, for you know them all already, and the deep interest I, and all of us, take in your happiness and welfare, and that we cannot wish any good for you that is not reflected doubly on ourselves. Today is a holiday. I rejoice in thinking how cheerful you are at home; and when I repeat to you how happily I live here, I feel as if this were also a felicitation. For me, a period like this, when serious thought and enjoyment are

1. *Afterwards published under the name of "Overture to the Hebrides".*

combined, is genuinely stimulating and altogether does me good. Every time I enter my room I rejoice that I am not obliged to pursue my journey on the following day—that I may quietly postpone many things till the morrow—and that I am in Rome!

Up to now, everything that passed through my brain was immediately swept away by fresh ideas, and every impression was crowded out by another, while here they all have a chance to develop. I never remember having worked with so much zeal; and if I am to complete everything that I have planned, I will have to work at it all winter long. It is true that I am deprived of the great delight of showing my finished compositions to one who could take pleasure in them, and enter into them along with me; but that very fact drives me back to my labours, which please me most when I am fairly in the midst of them. And now this has to be combined with the various solemnities and festivals of every kind which will supplant my work for a few days. But as I have resolved to see and to enjoy all I possibly can, I will not allow my work to hinder me, but will return with fresh zeal to my composing.

This is a truly glorious life! My health is excellent, only the hot wind, called here the sirocco, is a strain on my nerves, and I find I must beware of playing the piano much, or at night; but it is easy for me to refrain for a few days, as for some weeks I had to play almost every evening. Bunsen, who is always warning me against playing if I find it is not good for me, gave a large party yesterday where, after all that, I was obliged to play. But it was a pleasure, because as a result, I made a number of new acquaintances, and because Thorwaldsen, in particular, spoke of me in so gratifying a manner that I felt quite proud, for I honour him as one of the greatest of men, and have always revered him. He is a man like a lion, and the very sight of his face is invigorating. One knows at once that he must be a fine artist; his eyes look so clear, as if with him everything must assume a definite form and image. Moreover he is very gentle, and kind, and mild, because his nature is so superior; and yet I believe that he can enjoy every trifle. It is a source of genuine satisfaction to see a great man, and to know that the creator of works that will endure for ever stands before you in person, and is a man like others.

. . . It always makes me furious when men who have no pursuit presume to judge others who wish to achieve something, however small. I therefore took the liberty recently of rebuking a certain musician in society here. He began to speak of Mozart, and as Bunsen and his sister love Palestrina, he tried to flatter their tastes by asking me, for instance, what I thought of the worthy Mozart, and all his sins. I replied, however, that as far as I was concerned, I should be only too happy to renounce all my virtues in exchange for Mozart's sins; but that of course I could not venture to determine the extent of his virtues. The people all laughed, and were much amused. To think that such a person should have no awe of so great a name!

It is some consolation, however, that it is the same with all the arts, as the painters here are quite as bad. They are formidable to look at, sitting in their Café Greco. I scarcely ever go there, for I have such a horror both of them and their favourite resort. It is a small dark room, about eight feet square, where on one side you may smoke, but not on the other; so they sit around on benches, with their broadbrimmed hats on their heads, and their huge mastiffs beside them; their cheeks and throats, in fact the whole of their faces, covered with hair, puffing forth clouds of smoke (only on one side of the room), and saying rude things to each other, while the mastiffs see to the spreading of vermin. A neckcloth or a proper coat would be innovations. Any part of the face visible through the beard is hidden by spectacles; so they drink coffee, and speak of Titian and Pordenone, just as if they were sitting beside them, and also wore beards and wide-awakes! Moreover, they paint such sickly Madonnas and feeble saints, and such milksop heroes, that I feel the strongest inclination to hit out. These judges of Hades do not even shrink from discussing Titian's picture in the Vatican, about which you asked me; they say that it has neither subject nor meaning; yet it never seems to occur to them that a master, who has worked so long on a picture with love and devotion, must have had quite as much insight into the subject as they are likely to have, even with their coloured spectacles. If, in the course of my life, I never achieve anything else, I am at all events determined to be unutterably rude to all those who show no reverence for their masters, and then I shall have performed at least one good work. But there they stand, and see all the splendour of those creations for which they haven't an iota of comprehension, and yet dare to criticise them.

. . . I have this moment received your letter of the 27th, and am pleased to find that I have already answered many of your questions. There is no hurry about the letters I asked for, as I have now made almost more acquaintances than I wish; besides, late hours and so much playing do not suit me in Rome, so I can await the arrival of these letters very patiently; it was not so at the time I urged you to send them. I cannot, however, understand what you mean by your allusion to coteries which I ought to have outgrown, for I know that I, and all of us, invariably dreaded and detested what is usually meant by that, namely, a frivolous, exclusive circle of society, clinging to empty outward forms. Among persons, however, who see each other daily, without their interest undergoing any change, who have no sympathy with public life (and this is certainly the case in Berlin, with the exception of the theatre), it is only natural that they should develop a gay, cheerful, and original mode of treating passing events, and that this should give rise to a peculiar, and perhaps monotonous style of conversation. But this by no means constitutes a coterie. I feel convinced that I shall never belong to one, whether I am in Rome or Wittenberg. I am glad that the last words I was writing when your letter arrived, chanced to be that in Berlin you must take refuge in society from your surroundings; thus proving that I had no spirit of coterie, which invariably estranges men from one another. I should deeply regret your observing anything of the kind in me or in any of us, for more than a passing moment. Forgive me, my dear father, for defending myself so warmly, but this word is most repugnant to my feelings, and you say in your letters that I am always to speak right out what is on my mind, so pray do not take this amiss.

I was in St. Peter's today, where the grand solemnities called the absolutions have begun for the Pope, and which last until Tuesday, when the Cardinals assemble in conclave. The building surpasses all powers of conception. It appears to me like some great work of nature, a forest, a mass of rocks, or something similar; for I always lose the realisation that it is the work of man. You think of looking at the ceiling as little as you would at the sky. You lose your way in St. Peter's, you take a walk in it, and ramble till you are quite tired; when divine service is performed and chanted there, you are not aware of it till you come quite close. The angels in the baptistry are monstrous giants; the doves, colossal birds of prey; you lose all idea of measurement with the eye, or of proportion; and yet who does not feel his heart expand when standing under the dome and gazing up at it? At present a monstrous catafalque has been erected in the nave in this shape.[1] The coffin is placed in the centre under the pillars; the thing is totally devoid of taste, and yet it has a wondrous effect. The upper circle is thickly studded with lights, so are all the ornaments; the lower circle is lighted in the same way, and over the coffin hangs a burning lamp, and innumerable lights are blazing under the statues. The whole structure is more than a hundred feet high, and stands exactly opposite the entrance. The guards of honour, and the Swiss, march about in the quadrangle; in every corner sits a Cardinal in deep mourning, attended by his servants, who hold large burning torches, and then the singing commences with responses, in the simple and monotonous tone you no doubt remember. It is

1. *A little sketch of the catafalque was enclosed in the letter.*

the only occasion on which there is any singing in the middle of the church, and the effect is wonderful.

. . . I have just received your letter, which brings me word of Goethe's illness. What I feel personally at this news I cannot express. The whole evening his words, "I must try to keep all right till your return", have sounded continually in my ears, to the exclusion of every other thought: when he is gone, Germany will assume a very different aspect for artists. I have never thought of Germany without heartfelt joy and pride in the fact that Goethe lived there; and the rising generation seems for the most part so weak and feeble that it makes my heart sink within me. He is the last, and with him closes a happy, prosperous period for us! This year ends with frightening solemnity.

TO CARL FRIEDRICH ZELTER

Rome, December 18, 1830.

Dear Professor Zelter!

May this letter bring you my best wishes for your birthday, for Christmas and for the New Year at the same time. You know that my thoughts are always with you, and so are my hopes for your cheer and happiness. I will say no more at this time; at the close of such an eventful and solemn year one is almost afraid to write a letter which will take weeks to reach its destination, when so many things can have changed in the meantime! I prefer to send you some music which cannot change before it gets into your hands; will you please give it a kind welcome. It is a chorale which I composed in Venice. I would much rather have sent you some-

thing from my new works because there is much better stuff in them. But they would have been too bulky, and I decided to limit myself to two sheets only. Moreover, you mentioned once that the Academy as well as yourself deplored that no music was being composed for four parts, only for nothing less than double choirs or eight parts. As this piece conforms more or less to the form you spoke of and insofar, perhaps, corresponds to your wishes, I have copied it out for you. If you think it deserves to be performed at the Academy, I would, of course, be only too delighted. In any case, I beg you to write me fully about it, and also—as I have the score here—to indicate the measures and the bars of which you approve; I am uncertain about several places and would have altered them if new work had not piled up here.

Besides this I have completed an Ave Maria, a Lutheran chorale for eight parts, a capella, one psalm, "Non nobis, Domine", a German chorale, "O Haupt voll Blut und Wunden" for choir and orchestra, and finally an overture for orchestra. In your last letter you seemed to be anxious lest, following my predilection for one of the great masters, I might devote myself too much to church music and be led into imitation. Such, however, is certainly not the case; for I believe that nowhere can one so swiftly outgrow the belief in the mere name as here, nor, on the other hand, feel a deeper reverence and esteem for what has been accomplished. What we know and revere is strange and unknown here; one almost admits that things must be that way. And then one finds immortal monuments which have come to light after centuries, without the possibility of discovering the names of their creators. So that nothing is valid except what has sprung from the deepest faith of the innermost soul. And though the aesthetes and scholars struggle to prove why this is beautiful and that less so, by means of purely external qualities like epochs, style, and whatever else their pigeon holes may be called, I believe that that is the only immutable criterion for architecture, painting, music, and everything else. If the object alone has not inspired creation, it will never speak from "heart to heart", and imitation is then nothing but the most superficial product of the most alien thoughts. Naturally, nobody can forbid me to enjoy the inheritance left by the great masters nor to continue to work at it, because not everybody has to begin at the beginning. But then it must be continued creation according to one's ability, and not a lifeless repetition of what is already there. And nowhere is it more wonderfully clear than in Rome that every genuinely personal and sincere work will find its appropriate place, however long it may take. And that is the thread to which I cling through the maze of the rich museums, galleries, and other beauties. Everything new that I see each day (for I still make a practice of becoming acquainted with at least one new object every day) confirms me in this opinion. So I know beforehand just what impression I will have, and it is a pleasant sensation to find what you expect and be surprised at the same time.

The Cardinals are now in conclave, the ceremonies have come to a close, and I have listened daily to the Papal Choir. There again it struck me particularly how extraordinary everything is here. They did not sing particularly well, the compositions were poor, the congregation was not devout, and yet the whole effect was heavenly. This was only due to the fact that they were singing in the central nave of St. Peter's; the sounds are reflected from above and from every corner, they mingle, die away, and produce the most wonderful music. One chord melts into the other, and what no musician would dare, St. Peter's Church achieves. Here again it is the same as with everything else in this place; they may do as they like, build the most execrable houses, plant gardens in the worst taste, perform mediocre music; nature and the past are so rich that everything becomes beautiful and admirable. But therefore everything depends upon them, and if one cannot supply what is necessary for the present one's self, then certainly one finds much to be desired at every turn. When I see the young musicians wandering around here and complaining that there is nothing for them to gain musically, and that they had expected something quite different, and however their litany continues, I always want to rub their noses on the capital of a column, for that is where they will find music.

What do I care that the wretched bassoonist squeaks in the orchestra, or that the Italians do not genuinely enjoy either painting or music, or anything else? I enjoy them quite enough myself, and there are more divine things here than one can grasp in a lifetime. And so the bad music disturbs me very little; though for the sake of truth I must confess that it is really bad.

So with one thing and another the winter is quietly slipping away; for today I saw oranges hanging in the sun. And since I told you about the serious aspect of Roman life, I must not suppress the fact that the day before yesterday I went to a great ball and did more dancing and had more fun than ever before in my life.

So I am enjoying the most wonderful combination of gaiety and seriousness, such as can be found only in Rome. Remember me affectionately to your family. Farewell and be as happy as I wish you to be.

Your devoted

Felix.

FROM LETTERS TO HIS FAMILY

Rome, January 17, 1831.

For a week past we have had the loveliest spring weather. Young girls are carrying about nosegays of violets and anemones, which they gather early in the morning at the Villa Pamfili. The streets and squares swarm with gaily attired pedestrians; the Ave Maria has already been advanced twenty minutes—but what has become of the winter? Some little time ago it reminded me again of my work, to which I now mean to apply myself steadily, for I own that during the gay social life of the previous weeks, I rather neglected it. I have nearly completed the arrangement of "Solomon", and also my Christmas anthem, which consists of five numbers; the two symphonies also begin to assume a more definite form, and I particularly wish to finish them here. Probably I shall be able to accomplish this during Lent, when parties cease (especially balls) and spring begins. Then I shall have both time and inclination to compose, in which case I hope to have a good store of new works. Any performance of them here is quite out of the question. The orchestras are worse than anyone could believe; both musicians, and the right feeling for music, are wanting. The few violinists play according to their individual tastes, and make their entrances as and when they please; the wind instruments are tuned either too high or too low; and they execute flourishes like those we are accustomed to hear in farm-yards, but hardly as good; in short, altogether they make a tin-pan orchestra, and this applies even to compositions with which they are familiar.

The question is, whether all this could be radically reformed by introducing other people into the orchestra, by teaching the musicians to count time, and by instructing them in the first principles. I think, in that case, the people would no doubt take pleasure in it; as long as this is not done, however, no improvement can be hoped for, and everyone seems so indifferent about it that there is not the slightest prospect of such a thing. I heard a flute solo in which the flute was more than a quarter of a tone too high; it set my teeth on edge, but no one noticed it, and as there was a trill at the end they applauded mechanically. If it were even a shade better with regard to singing! The great singers have left the country. Lablache, David, Lalande, Pisaroni, etc., sing in Paris, and the minor ones who remain, copy their inspired moments, which they caricature in the most insupportable manner.

We in Germany may perhaps wish to accomplish something

false or impossible, but it is, and always will be, quite dissimilar. Just as, to me, a Cicisbeo will always be something mean and low, so will Italian music. I may be too obtuse to appreciate either; but that isn't the point. Recently in the filharmonica, after all the Pacini and Bellini, Cavaliere Ricci asked me to accompany him in "Non più andrai"; the very first notes showed how fundamentally different and worlds apart they were from everything else. I realised then, perfectly clearly, that the gap can never be bridged as long as there are such blue skies and delightful winters here as these. By the same token, the Swiss cannot paint beautiful scenery, precisely because they have it the whole day before their eyes. "Les Allemands traitent la musique comme une affaire d'état," says Spontini, and I accept the dictum. I recently heard some musicians here talking of their composers, and I listened in silence. One quoted H, but the others interrupted him, saying he could not be considered an Italian, for the German school still clung to him and he had never been able to get rid of it; consequently he had never been at home in Italy. We Germans say precisely the reverse of him, and it must be not a little trying to find yourself so entre deux, without any fatherland. As far as I am concerned I stick to my own colours, which are quite honourable enough for me.

Night before last a theatre that Torlonia has taken over and organised, was opened with a new opera of Pacini's. There was a great crowd, and every box was filled with handsome, well-dressed people; young Torlonia appeared in a stage-box with his mother, the old Duchess, and they were both immensely applauded. The audience called out "Bravo, Torlonia, thank you, thank you!" Opposite to him was Jerome, with his suite, and covered with orders; in the next box Countess Samoilow, etc. Over the orchestra is a picture of Time pointing to the dial of the clock, which revolves slowly, and is enough to make anyone melancholy. Pacini then appeared at the piano, and was greeted. He had prepared no overture, so the opera began with a chorus, accompanied by strokes on an anvil tuned in the proper key. The Corsair came forward, sang his aria, and was applauded, on which the Corsair above, and the Maestro below, bowed (this pirate is a contralto, and sung by Mademoiselle Mariani); a variety of airs followed, and the piece became very tiresome. This seemed to be the opinion of the public also, for when Pacini's grand finale began, the whole pit stood up, talking to each other as loudly as they could, laughing and turning their backs on the stage. Madame Samoilow fainted in her box, and was carried out. Pacini disappeared from the piano, and at the end of the act, the curtain fell amid great tumult. Then came the grand ballet of Barbe Bleue, followed by the last act of the opera. As the audience were now in a mood for it, they hissed the whole ballet from the beginning, and accompanied the second act of the opera also with hooting and laughter. At the close Torlonia was called for, but he would not appear.

This is the matter-of-fact narrative of a first performance at the opening of a theatre in Rome. I had anticipated much amusement, so I came away considerably out of humour. Nevertheless, if the music had made a furore, I should have been very indignant, for it is so wretched that it is really beneath all criticism. But that they should turn their backs on their favourite Pacini, whom they wished to crown in the Capitol, that they should parody his melodies, and sing them in a ludicrous style, this does, I confess, provoke me not a little, and is likewise a proof of how low such a musician stands in public opinion. Some other time they will carry him home on their shoulders; but that is no compensation. They would not treat Boiëldieu like this in France; quite apart from all love of art, a sense of propriety would prevent them. But enough of this subject, it is too depressing.

Why should Italy still insist on being the land of art, while in reality it is the land of nature, and so delights every heart! I have already described to you my walks to the Monte Pincio. I continue them daily. I went lately with the Vollards to Ponte Nomentano, a solitary dilapidated bridge in the spacious green Campagna. Many ruins from the days of ancient Rome, and many watch-

towers from the Middle Ages, are scattered over this long succession of meadows; chains of hills rise toward the horizon, now partially covered with snow and fantastically varied in form and colour by the shadows of the clouds. And there is also the enchanting, vapoury vision of the Alban Hills, which change like a chameleon, as you gaze at them—where for miles you can see little white chapels glittering on the dark ground of the hills, up to the Passionist Convent on the summit—from which you can trace the road winding through thickets, and the hills sloping downwards to the Lake of Albano, with a hermitage peeping through the trees. The distance is equal to that from Berlin to Potsdam, say I, as a good Berliner; but that it is a lovely vision, I say in earnest. No lack of music there; it echoes and vibrates on every side; not in the vapid, tasteless theatres. So we rambled about, chasing each other in the Campagna, and jumping over the fences; and when the sun went down we drove home, feeling so weary, and yet as self-satisfied and pleased, as if we had done great things; and so we have, if we properly appreciated it.

I have taken up sketching again, and have even begun to paint, because I would like to be able to recall some of the play of colours, and practice quickens the perceptions. I must now tell you, dear mother, of a great, a very great pleasure I recently enjoyed, because you will enjoy it with me. Two days ago I was at a small party at Horace Vernet's for the first time, and played there. He had previously told me that "Don Juan" was his real favourite in music, and that he especially loved the duel scene and the Commendatore at the end. I highly approved of such sentiments on his part, so while playing a prelude to Weber's Concert-Stück, I imperceptibly glided further into extemporising. Thinking I would please him by taking these themes, I worked them up enthusiastically for some time. This delighted him to a degree that I have rarely seen achieved by my music, and we at once became more intimate. Afterwards he suddenly came up to me and whispered that we must make an exchange, for he could also improvise; and when I was naturally curious to know what he meant, he said it was his secret. He is like a small child, however, and could not conceal it for more than a quarter of an hour. Then he came in again, and taking me into the next room, asked if I had any time to spare, as he had stretched and prepared a canvas, and wanted to paint my portrait, which I was to keep in memory of this day, either roll it up and send it to you, or take it with me, just as I chose. He said he would have no easy task with his improvisation, but at all events he would attempt it. I was only too glad to say yes, and cannot tell you how pleased I was with the delight and enthusiasm he evidently felt for my playing.

It was in every respect a happy evening; as I ascended the hill with him, everything was so still and peaceful, and only one window was lighted up in the large dark villa. Fragments of music floated on the air, and its echoes in the dark night, mingled with the murmuring of fountains, were sweeter than I can describe. Two young students were drilling in the anteroom, while the third acted the part of lieutenant, and commanded in good form. In another room my friend Montfort, who won the prize for music in the Conservatory, was seated at a piano, and others were standing round, singing a chorus; but it went very badly. They urged another young man to join them, and when he said that he did not know how to sing, his friend rejoined, "Qu'est-ce que ça fait? c'est toujours une voix de plus!" I helped them as best I could, and we had a very good time. Afterwards we danced, and I wish you could have seen Louisa Vernet dancing the Saltarella with her father. When at length she was forced to stop for a few moments, she snatched up a tambourine, playing with spirit, and relieving us, who really could scarcely move our hands any longer. I wished I had been a painter, for what a superb picture she would have made! Her mother is the kindest creature in the world, and the grandfather, Charles Vernet (who paints such splendid horses), danced a quadrille the same evening with so much ease, making so many entrechats, and varying his steps so gracefully, that it is a great pity he should actually be seventy-two years old. Every day he rides and tires out two horses, then he paints and draws a little, and spends the evening in society.

In my next letter I must tell you of my acquaintance with Robert, who has just finished an admirable picture, "The Harvest", and also describe my recent visits with Bunsen to the studios of Cornelius, Koch, Overbeck, etc. My time is fully occupied, for there is plenty to do and see; unluckily I cannot make time elastic, however much I may try to extend it. I have as yet said nothing of Raphael's portrait as a child, and Titian's "Nymphs Bathing", who, piquantly enough, are designated "Sacred and Profane Love", one being in full gala costume, while the other is devoid of all drapery; or of my exquisite "Madonna di Foligno", or of Francesco Francia, the most guileless and devout painter in the world; or of poor Guido Reni, whom the bearded painters of the present day treat with such contempt, and yet he painted a certain Aurora, and many other splendid objects besides; but what avails description? It is well for me that I can revel in the sight of them. When we meet, I may perhaps be able to give you a better idea of them.

Your

Felix.

Rome, February 8, 1831.

The Pope is elected; the Pope is crowned. He performed mass in St. Peter's on Sunday, and conferred his benediction; in the evening both the dome and the girandole were lighted up; the carnival began on Saturday, and pursues its headlong course in the most motley forms. The city has been illuminated every evening. Last night there was a ball at the French Embassy; today the Spanish ambassador gives his grand entertainment. Next door to me they sell confetti, and shout! And now I might as well stop, for why attempt to describe what is, in fact, indescribable? You must make

Hensel tell you all about these wonderful festivals; their pomp, brilliance, and animation surpass anything, and my sober pen is not equal to the task. What a different aspect everything has assumed during the last eight days, for now the mildest and warmest sun is shining, and we remain on the balcony enjoying the air till after sunset. Oh, that I could enclose in this letter only one quarter of an hour of all this pleasure, or convey to you how life actually flies in Rome, every minute bringing its own memorable delights! Giving festivals here is an easy matter; they have only to illuminate the simple architectural outlines and the dome of St. Peter's burns in the dark violet air, glowing quite still. If there are fireworks, they brighten the gloomy solid walls of the Castle of St. Angelo, and fall into the Tiber; when they commence their fantastic festivals in February, the most brilliant sun shines down on them and beautifies everything. It is an incredible land.

But I must tell you how I came to spend my birthday so differently from the way I expected. But I must be brief, for in an hour I go to join the carnival in the Corso. My birthday had three celebrations—the eve, the birthday itself, and the day after. On the second of February, Santini was sitting in my room in the morning, and in answer to my impatient questions about the Conclave, he replied with a diplomatic air, that there was little chance of a pope being elected before Easter. Mr. Brisbane also called, and told me that after leaving Berlin, he had been in Constantinople, and Smyrna, etc., and inquired after all his acquaintances in Berlin, when suddenly the report of a cannon was heard, and then another, and the people began to rush across the Piazza di Spagna, shouting with all their might. We three scattered, heaven knows how, and arrived breathlessly at the Quirinal, just in time to see the man leaving the unbricked window through which he had shouted—"Annuncio vobis gaudium magnum; habemus Papam R. E. dominum Capellari, qui nomen assumsit Gregorius XVI". All the Cardinals now crowded onto the balcony, breathed the fresh air, and laughed together. It was the first time they had been in the open air for fifty days, and they looked so gay, their red caps shining brightly in the sun. The whole piazza was filled with people, who clambered onto the obelisk, and on the horses of Phidias, and the statues projected far above in the air. Carriage after carriage drove up, amid jostling and shouting. Then the new Pope appeared, and before him was borne the golden cross, and he blessed the crowd for the first time, while the people at the same moment prayed and cried "Hurrah!" All the bells in Rome were ringing, and there was firing of cannons, and flourishes of trumpets, and military music. This was the eve of my birthday.

Next morning I followed the crowd down the long street to the Piazza of St. Peter's, which looked finer than I had ever seen it, bright in the sunshine and swarming with carriages; the Cardinals in their red coaches, driving in state to the sacristy, with servants in embroidered liveries, and innumerable people of every rank, nation, and condition; and high above them the dome and the church, seeming to float in blue vapour, for there was considerable mist in the morning air. And I thought that Capellari would probably appropriate all this to himself when he saw it; but I knew better. It was all to celebrate my birthday; and the election of the Pope, and the homage, were simply a spectacle in honour of me; but it was well and naturally performed and as long as I live, I shall never forget it.

The Church of St. Peter's was crowded to the doors. The Pope with his fans of peacocks' feathers carried before him was borne in, and set down on the high altar, and the papal singers intoned, "Tu es sacerdos magnus". I only heard two or three chords, but that was sufficient; just the sound. Then came one Cardinal after the other and kissed the Pope's foot and his hands, and he in turn embraced them. When one has watched this for a while, standing in a crowd so squeezed that one cannot move, and then suddenly looks up at the dome, as far up as the lantern, it gives one a strange feeling. I stood with Mr. Diodati, in a throng of Capuchins. These saintly men are far from being devotional on an occasion of this kind, and by no means cleanly. But I must hurry; the carnival is beginning, and I must not miss any of it.

At night (in honour of my birthday) barrels of pitch were burned in all the streets, and the Propaganda (building of the Society of the Propagation of the Faith) illuminated. The people thought this was owing to its being the former residence of the Pope, but I knew it was because I lived exactly opposite, and I had only to lean out of my window to enjoy it all. Then came Torlonia's ball, and in every corner were seen glimpses of red caps above, and red stockings below.

The following day they worked very hard at scaffoldings, platforms, and stages for the carnival; edicts were posted up about horse-racing, and samples of masks were displayed at the windows, and (in celebration of the day following my birthday) the illumination of the dome, and the girandole were fixed for Sunday. On Saturday all the world went to the Capitol to see the ritual of the Jews' supplication to be suffered to remain in the Sacred City for another year; a request which is refused at the foot of the hill, but after repeated entreaties, granted on the summit, and the Ghetto is assigned to them. It was very boring; we waited two hours, and after all, understood the oration of the Jews as little as the answer of the Christians. I came down again in very bad humour, and thought that the carnival had commenced unpropitiously. So I arrived in the Corso and was driving along, not even thinking, when I was suddenly assailed by a shower of sugar comfits. I looked up; they had been flung by some young ladies whom I had seen occasionally at balls, but scarcely knew, and when in my embarrassment I took off my hat to bow to them, the pelting began in good earnest. Their carriage drove on, and in the next was Miss T, a delicate young Englishwoman. I tried to bow to her, but she pelted me too, so I became quite desperate, and clutch-

ing the confetti, I flung it back bravely; there were swarms of my acquaintances, and my blue coat was soon as white as that of a miller. The B.s were standing on a balcony, flinging confetti like hail at my head; and thus pelting and being pelted, amid a thousand jests and jeers, and the most extravagant masks, and the horse-races, the day came to an end.

The following day there was no carnival, but as compensation, the Pope conferred his benediction from the Loggia in St. Peter's Square; he was consecrated as Bishop in the Church, and at night the dome was lighted up. How the lighting of the building was changed in an instant, you must ask Hensel to paint or to describe, as he prefers. To me, especially, the sudden and surprising vision, of so many hundred human beings, previously invisible, and now climbing about and working in the air, was quite dizzying—and the glorious girandole! But who can picture it? Now the gaieties are recommencing. Farewell! in my next letter I mean to continue my description. Yesterday, at the carnival, flowers and bonbons were indiscriminately thrown, and a mask gave me a bouquet, which I have dried, and intend to bring home for you. All idea of work is out of the question at present; I have only composed one little song; but when Lent comes, I intend to be more industrious. Who can think either of writing or music at such a moment? I must go out, so farewell, dear ones.

FELIX.

Rome, February 22, 1831.

Listen and wonder! Since I left Vienna I have half composed Goethe's "First Walpurgis Night", and have not courage to write it down. The composition has now taken shape, and become a grand cantata, with full orchestra, and may turn out quite amusing, for at the beginning there are songs of spring, and plenty of other similar things. Then, when the watchmen with their pitchforks, pronged sticks and owls, make a noise, the witches come, and you know that I have a particular foible for them; the sacrificial Druids then appear—in C major—with trombones—after which the watchmen come in again in alarm, and here I mean to introduce a tripping, mysterious chorus; and lastly to conclude with a grand sacrificial hymn. Do you not think that this might develop into a new style of cantata? An instrumental introduction I have gratis, and the effect of the whole is very spirited. I hope it will soon be finished. I have once more begun to compose with fresh vigour, and the Italian symphony makes rapid progress; it will be the most amusing piece I have yet composed, especially the last movement. I have not yet decided on the adagio, and think I shall reserve it for Naples. "Verleih uns Frieden" is completed, and "Wir glauben all" will also be ready in a few days. The Scotch symphony alone is not yet quite to my liking; if any brilliant idea occurs to me, I will seize it at once, quickly write it down, and finish it fast.

Felix.

Rome, March 29, 1831.

In the midst of Holy Week. Tomorrow for the first time I am to hear the Miserere, and whilst you last Sunday were performing "The Passion", the Cardinals and all the priesthood here received beautiful plaited palms and olive-branches. The Stabat Mater of Palestrina was sung, and there was a grand procession. My work has got on badly during the last few days. Spring is in her bloom; there is a warm blue sky outdoors, such as we at most only dream of, and the journey to Naples in every thought; so the requisite quiet for writing is not to be found. C, who is otherwise a phlegmatic fellow, has written me an intoxicated letter from Naples! The most prosaic people wax poetic when they speak of it. The finest season of the year in Italy is from the 15th of April to the

15th of May. Who can wonder that I find it impossible to return to my Scottish, misty mood? I have therefore had to lay aside the Scotch symphony for the present, but hope to write out the "Walpurgis Night" here. I shall manage to do so if today and tomorrow are "good days", and if we have bad weather, for really a fine day is too great a temptation. The moment my work ceases to progress, I always hope to find some resource in the open air, so I go out but think of anything and everything except my work, and do nothing but wander about, and when the church bells begin to ring, it is already the Ave Maria. But all I want now is a short overture; if that occurs to me, the thing is complete, and I can write it out in a couple of days. Then I shall leave all notes and their requisite music-paper here, go off to Naples, where, please God, I mean to do nothing.

"Frühlingslied", song, written in 1830.
(Original manuscript, private collection.)

Rome, April 4, 1831.

Holy Week is over, and my passport to Naples obtained. My room begins to look empty, and the winter in Rome belongs among reminiscences. I intend to leave here in a few days, and my next letter (God willing) will be from Naples. Interesting and amusing as the winter in Rome has been, it has closed with a truly memorable week; for what I have seen and heard far surpassed my expectations, and being the conclusion, I will endeavour in this, my last letter from Rome, to give you a full description of it all. People have often both zealously praised and censured the ceremonies of Holy Week, and yet omitted, as is often the case, the chief point, namely a complete whole. My father will probably remember the description of Mlle. de R.—who after all only did what most people do who write or talk about music and art—when, in a hoarse and prosaic voice, she attempted at dinner to give us some idea of the fine, clear Papal Choir. Many others have taken just the music and then found fault with it, because the external adjuncts it requires to produce the full effect, were lacking. Those people may be in the right; still, so long as these indispensable externals are there, and especially in such perfection, just so long will it produce its effect. And the more convinced I am that place, time, order, and the vast crowd of human beings awaiting, in the most profound silence, the moment for the music to begin, contribute largely to the effect, the more odious I find it to have a part deliberately separated from what is indivisible, in order to depreciate it. That man must be unhappy, indeed, in whom the devotion and reverence of a vast assemblage did not arouse similar feelings of devotion and reverence, even if they were worshipping the Golden Calf; he alone may destroy this, who can replace it with something better.

Whether one person repeats it from another, whether it is owing to its great reputation or is merely due to imagination, is all *the same. It suffices that we have a perfect totality which has exercised the most powerful influence for centuries past, and still exercises it, and therefore I reverence it as I do every species of real perfection. I leave it to theologians to judge its religious influence, for the various opinions on that point are of no great value. There is more to it than the mere ceremonies; in order to win my respect, it is sufficient, as I have already said, for any project—whatever its sphere—to be carried out with fidelity and consciousness as far as ability will permit. Thus you must not expect from me a formal criticism of the singing, as to whether they intoned correctly or incorrectly, in tune or out of tune, or whether the compositions are good. I would rather try to show you that the affair as a whole makes a great impression, and that everything contributes to this end. And as, last week, I enjoyed music, formalities and ceremonies without dissecting them, but revelled in the perfect whole, so I do not intend to dissect them in this letter. The technical part, to which I naturally paid particular attention, I mean to detail to Zelter.*

The first ceremony was on Palm Sunday. The concourse of people was so great that I could not reach my usual place on what is called the Prelate's Bench, but was forced to stand among the Guard of Honour. There, although I had a good view of the solemnities, I could not follow the singing properly, as they pronounced the words very indistinctly, and on that day I still had no book. The result was that on this first day the various antiphonies, gospels, and psalms, and the custom of chanting which is followed here, made the most confused and singular impression on me. I had no clear conception of what rule was being followed in the various cadences. I took particular pains to discover that rule and succeeded so well, that at the end of Holy Week, I could have sung with them. Thus I also avoided the weariness, so universally complained of during the endless psalms before the Miserere; for I observed the variety in the monotony, and when perfectly certain of any particular cadence, I instantly wrote it down. So by degrees

I made out the melodies of eight psalms correctly. I also noted down the antiphonies, etc. and was thus constantly occupied and interested.

The first Sunday, however, as I have told you, I could not make it all out satisfactorily; I only knew that they sang the chorus, "Hosanna in Excelsis", and intoned various hymns, whilst twisted palms were offered to the Pope, which he distributed among the Cardinals. These palms are long staffs, decorated with many ornaments (buttons, crosses and crowns), all made entirely of dried palm leaves, which look like gold. The Cardinals, who are seated in the chapel in the form of a quadrangle, with the abbots at their feet, now advance, each in turn, to receive their palms, with which they return to their places. Then come the bishops, monks, abbots and the rest of the ecclesiastics, the papal singers, the knights, and others, who receive olive branches entwined with palm leaves. This makes a long procession, during which the choir continues to sing uninterruptedly. The abbots who have held the long palms of their Cardinals like sentinels' lances, lay them on the ground before them, and at this moment there is a brilliance of colour in the chapel such as I have never before seen at any ceremony. There were the Cardinals in their gold-embroidered robes and red caps, and the purple abbots in front of them with golden palms in their hands; then there were the gaudy servants of the Pope, the Greek priests and the Greek patriarchs in the most gorgeous attire; the Capuchins with long, white beards, and all the other monks; then, again, the Swiss in their popinjay uniforms, all carrying green olive branches; and all this time singing is going on. It is, of course, hardly possible to distinguish what is being sung; one just enjoys the sound.

Then they carry in the Pope's throne, on which he is elevated in all processions, and where I saw Pius VIII enthroned on the day of my arrival (vide the "Heliodorus" of Raphael's where he is portrayed). The Cardinals, two by two, with their palms, head the procession, and the folding doors of the chapel being thrown open, they slowly file through. The singing, which up to now has enveloped one like an element, becomes fainter and fainter, for the singers also walk in procession, and at length it is only heard softly from the distance. Then the choir in the chapel bursts forth very loudly with a query, to which the distant one responds, and so it goes on for a time, till the procession again draws near and the choirs reunite once more. Whatever they may be singing, it produces a marvellous effect; and though it is true that the hymns, sung in unison, are monotonous and even formless, that they are without any proper connection and are sung fortissimo throughout, I still base my appeal on the impression which the whole must make on everyone. After the procession, the gospel is chanted in the most singular tone, and is succeeded by the Mass. I must also mention my favourite moment, the Credo. The priest takes his place for the first time in the centre, before the altar, and after a short pause intones in his hoarse, old voice, the Credo of Sebastian Bach. When he has finished, the priests stand up, the Cardinals leave their seats and advance into the middle of the chapel, form a circle and all repeat the responses in loud voices, "Patrem omnipotentem", etc. The choir then chimes in, singing the same words. When I heard my well-known

for the first time, and all the grave monks around me began to recite in loud, eager tones, it gave me quite a start; this is the moment I still like best of all. After the ceremony, Santini made me a present of his olive branch, which I carried in my hand the whole day when I was walking about—for the weather was beautiful. The Stabat Mater, which succeeds the Credo, created the least effect. They sang it poorly, out of tune and abridged. The Singakademie does it infinitely better.

There was nothing on Monday or Tuesday; but on Wednesday,

at half-past four, vespers began. The psalms are sung in alternate verses by two choirs, although invariably by one class of voice, basses or tenors. For an hour and a half, therefore, nothing but the most monotonous music is heard; the psalms are only once interrupted by the lamentations, and this is the first moment when, after a long time, a full chord is heard. This chord is very softly intoned, and the whole piece is sung pianissimo, whilst the psalms are shouted as loudly as possible, and always on one note, on which the words are uttered with the utmost rapidity. A cadence occurs at the end of each verse, which defines the different characteristics of the various melodies. It is therefore not surprising that the mere softness of the sound in the first lamentation (in G major) should produce so touching an effect. Then it goes on again in a monotone. A wax light is extinguished at the end of each psalm, so that in the course of an hour and a half, the fifteen lights around the altar are all out. Six large-sized candles still burn in the vestibule high over the entrance. The whole strength of the choir with alti, soprani, etc. intone (fortissimo and in unison) a new melody, the "Canticum Zachariae", in D minor, singing it very slowly and solemnly in the twilight; the last remaining candles are then extinguished. The Pope leaves his throne and falls on his knees before the altar, and all around do the same, repeating a Paternoster sub silentio; that is, a pause follows, during which you know that each Catholic present is saying the Lord's Prayer, and immediately afterwards the Miserere begins pianissimo thus:

To me this is the most sublime moment of the whole ceremony. You can easily picture to yourself what follows, but not this commencement. The continuation, which is the Miserere by Allegri,

Neuchâtel, Switzerland.
Drawing by Mendelssohn, 1821.

Organ in the Church of the Holy Spirit in Heidelberg.
Drawing by Mendelssohn, 1826.

is a simple sequence of chords on which embellishments have been superimposed. This is either traditional or—what seems to me far more probable—the work of some clever maestro who had a few fine voices at his disposal, and in particular a very high soprano. These embellishments always recur on the same chords, and as they are cleverly devised and beautifully adapted to the voice, one always enjoys hearing them. I could not detect anything unearthly or mysterious in the music; indeed I am perfectly contented to have its beauty earthly and comprehensible. Again I refer you, dearest Fanny, to my letter to Zelter . . .

On Thursday, at nine o'clock in the morning, the solemnities recommenced, and lasted until one o'clock. There was High Mass and afterwards a procession. The Pope conferred his benediction from the loggia of the Quirinal, and washed the feet of thirteen priests, who are supposed to represent the pilgrims, and who were seated in a row, wearing white gowns and white caps, and who afterwards dined. The crowd of English ladies was extraordinary. I disliked the whole affair. The psalms began again in the afternoon and lasted this time until half past seven. Some portions of the Miserere were taken from Baini, but the greater part was from Allegri. It was almost dark in the chapel when the Miserere commenced. I clambered up a tall ladder standing there by chance, and so I had the whole chapel—crowded with people, and the kneeling Pope and his Cardinals, and the music—beneath me. It made a splendid effect. On Friday forenoon the chapel was stripped of all its decorations, and the Pope and Cardinals were in mourning. The history of the Passion, according to St. John and composed by Vittoria, was sung; then Palestrina's "Improperia", during which the Pope and all the others take off their shoes, advance to the cross and adore it. In the evening they did Baini's Miserere, which they sang infinitely the best.

Early on Saturday, in the baptistry of the Lateran, heathens, Jews and Mohammedans were baptised—all represented by a small child which kept wailing—and subsequently some young priests received their first consecration. On Sunday, the Pope himself performed High Mass in the Quirinal, and pronounced his benediction on the people, and then it was all over. Now it is Saturday, April 9th, and tomorrow, at the earliest hour, I will get into a carriage and set off for Naples, where a new beauty awaits me. You will perceive by the end of this letter that I am writing in haste. This is my last day and there is a great deal yet to be done. I will therefore not finish my letter to Zelter, but will send it off from Naples. My description has to be correct, and my approaching journey greatly distracts me. And so off to Naples! The weather is clearing up and the sun is shining for the first time in several days. My passport is ready, the carriage is ordered, and I am looking forward to the months of spring.

Farewell!

Felix.

TO HIS SISTERS

Naples, May 28, 1831.

My dear Sisters,

As my journal has become too thin and poor to send you, I must at least supply you with an abrégé of my story. Know, then, that on Friday, the 20th of May, we breakfasted in corpore in Naples, on fruit, etc.; this in corpore includes the travelling party to the islands, consisting of Ed. Bendemann, T. Hildebrand, Carl Sohn, and Felix Mendelssohn-Bartholdy.

My knapsack was not very heavy, for it contained nothing important but Goethe's poems, and three shirts. So we packed our-

selves into a hired carriage, and drove through the grotto of Posilippo to Pozzuoli. The road runs along the sea, and nothing can be gayer. That makes it all the more painful to witness the horrible crowd of cripples, blind men, beggars, and galley slaves, in short, wretches of every description who there await you, surrounded by the holiday aspect of nature.

I seated myself quietly on the mole and sketched, whilst the others plodded through the Temples of Serapis, the theatres, the hot springs and extinct volcanoes, which I had already seen to satiety on three occasions. Then, like youthful patriarchs or nomads, we collected all our goods and chattels, cloaks, knapsacks, books and portfolios on donkeys, and adding ourselves on the top, we made the tour of the Bay of Baiae to the Lake of Avernus, where you are obliged to buy fish for dinner; we crossed the hill to Cumae (vide Goethe's "Wanderer") and descended on Baiae, where we ate and rested. Then we looked at more ruined temples, ancient baths, and other things of the same kind, and thus evening had arrived before we crossed the bay . . .

I see by some newspapers my friends have sent me, that my name is not forgotten, and so I hope when I return to London to be able to work steadily, which I was previously unable to do, being forced to go to Italy. If they make any difficulty in Munich about my opera, or if I cannot get a libretto that I like, I shall compose an opera for London. I know that I could get a commission there, as soon as I choose. I am also bringing some new pieces with me for the Philharmonic, and so I shall have made good use of my time.

As my evenings here are at my own disposal, I read a little French and English. The "Barricades" and "Les Etats de Blois" particularly interested me, for whilst I read them I was moved with horror by a period which we have often heard extolled as a vigorous epoch and one which has too soon passed away. Though these books seem to me to have many faults, yet the delineation of the two opposite leaders is only too correct; both were weak, irresolute, miserable hypocrites, and one thanks God that the so highly-prized Middle Ages are gone never to return. Say nothing of this to any disciple of Hegel's, but it is true, nevertheless; and the more I read and think on the subject, the more I feel this to be true. Sterne has become a great favourite of mine. I remembered that Goethe once spoke to me of the "Sentimental Journey", and said that it was impossible for any one to give a better picture of what a stubborn and despondent object the human heart can be.

There are very few German books to be had here. I am therefore restricted to Goethe's poems, and, by God, there is enough food for thought in them, and they are eternally new. I feel especially interested in the poems which he evidently composed in or near Naples, such as "Alexis and Dora"; for I see daily from my window how this wonderful work originated. In fact, as is the case with every masterpiece, I often suddenly and involuntarily think that the very same ideas might have occurred to me on a similar occasion, and it seems as if it was only by chance that Goethe uttered them first.

With regard to the poem, "Gott segne dich, junge Frau", I even maintain that I have discovered its locality and dined with the woman herself; but of course she ought to have grown old by now, and the boy she was then nursing might have become a stalwart vine-dresser. Her house lies between Pozzuoli and Baiae, "eines Tempels Trümmern", and is fully three miles from Cumae. You may imagine how new, therefore, these poems seem, and how different and fresh the feeling with which I now regard and study them. I say nothing of Mignon's song at present. But it is just amazing that Goethe and Thorwaldsen are still living, that Beethoven died only a few years ago, and yet H. declares that German art is as dead as a rat. Quod non! So much the worse for him if he really feels thus; but when I reflect for a time on his conclusions, they appear to me very shallow. Apropos! Schadow, who returns to Duesseldorf in a few days, has promised to extract some new songs for me from Immermann, which gives me much cause for rejoicing. That man is a true poet; it is proved by his letters, and everything that he has written. Count Platen is a small, shrivelled, wheezing old man, with gold spectacles, yet not more than five-and-thirty! He quite scared me. The Greeks look very different! He abuses the Germans terribly, forgetting however that he does so in German. But I am getting too deep into gossip; so farewell for today.

Felix.

TO HIS PARENTS

Rome, June 6, 1831.

My dear Parents,

It is high time that I write you a sensible, methodical letter; I doubt whether any of those from Naples was worth much. It seemed as if the atmosphere there prevented everyone from thinking seriously. I, at least, very seldom succeeded in collecting my thoughts. Now, although I have been here only a few hours, that old Roman comfort and serene gravity, to which I alluded in my former letters from this place, have again taken possession of me. I cannot express how infinitely I prefer Rome to Naples. People say that Rome is dull, monotonous in colour, melancholy and solitary. It is certainly true that Naples is more like a great European city, livelier and more varied—more cosmopolitan. But I may tell you confidentially that I am beginning to feel a particular aversion to everything cosmopolitan. I dislike it as I dislike many-sidedness, in which, moreover, I begin to think I have not much faith. Anything that aspires to be distinguished and beautiful and great must be one-sided. But then this one-sidedness must be developed to a state of consummate perfection, and no one can deny that such is the case in Rome.

Naples seems to me too small to be called a great city with propriety . . . All the life and bustle are confined to two large thoroughfares: the Toledo and the coast from the harbour to the Chiaja. Naples does not, to my mind, fulfil the requirements of a centre of a great nation, as London does so consummately; and that is chiefly because she lacks people. For I cannot class the fishermen and lazzaroni among people; they are more like savages and their habitat is not Naples but the sea. The middle classes—tradesmen and workers—who form the basic population of the great towns, are quite subordinate, one might almost say that such a class does not exist there. It was this that so often prevented me from enjoying my stay in Naples. But as this lack of enjoyment persisted, I thought at last that it might be due to something within me. I cannot say that I was precisely unwell during the incessant sirocco, but it was more disagreeable than an indisposition which passes away in a few days. I felt languid, disinclined for everything serious—in fact, apathetic. I lounged about the streets all day with a long face, and would have preferred to stretch myself on the ground, without thinking, or wishing, or doing anything. Then it suddenly occurred to me that the principal classes in Naples really live in precisely that way; and that consequently the source of my depression did not originate in me, as I had feared, but in the whole combination of air, climate, etc. The atmosphere is suitable for a grandee who rises late, is never required to go out on foot, who never thinks (for this makes one hot), who sleeps away a couple of hours on a sofa in the afternoon, then eats his ice cream and drives to the theatre at night, where again he finds nothing to think about, but simply makes and receives calls. On the other hand, the climate is equally suitable for a fellow in a shirt, with naked legs and arms, and who likewise has no occasion to move about—who begs for a few grani when he has nothing left to live on and who takes his afternoon's siesta stretched on the ground, or on the quay, or on the stone pavement (the pedestrians step over him, or shove him aside if he lies right in the middle). He fetches his frutti di mare himself out of the sea, and sleeps wherever he may chance to find himself at night; in short, he spends every moment doing what he likes best, the same as an animal.

These are the two principal classes in Naples. By far the largest portion of the population of the Toledo there consists of gaily dressed ladies and gentlemen, or of husbands and wives driving together in handsome carriages, and of those olive sans-culottes who sometimes carry about fish for sale, bawling horribly, or carrying burdens when they have no money left. I believe there are few indeed who have any settled occupation, or follow any pursuit with zeal and perseverance, or who like work for the sake of working. Goethe says that the misfortune of the north is that people there always wish to be doing something, and striving for some end, and that he approves of an Italian who advised him not to think so much, for it would only give him a headache. But he must have been jesting; at all events, he did not act this way himself, but rather like a genuine northerner. If, however, he means that the difference in character is produced by nature, and due to her influence, then there is no doubt that he is right. I can see why this must be so, and why wolves howl; still it is not necessary to howl along with them. The proverb should be exactly reversed. Those who, owing to their positions, are obliged to work, and must consequently both think and bestir themselves, treat this situation as a necessary evil, which brings in money; and when they have it, they, too, live like the great—or the naked—gentlemen. Thus there is no shop where you are not cheated. Natives of Naples, who have been customers for many years, are obliged to bargain and to be as much on their guard as foreigners; and one of my acquaintances, who had dealt at the same shop for fifteen years, told me that during the whole of that period there had been invariably the same battle about a few scudi, and that nothing could stop it.

That is why there is so little industry and competition; and why Donizetti finishes an opera in ten days; it is sometimes hissed, but that does not matter, for he has been paid all the same, and he can go about amusing himself. But should his reputation eventually suffer, he would be forced to do real work, which might be disagreeable. That is why he sometimes spends three weeks on an opera, bestowing considerable pains on a couple of arias in it, so that they may please the public. Then he can afford to amuse himself once more, and once more write trash. Their painters, by the same token, paint the most incredibly bad pictures, pictures that are inferior even to their music. Their architects also erect buildings in the worst taste; among others, an imitation, on a small scale, of St. Peter's in Chinese style. But what does it matter? The pictures are brightly coloured, the music makes plenty of noise, the buildings give plenty of shade, and the Neapolitan grandees ask no more.

Now as my physical mood became similar to theirs, everything conspired to keep me idle, and to make me lounge about, and sleep. And yet I constantly said to myself that this was wrong; and strove to busy myself, and to work, but it was impossible. Hence arose the querulous tone of some of the letters I wrote you, and I could only escape from such a mood by rambling over the hills, where nature is so divinely beautiful that every man ought to feel grateful and cheerful. I did not neglect meeting musicians, and we had a great deal of music. But I actually cared little for their flattering encomiums.

Now however I am once more in old Rome, where life is very different. There are daily processions, for last week was the Corpus Domini; and just as I left the city during the closing celebration of Holy Week, so I now return to find it engaged in the same manner for Corpus Domini. It made a singular impression on me to see that in the interim the streets had assumed such an aspect of summer; on all sides booths with lemons and iced water, the people *in light dresses, the windows open, and the shutters closed. You sit at the doors of coffee-houses and eat ices in quantities; the Corso swarms with carriages, for people no longer walk much, and though in reality I miss no dear friends nor relatives, yet I felt quite moved when I once more saw the Piazza di Spagna, and the familiar names written up on the corners of the streets. I shall stay here for about a week, and then proceed northwards.*

The Infiorata is on Thursday, but it is not yet quite certain that it will take place, because there are some apprehensions of a revolution; but I have hopes. I mean to take advantage of this opportunity to see the hills once more, and then to set off for the north. Wish me a good journey, for I am on the eve of departure. It is a year this very day since I arrived in Munich, heard "Fidelio", and wrote to you. We have not met since. But, please God, it will not be so long again.

Felix.

TO CARL FRIEDRICH ZELTER

Rome, June 16, 1831.

Dear Professor,

It was my intention some time ago to write you a description of the music during Holy Week, but my journey to Naples intervened, and during my stay there, whilst most of my time was spent wandering among the mountains, and in gazing at the sea, I found no real leisure for writing; hence the delay for which I now apologise. Since then I have not heard a single note worth remembering;

in Naples the music is most inferior. From the last months, therefore, I have no musical reminiscences to send you, save those of Holy Week, which, however, made so indelible an impression that they will always be fresh in my memory. I have already described to my parents the effect of the ceremonies as a whole, and they probably sent you the letter.

It was fortunate that I resolved to listen to the various Offices with cool and close attention, for nonetheless, from the very first moment I felt sensations of reverence and piety. I consider such a mood indispensable for the reception of new ideas, and no portion of the general effect escaped me, although I took care to observe each separate detail.

The ceremonies commenced on Wednesday, at half-past four, with the antiphony "Zelus domus tuae". A little book containing the Offices for Holy Week explains the sense of all the solemnities. "Each Vesper contains three psalms, signifying that Christ died for the virgins, the wives, and the widows, and also symbolical of the three laws, the natural, the written, and the evangelical. The "Domine labia mea" and the "Deus in adjutorium" are not sung on this occasion, when the death of our Saviour and Master is deplored, as slain by the hands of wicked godless men. The fifteen lights represent the twelve apostles and the three Maries. (In this manner the book contains much curious information on this subject, so I mean to bring it along for you.) The psalms are chanted fortissimo by all the male voices of two choirs. Each verse is divided into two parts, like question and answer, or rather, classified into A and B; the first chorus sings A, and the second replies with B. All the words, except the last, are sung with extreme rapidity on one note, but on the last they make a short "melisma" which is different in the first and second verse. The whole psalm, with all its verses, is sung on this melody, or tono as they call it, and I wrote down seven of these toni, which were employed during the three days. You cannot conceive how tiresome and monotonous the *effect is, and how harshly and mechanically they chant through the psalms. The first tonus which they sang was*

Thus the whole forty-two verses of the psalm are sung in precisely the same manner; one half of the verse ending in G, A, G, the other in G, E, G. They sing with the accent of a number of men quarrelling violently, and it sounds as if they were shouting the same thing furiously at each other. The closing words of each psalm are chanted more slowly and impressively, a long triad being substituted for the "melisma" sung piano. For instance, this is the first:

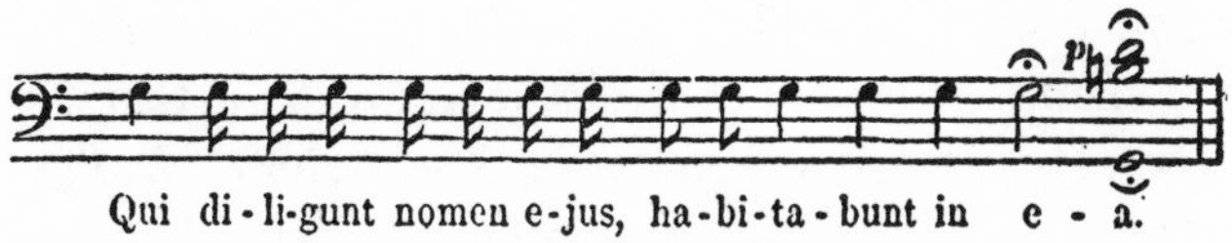

An antiphony, and sometimes more than one, serves as an introduction to each psalm. These are generally sung by two contralto voices, in canto fermo, in harsh, hard tones; the first half of each verse in the same style, and the second responded to by the chorus of male voices that I already described. I have kept the several antiphonies that I wrote down, that you may compare them with the book. On the afternoon of Wednesday, the 68th, 69th, and 70th psalms were sung. (By the bye, this division of the verses of the psalms sung in turns by each chorus is one of the innovations that Bunsen has introduced into the Evangelical Church here; he also ushers in each chorale by an antiphony composed by Georg—a musician who lives here—in the styles of canti fermi, first sung

by a few voices, joined by a chorale, such as "Ein' feste Burg ist unser Gott".) After the 70th psalm comes a paternoster sub silentio—that is, all present stand up, and there is a short silent pause.

Then the first Lamentation of Jeremiah commences, sung in a low subdued tone, a solemn and fine composition of Palestrina's in the key of G major. When it follows the frightful uproar of the psalms, and is sung without basses—only by high sopranos and tenors—with the most delicate swelling, subsiding and occasional dying away, and each tone and chord slowly blends into the succeeding one, the effect is truly heavenly. It is rather unfortunate, however, that those very parts which they sing with the deepest emotion and reverence, and which have evidently been composed with peculiar fervour, should chance to be merely the titles of the chapter or verse, aleph, beth, gimel, etc., and that the beautiful opening, which sounds as if it came direct from Heaven, should be precisely on the words, "Incipit Lamentatio Jeremiae Prophetae Lectio I". This must be not a little repulsive to a Protestant heart, and if there should be any design to introduce a similar mode of chanting into our churches, it seems to me that this will always be a stumbling-block; for any one who sings "chapter first" cannot possibly feel any pious emotions, however beautiful the music may be.

Indeed my little book says, "Vedendo profetizzato il crocifiggimento con gran pietà, si cantano eziandio molto lamentevolmente aleph, e le altre simili parole, che sono le lettere dell' alfabeto Ebreo, perchè erano in costume di porsi in ogni canzone in luogo di lamento, come è questa. Ciascuna lettera ha in se, tutto il sentimento di quel versetto che la segue, ed è come un argomento di esso"; [1] but this does not help much. After this, the 71st, 72nd, and

1. *After the crucifixion is announced, with great devotion, the word "Aleph" and other similar words which represent the letters of the Hebrew alphabet are sung in a very sorrowful mood, because it has been the ancient custom to use these instead of lamentations in each such chant. Each letter is itself charged with all the sentiment of the verse which follows it, and figures as its argument.*

73rd psalms are sung in the same manner, with their antiphonies. These are apportioned arbitrarily to the various voices. The soprano begins, "In monte Oliveti", on which the bass voices join in forte, "Oravit ad Patrem: Pater", etc. Then follow the lessons from the treatise of Saint Augustine on the psalms. The strange manner in which these are chanted appeared to me most extraordinary when I heard them for the first time on Palm Sunday, without knowing what it meant. A solitary voice is heard reciting on one note, not as in the psalms, but very slowly and impressively, making the tone ring out clearly.

There are different cadences employed for the different punctuation of the words, to represent a comma, interrogation, and full stop. Perhaps you are already acquainted with these. To me they were a novelty, and seemed very singular. The first, for example, was chanted by a beautiful bass voice in G. If a comma occurs, he sings this way on the last word: 

an interrogation thus: 

a full-stop: 

For example: 
con - jun - ga - mus o - ra - ti - o - nem.

I cannot describe to you how strange the falling cadence from A to C sounds; especially when the bass is followed by a soprano who begins on D, and makes the same falling cadence from E to G; then an alto does the same in his key; for they sang three different lessons alternately with the canto fermo. I send you a specimen of the mode in which they render the canto fermo, regardless both of the words and the sense. The phrase "better he had never been born" was sung thus:

quite fortissimo and monotonously. Then came the psalms 74, 75, and 76, followed by three lessons, succeeded by the Miserere, sung in the same style as the preceding psalms, in the following tonus:

You may well rub your ears before you can improve on this. Then followed psalms 8, 62, and 66, "Canticum Moysi" in its own key. Psalms 148, 149, and 150 came next, and then antiphonies. During this time the lights on the altar are all extinguished, save one which is hidden behind the altar. Six wax candles still continue to burn high above the entrance, the rest of the space is already dim, and now the whole chorus intones in unison and with full volume the "Canticum Zachariae", during which the last remaining lights are extinguished. The mighty forte in the gloom, and the solemn vibration of so many voices are wonderful.

The melody (in D minor) is also very beautiful. At the close all is profound darkness. An antiphony begins on the sentence, "Now he that betrayed him gave them a sign", and continues to the words "that same is he, hold him fast". Then all present fall on their knees, and one solitary voice sings softly, "Christus factus est pro nobis obediens usque ad mortem"; on the second day is added, "mortem antem crucis"; and on Good Friday, "propter quod est super omne nomen". A pause ensues, during which each person repeats the Paternoster to himself. During this silent prayer, a death-like silence prevails in the whole church; presently the Miserere commences, with a chord softly breathed by the voices, and gradually branching off into two choirs. This beginning, and its first harmonious vibration, certainly made the deepest impression on me. For an hour and a half previously, one voice alone had been heard chanting almost without any variety; after the pause comes an admirably constructed chord (this is wonderful) causing every one to feel in his heart the power of music; it is this, indeed, that makes such an impression. The best voices are reserved for the Miserere, which is sung with the greatest variety of effect, the voices swelling and dying away and rising again from the softest piano to the full strength of the choir. No wonder that it excites deep emotion in every listener. Moreover, they do not neglect the power of contrast; verse after verse is chanted by all the male voices in unison, forte, and harshly. At the beginning of the subsequent verses, one hears the lovely, rich, soft sounds of the other voices; they last only for a short space, and are again succeeded by the male chorus. During the verses sung in a monotone, every one knows how beautiful the softer choir is going to sound; soon they are heard again, again to die away too quickly, and before you can collect your thoughts, the service is over.

On the first day, when the Miserere of Baini, in the key of B minor was given, they sang thus: "Miserere mei Deus" to "misericordiam tuam" from the music, with solo voices, two choirs singing with all their strength; then all the bass singers commenced tutti forte on F-sharp, chanting on that note "et secundum multitudinem" to "iniquitatem meam" which is immediately succeeded by a soft chord in B minor, and so on, to the last verse of all, which they sing with their entire strength; a second short, silent prayer ensues; then all the Cardinals scrape their feet noisily on the pavement, which betokens the close of the ceremony. My little book says, "This noise is symbolical of the tumult made by the Hebrews in seizing Christ". It may be so, but it sounded exactly like the commotion in the pit of a theatre, when the beginning of a play is delayed, or when it is finally condemned. The single taper still burning, is then brought from behind the altar, and all silently disperse by its solitary light.

Here I must mention the striking effect of the blazing chandelier which lights up the great vestibule when the Cardinals and their attendant priests traverse the illuminated Quirinal through ranks of Swiss Guards. The Miserere sung on the first day was Baini's, a composition devoid of life or strength, like all his works; still it had chords and music, and so it made an impression.

On the second day they gave some pieces by Allegri and Bai, on Good Friday—all was Bai's. As Allegri composed only one verse, on which the rest are chanted, I heard each of the three compositions which they gave on that day. However, it is quite immaterial which they sing, for the embellishments are pretty much the same in all three. Each chord has its embellishments, and thus very little of the original composition can be detected. How these embellishments have crept in, no one will say. It is maintained that they are traditional; but this I entirely disbelieve. In the first place no musical tradition can be relied on; besides, how is it possible to carry a five-part movement down to the present time, from mere hearsay? It does not sound like it. It is evident that they have been added more recently; and it appears to me that the director, having had good high voices at his command, and wishing to use them during Holy Week, wrote some ornamental phrases for them, founded on the simple unadorned chords, to enable them to give full scope and effect to their voices. They certainly are not of ancient date, but are composed with talent and taste, and their effect is admirable. One in particular is often repeated, and makes

Mendelssohn's sisters.
Drawing by Wilhelm Hensel, 1828.

Scottish landscape, from the diary of Mendelssohn and Karl Klingemann.
Sketch by Mendelssohn, 1829.

so deep an impression that when it begins, visible excitement pervades all present; indeed, in any discussion about the manner of performing this music, and whenever people say that the voices do not sound like the voices of men, but of angels from on high, and that these sounds can never be heard elsewhere, it is this particular embellimento to which they invariably allude. For example, in the Miserere, whether that of Bai or Allegri (for they have recourse to the same embellimenti in both) these are the consecutive chords:

Instead of this, they sing it thus:

The soprano intones the high C in a pure, soft voice, allowing it to vibrate for a time, then slowly glides down, while the alto holds the C steadily, so that at first I was under the delusion that the high C was still held by the soprano; the skill, too, with which the harmony is gradually developed, is truly admirable. The other embellimenti are adapted in the same way to the consecutive chords; but the first one is by far the most beautiful. I can give no opinion as to the particular method of performing the music; but something I once read, namely, that some particular acoustic contrivance caused the continued vibration of the sounds, is an entire fable, quite as much so as the assertion that they sing according to tradition, and without any fixed beat; one voice simply following the other. I saw plainly enough the shadow of Baini's long arm moving up and down; indeed he sometimes struck his music-desk quite audibly. There is no lack of mystery, either, on the part of the singers and others; for example, they never say beforehand what particular Miserere they intend to sing, but that it will be decided at the moment, etc., etc. The key in which they sing depends on the purity of the voices. The first day it was in B minor, the second and third in E minor, but each time they finished almost in B-flat minor.

The chief soprano, Mariano, came from the mountains to Rome expressly to sing on this occasion, and it is to him I owe hearing the embellimenti with their highest notes. However careful and attentive the singers may be, still the negligence and bad habits of the whole previous year have their revenge, consequently one sometimes hears the most fearful dissonance.

I must not forget to tell you that on the Thursday, when the Miserere was about to begin, I clambered up a ladder leaning against the wall, and was therefore placed close to the roof of the chapel, so that I had the music, the priests, and the people far beneath me in gloom and shadow. Seated thus alone, without the vicinity of any obtrusive stranger, the impression on me was very profound. But to proceed: you must have had more than enough of Misereres in these pages, and besides, I intend to bring you more particular details, both verbal and written.

On Thursday, at half-past ten, High Mass was celebrated. They sang an eight-part composition of Fazzini's, in no way remarkable. I reserve for you some canti fermi and antiphonies, which I wrote down at the time, and my little book describes the order of the various services and the meaning of the different ceremonies. At the "Gloria in Excelsis" all the bells in Rome peal forth, and are not rung again till after Good Friday. The hours are marked in the churches by wooden clappers. It was fine when the words of the "Gloria", the signal for all the strange tumult of bells, were chanted from the altar by old Cardinal Pacca in a feeble trembling voice, and he was followed by the choirs and all the bells. After the Credo they sang the "Fratres ego enim" of Palestrina, but in the most unfinished and careless manner. Then came the washing of the pilgrims' feet, and a procession in which all the singers joined, Baini beating time from a large book carried before him, making signs first to one, and then another, while the singers pressed forward to look at the music, counting the time as they walked, and then chiming in—the Pope being borne aloft in his chair of state. All this I have already described to my parents.

In the evening there were psalms, lamentations, lessons, and the Miserere again, scarcely differing from those of the previous day. One lesson was chanted by a soprano solo in a peculiar melody that I mean to bring home with me. It is an adagio, in long-drawn notes, and lasts a quarter of an hour at least. There is no pause in the music, and the melody lies very high, and yet it was executed with the purest, clearest, and most even intonation. The singer did not break his tone so much as a single comma, the very last notes swelling and dying away as evenly and as full as at the beginning; it was a masterly performance. I was struck with the meaning they attach to the word appoggiatura. If the melody goes from C to D, or from C to E, they sing thus: 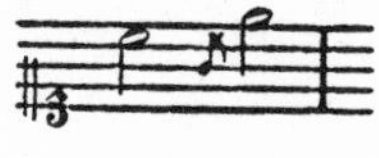

Or:  Or: 

and this they call an appoggiatura. Whatever they may choose to call it, the effect is most disagreeable, and it must require long *habit not to be discomposed by this strange practice which reminds me very much of our old women at home in church; moreover the effect is the same. I saw in my book that the "Tenebrae" was to be sung, and thinking that it would interest you to know how it is given in the Papal Chapel, I was on the watch with a sharp-pointed pencil when it commenced, and send you herewith the principal parts. It was sung very quickly, and forte throughout, with no exception. The beginning was:*

I cannot help it; it does irritate me to hear the most holy and beautiful words sung to such dull, drawling music. They say it is canto fermo, Gregorian, etc.; no matter. If at that period there was neither the feeling nor the capacity for writing in a different style, at all events we have the power to do so now, and certainly

one cannot find this mechanical monotony in the words of the scriptures. They are all truth and freshness, and, moreover, expressed in the simplest and most natural manner. Why then make them sound like a mere formula? For, in truth, such singing as this is nothing more! The word "Pater" with a little flourish, the "meum" with a little shake, the "ut quid me"—can this be called sacred music? There is certainly no false expression in it, because there is none—of any kind; but does not this very fact prove the desecration of the words? A hundred times during the ceremony I was driven wild by such things as these; and then came people in a state of ecstasy, saying how splendid it had all been. It sounded to me like a bad joke, but they were in earnest!

At Mass early on Friday morning, the chapel is stripped of all its decorations, the altar uncovered, and the Pope and Cardinals in mourning. The "Passion" from St. John was sung, composed by Vittoria, but only the words of the people in the chorus are his, the rest are chanted according to an established formula; but more of this hereafter. The whole appeared to me too trivial and monotonous. I was quite out of humour, and in fact dissatisfied with the affair altogether. One of the two following methods ought to be adopted. The "Passion" ought either to be recited quietly by the priest, as St. John relates it, in which case there is no occasion for the chorus to sing "Crucifige eum", nor for the alto to represent Pilate; or else the scene ought to be so completely reproduced, that it would make me feel as if I were actually present, and saw it all myself. In that event, Pilate ought to sing just as he would have spoken, the chorus shout out "Crucifige" in a tone anything but sacred; and then, through the impress of complete truth, and of the subject portrayed, the singing would become sacred music.

For I require no underlying thought when I hear music—which to me is not "a mere medium to elevate the mind to piety", as they say here, but a distinct language which speaks clearly; and the sense is expressed by the words. This is the case with the "Passion" of Sebastian Bach; but as they sing it here, it is very imperfect, being neither a simple narrative, nor yet a grand, solemn, dramatic truth. The chorus sings "Barabbam" to the same sacred chords as "et in terra pax". Pilate speaks in exactly the same manner as the Evangelist. The voice that represents Jesus always commences piano, in order to have one definite distinction, but when the chorus breaks loose, shouting out the sacred chords, one does not know what it is all about.

Forgive these strictures, I now proceed to simple narration again. The Evangelist is a tenor, and the manner of chanting is the same as that of the lessons, with a peculiar falling cadence at the comma, interrogation, and full stop. The Evangelist intones on D, and sings thus at a full stop:

at a comma:

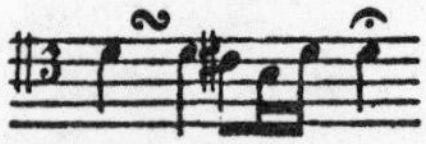

and at the conclusion, when another personage enters, thus:

Christ is a bass, and always commences like this:

I could not catch the formula, though I noted down several parts, which I can show you when I return; among others, the words spoken on the cross. All the other personages, Pilate, Peter, the Maid, and the High Priest, are altos, and sing this melody only:

The chorus sings the words of the people from its place above, whilst everything else is sung from the altar. I really must mark down here, as a curiosity, the "Crucifige", just as I noted it:

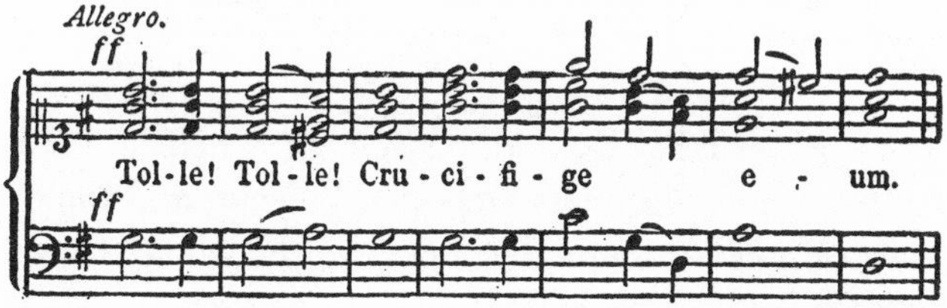

The "Barabbam" too is singular; very tame Jews indeed! But my letter is already too long, so I shall discuss the subject no further. Prayers are then offered up for all nations and institutions, each separately designated. But when the prayer for the Jews is uttered, no one kneels, as they do for all the others, nor is Amen said. They pray pro perfidis Judaeis, and the author of my book has discovered an explanation for this, also. Then follows the Adoration of the Cross. A small crucifix is placed in the centre of the chapel, and all approach barefooted (without shoes), fall down before it and kiss it; during this time the "Improperia" are sung. I have only once heard this composition, but it seems to me to be one of Palestrina's finest works, and they sing it with remarkable enthusiasm. There is surprising delicacy and harmony in its execution by the choir; they are careful to place every passage in its proper light, and to render it sufficiently prominent without making it too conspicuous—one chord blending softly with the other. Moreover, the ceremony is very solemn and dignified, and the most profound silence reigns in the chapel. They sing the oft-recurring Greek "Holy" in the most admirable manner, each time with the same smoothness and expression. You will be not a little surprised, however, when you see it written down, for they sing as follows:

Such passages as that at the commencement, where all the voices sing the same embellishment, repeatedly occur, and the ear becomes accustomed to them. The effect of the whole is undoubtedly superb. I only wish you could hear the tenors in the first chorus, and the way they take the high A on the word "Theos"; the note is long-drawn-out and has such a ringing quality, though hardly louder than a breath. It is extremely touching. This is repeated again and again till everyone in the chapel has performed the Adoration of the Cross; but as on this occasion the crowd was not large, I unfortunately had not the opportunity of hearing it as often as I could have wished.

I quite understand why the "Improperias" produced the strongest effect on Goethe, for they are the most nearly perfect of all, both as music and ceremonial; and everything connected with them is in complete harmony. A procession follows to fetch the Host, which had been exposed and adored on the previous evening in another chapel of the Quirinal, lighted up by many hundreds of wax-lights. The morning service closed at half-past one with a hymn in canto fermo. At half-past three in the afternoon the first vesper began, with the psalms, lessons, etc. I corrected what I had written down, heard the Miserere of Baini, and about seven o'clock followed the Cardinals home through the illuminated vestibule—so everything had been seen, and everything was over.

I was anxious, dear Professor, to describe Holy Week to you minutely, as they were memorable days to me, every hour realising something long anticipated. I also particularly rejoiced in the fact that, despite the excitement and the numerous discussions, praising or finding fault, the solemnities made as vivid an impression on me as if I had been entirely free from all prejudice or prepossession. I thus saw the truth confirmed, that perfection, even in a sphere entirely foreign to us, leaves its own stamp on the mind. May you read this long letter with even half the pleasure I feel in recalling the period of Holy Week in Rome.

Yours faithfully,

Felix Mendelssohn Bartholdy.

FROM A LETTER TO EDWARD DEVRIENT

Milan, July 15, 1831.

You reproach me with being two-and-twenty without having yet acquired fame. To this I can only reply, that had it been the will of God that I should be renowned at the age of two-and-twenty, I no doubt should have been so. I cannot help it, for I can no more write to win a name, than to obtain a conductor's position. It would be a good thing if I could secure both. But so long as I do not actually starve, so long is it my duty to write only as I feel, and according to what is in my heart, and to leave the results to Him who disposes of other and greater matters. Every day I am more sincerely anxious to write exactly as I feel, and to have even less regard than ever for outside opinions; and when I have composed a piece just as it sprang from my heart, then I have done my duty; whether hereafter it brings fame, honour, decorations, or snuff-boxes, etc., is a matter of indifference to me. If you mean, however, that I have neglected, or delayed, perfecting myself, or my compositions, then I beg you will say, distinctly and clearly, in what respect and wherein I have done so. This would indeed be a serious reproach.

You wish me to write only operas, and think I am unwise not to have done so long ago. I answer: place the right libretto in my hands and in a few months it will be composed, for every day I long more eagerly to write an opera. I know that it is more likely to be fresh and gay, if I find it now; but I have no words. And I assuredly will never write music for any poetry that does not inspire me. If you know a man capable of writing the libretto of an opera, for heaven's sake tell me his name; that is all I want. But till I have the words, you would not wish me to be idle—even if it were possible for me to be so.

I have recently written a good deal of sacred music; that is quite as much of a necessity to me as is the study of some particular book, such as the bible or some other, to people who have that impulse, and who care for no other reading at that time. If it bears any resemblance to Sebastian Bach, it is again no fault of mine, for I wrote it just according to the mood I was in; and if the words inspired me with a mood akin to that of old Bach, so much the better. I am sure you do not think that I would merely copy his form, without the substance; if it were so, I should feel such disgust and such a void, that I could never again finish a composition. Since then I have written a grand piece of music which will probably impress the public at large—the first "Walpurgis Night" of Goethe. I began it simply because it pleased me, and inspired me, and gave no thought to its performance. But now that it lies finished before me, I see that it is quite suitable for a great Concertstück, and you must sing the bearded Pagan Priest at my first subscription concert in Berlin. I wrote it expressly to suit your voice; and as I have hitherto found that the pieces I have composed with least reference to the public are precisely those which they liked best, no doubt it will be the same with this, too. I only mention this to prove to you that I do not neglect the practical. To be sure this is invariably an after-thought, for who the deuce could write music, the most unpractical thing in the world (the very reason why I love it so dearly) and yet think all the time of the practical! It is just as if one were to bring a declaration of love to his mistress in rhyme and verse, and recite it to her.

I am going to Munich, where they have offered me an opera, to see if I can find a man there who is a poet, for I will only have a man who has a certain amount of fire and a genuine gift. I do not expect a giant, and if I fail to find anyone there, I shall probably make Immermann's acquaintance for this express purpose; and if he is not the man either, I shall try for one in London. I always fancy that the right fellow has not yet appeared; but what can I do to find him? He certainly does not live in the Reichmann Hotel, nor next door; but where else? Do write to me on this subject. Although I firmly believe that a kind Providence sends us all things in due time, and therefore also libretti; still we must do our duty and look around us—and I do wish the libretto were found.

In the meantime I write as good music as I can, and hope to make progress. And we already agreed when discussing this affair in my room that, as I said before, I am not responsible for the rest. But enough now in this dry vein. I really have become almost morose and impatient once more, and yet I had so firmly resolved never again to be so!

TO HIS PARENTS

A l'Union, Prieuré de Chamonix, End of July, 1831.

My dear Parents,

From time to time I have to write to thank you for my wondrously beautiful journey; and even though I have done so before, I must do it again now, for I have never experienced more delightful days than those on my journey hither, and during my stay here. Fortunately you already know this valley, so I need not describe it to you; indeed, how could I? But let me say this: that nowhere has nature in all her glory greeted my eyes with such brilliance as here, and not only when I saw it with you for the first time, but now, as well. And if everyone who sees it should thank God for having given him faculties to comprehend and appreciate such grandeur, so must I also thank you for having supplied me with the means of enjoying such a pleasure.

I was told that I had exaggerated the shapes of the mountains in my imagination; but yesterday, at sunset, I was pacing up and down in front of the house, and each time that I turned my back on the mountains, I endeavoured vividly to represent these masses to myself, and each time when I again faced them, they far exceeded my conceptions. Just like the morning that we drove away from here, when the sun was rising (no doubt you remember it) the hills have been clear and lovely ever since I arrived. The snow pure and sharp and nearby in the dark blue atmosphere; the glaciers thundering unremittingly, as the ice melts. When clouds gather, they lie lightly around the base of the mountains, but the summits stand forth clearly above. Would that we could see them together!

I have passed this whole day here quietly, and entirely alone. I wished to sketch the outlines of the mountains, so I went out and found an admirable point of view, but when I opened my book, the paper seemed so very small that I hesitated to try it. I have succeeded in reproducing the outlines correctly (so-called), but every stroke looks so formal when compared with the grace and freedom which pervades nature everywhere here. And then the splendour of colour! In short, this is the highlight of my trip; and the whole of my excursion on foot, so solitary, free and unencumbered, is something new to me, and a hitherto unknown sensation.

I must however relate how I came here, otherwise my letter will contain nothing but exclamations. As I previously wrote you, I had the most odious weather on Lago Maggiore, and the Islands. It continued so incessantly stormy, cold, and wet, that the same evening I took my place in the diligence rather downheartedly, and drove on towards the Simplon. We had been journeying for scarcely half an hour, when the moon came out, the clouds dispersed, and next morning the weather was bright and beautiful. I felt almost embarrassed by such good fortune, but I could now thoroughly enjoy the glorious road, winding first through high green valleys, then through rocky ravines, through meadows, and at last past glaciers and snowy mountains. I had with me a little French book on the subject of the Simplon road, which both pleased and affected me; for it contained Napoleon's correspondence with the Directoire about the projected work, and the first report of the general who crossed the mountain. With what spirit and vigour these letters are written! And yet a little swagger too, but with such a glow of enthusiasm that it quite touched me as I was driven along this capital level highway by an Austrian postilion. I compared the fire and poetry displayed in every description contained in these letters (I mean those of the subaltern general) with the eloquence of the present day, which leaves you so terribly cold and is so odiously prosaic in all its philanthropic views, and so lame—where I notice plenty of fanfaronnade, but no genuine youth—and it seemed to me that a great epoch has passed away for ever. I was unable to divest myself of the idea that Napoleon never saw this work—one of his favourite projects—for he never crossed the completed Simplon and was therefore deprived of this gratification. High up, in the Simplon village, all is bleak, and I actually shivered from cold for the first time during the last year and a half. A neat, civil Frenchwoman keeps the inn on the summit, and it would not be easy to describe how pleasant it was to find such thrifty cleanliness, which cannot be found in Italy.

We then descended into the Valais, as far as Brig, where I stayed all night, overjoyed to find myself once more among honest, natural people, who could speak German, and who plundered me, into the bargain, in the most infamous manner. The following day I drove through the Valais—an enchanting journey: the road, like those you have seen in Switzerland, ran all along between two lofty ranges of mountains (whose snowy peaks started up at intervals) and through avenues of green, leafy walnut trees, standing in front of pretty brown houses; below, the wild grey Rhone, past Lenk, and—every quarter of an hour—a village with a little church. From Martigny I travelled for the first time in my life literally on foot, and, as I found the guides too dear, I went on alone, with my cloak and knapsack on my shoulders. About a couple of hours later I met a stout peasant lad who became my guide and porter in one, and so we went on, past Forclas to Trient, a little dairy village, where I breakfasted on milk and honey, and thence up to the Col de Balme.

The whole valley of Chamonix and Mont Blanc, with all its precipitous glaciers, lay before me bathed in sunshine. A party of gentlemen and ladies (one of the latter very pretty and young) came from the opposite side on mules, with a number of guides; scarcely had we all assembled under one roof, when subtle vapours began to rise, shrouding first the mountain and then the valley, and at last thickly covering every object, so that soon nothing was to be seen. The ladies were afraid of going out into the fog (as if they were not already in the midst of it); but at last they set off, and from the window I watched the singular spectacle of the caravan leaving the house, all laughing, and talking loudly in French and English and patois. The voices presently became indistinct; then the figures likewise; and last of all I saw the pretty girl in her wide Scotch cloak; then only glimpses of grey shadows at intervals, and they all disappeared. A few minutes later I ran down the opposite side of the mountain with my guide; we soon emerged once more into sunshine, and entered the green valley of Chamonix with its glaciers; and at length arrived here at the Union. I have just returned from a ramble to Montanvert, the Mer de Glace, and to the source of the Arveiron. You know this splendid scenery, and so you will forgive me, if, instead of going to Geneva tomorrow, I first make the tour of Mont Blanc, that I may become acquainted with this personage from the southern side also, which is, I hear, more striking still. Farewell, dear parents! May we have a happy meeting!

Yours,

Felix.

TO HIS FAMILY

Engelberg, August 23, 1831.

My heart is so full that I must tell you about it. In this enchanting valley I have just taken up Schiller's "Wilhelm Tell", and read half of the first scene; there is surely no art like our German one! Heaven knows why it is so; but I do think that no other nation could fully comprehend such an opening scene, far less be able to compose it. This is what I call a poem, and an opening; pure, clear verse, in which the lake, smooth as a mirror, and everything else is so vividly described; and then the slow commonplace Swiss talk, and Baumgarten coming in—it is just too glorious! How fresh, how powerful, how exciting! We have no such work as this in music, and yet even that sphere ought one day to produce something equally perfect. It is so admirable, too, to have created an entire Switzerland for himself, although he never saw it, and yet all is so faithful and so strikingly truthful; life, people, scenery and nature. I was delighted when the old innkeeper here, in a solitary mountain village, brought me the book with the well-known characters and old familiar names from the monastery; but the opening again quite surpassed all my expectations. It is now more than four years since I read it; I mean presently to go over to the monastery, to work off my excitement on the organ.

Afternoon.

Do not be astonished at my enthusiasm, but read the scene through again yourself, and then you will understand me. Such passages as those where all the shepherds and hunters shout "Save him! save him!" at the close, at the Ruetli when the sun is about to rise, could indeed only have occurred to a German, and only to Schiller; and the whole piece is crowded with similar passages. Let me refer to that particular one at the end of the second scene where Tell comes with the rescued Baumgarten to Stauffacher, and the agitating conference closes in such tranquillity and firmness; this, along with the beauty of the thought, is so thoroughly Swiss. Then the beginning of the Ruetli—the symphony which the orchestra ought to play at the end I composed in my mind today, because I could do nothing satisfactory on the little organ.

Altogether a great many plans and ideas occurred to me. There is a vast deal to do in this world, and I mean to be industrious. The word Goethe used to me: that Schiller could have supplied two great tragedies every year, with its business-like tone, always inspired me with particular respect. But not till this morning did the full force of its significance become clear, and it has made me feel that I must pull myself together. Even the mistakes are captivating, and there is something grand in them; and though certainly Bertha, Rudenz, and old Attinghausen, strike me as great blemishes, still Schiller's idea is evident, and he had to do as he did; and it is consoling to find that even so great a man could for once commit such full-scale errors.

I have passed a most enjoyable morning, and I feel in the kind of mood which makes you long to recall such a man to life, in order to thank him, and I long one day to compose a work which will impress others with similar feelings.

Probably you do not understand what induced me to take up my quarters here in Engelberg. It happened thus: I have not had a single day's rest since I left Untersee, and therefore wished to remain for a day at Meiringen, but was tempted by the lovely weather in the morning to come on here. The usual rain and wind assailed me on the mountains, and so I arrived very tired. Now this is the nicest inn imaginable—clean, tidy, very small and rustic—an old white-haired innkeeper; a wooden house, situated in a meadow, a little apart from the road; and the people so kind and cordial that I feel quite at home. I think this sort of domestic comfort is only to be found among those who speak the German tongue; at all events, I never met with it anywhere else; and though other nations may not miss it or care about it, still I am a native of Hamburg, and so it makes me feel happy and at home. It is therefore not strange that I decided on taking my day's rest here with these worthy old people. My room has windows on every side, commanding a view of the valley: it is prettily panelled with wood;

some coloured texts and a crucifix are hanging on the walls; there is a bulky green stove, and a bench encircling it, and two lofty bedsteads. When I am lying in bed I have the following view:

I have failed again in my buildings, and in the hills too, but I hope to make a better sketch of it for you in my book, if the weather is tolerable, tomorrow. This valley will remain one of my favourites in all Switzerland. I have not yet seen the gigantic mountains by which it is enclosed, as they have been shrouded in mist all day; but the beautiful meadows, the numerous brooks, the houses, and the foot of the hills, so far as I could see them, are exquisitely lovely. The green of Unterwalden is more brilliant than in any other canton, and it is celebrated for its pastures even among the Swiss. The previous journey, too, from Sarnen was enchanting, and never did I see larger or finer trees, or a more fruitful country. Moreover the road is as easy as if you were walking in a large garden; the declivities are clothed with tall slender beeches; the stones overgrown by moss and herbs; there are springs, brooks, small lakes, and houses: on one side is a view of the Unterwalden and its green plains, and shortly after, a view of the whole valley of Hasli with the snowy mountains, and cataracts leaping from rocky precipices; the road is shaded the whole way by enormous trees.

Yesterday, early, as I told you, I was tempted by the bright sun to go up to the Joch and cross the Genthel valley, but on the summit the most dreadful weather set in; we were obliged to make our way through the snow, and sometimes the trip became unpleasant. However, we speedily emerged from the sleet and snow, and an enchanting moment followed, when the clouds broke while we were still standing in them, and far beneath us we saw through the mists, as through a black veil, the green valley of Engelberg. We soon made our way down, heard the silvery bell of the monastery ring out the Ave Maria, next saw the white building on the meadow, and arrived here after an expedition of nine hours. I need not say how welcome a comfortable inn is at such a time, how good the rice and milk tastes and how long you sleep next morning.

Today we again had disagreeable weather, so they brought me "Wilhelm Tell" from the library of the monastery, and the rest you know. I was much struck by Schiller's having so completely failed to portray Rudenz, for the whole character is feeble and without sufficient motive, and it seems as if he had resolved purposely to represent him throughout in the worst possible light. His words in the scene with the apple might tend to redeem him, but this is after the one with Bertha, and makes no impression. When he joins the Swiss, after the death of Attinghausen, it might be supposed that he has changed, but he instantly proclaims that his Bertha is carried off, so again he has as little merit as ever. It occurred to me that if he had uttered the same manly words against Gessler, without their having been preceded by the explanation with Bertha; and if such a result had then arisen in the following act, the character would have been much better, and the explanatory scene not just theatrical, as it is now. This is certainly very like the egg and the hen, but I should like to hear your opinion on the subject. I dare not speak to one of our learned men on such matters; they are much too clever. If, however, I chance some of these days to meet one of those youthful modern poets who condescend to Schiller, and only partly approve of him, so much the worse for him, for I shall crush him to death.

Now, good night; I must rise early tomorrow; there is to be a grand fête in the monastery, and a solemn religious service, and I am to play the organ for them. The monks were listening this morning while I was extemporising a little, and were so pleased, that they invited me to play in the fête and play it out tomorrow. The organist Father has also given me the subject on which I am to extemporise; it is better than any that would have occurred to an organist in Italy.

I shall see what I can make of this tomorrow. I played a couple of new pieces of mine on the organ this afternoon in the church, and they sounded rather good. When I came past the monastery the same evening, the church was closed, and hardly were the doors shut, when the monks began to sing vespers fervently, in the dark church. They intoned the low B, which vibrated splendidly, and could be heard far down the valley.

August 24.

This whole day I have done nothing but sketch and play the organ. In the morning I performed my duties as organist—it was a grand affair. The organ stands close to the high altar, next to the stalls for the "patres". So I took my place in the midst of the monks, a very Saul among the prophets. An impatient Benedictine at my side played the double bass, and others the violins; one of their dignitaries was first violin. The pater praeceptor stood in front of me, sang a solo, and conducted with a long stick as thick as my arm. The pupils of the monastery formed the choir, in their black cowls; an old, decayed rustic played on an old, decayed oboe, and at a little distance two more were puffing away composedly at two huge trumpets with green tassels. With all this the affair was *gratifying. It was impossible not to like the people, for they had plenty of zeal, and all worked away as well as they could. A Mass, by Emmerich, was given, and every note of it betrayed its "powder and pigtail". I played thorough-bass faithfully from my figured part, adding wind instruments from time to time, when I felt bored, made the responses, extemporised on the appointed theme, and at the end, by desire of the Prelate, played a march, in spite of my repugnance to doing this on the organ, and was then honourably dismissed. . . .*

It was time for the monks to go to complines, and we took leave of each other cordially. They wished to give me letters of introduction to some other places in Unterwalden, but I declined, as I intend to go to Lucerne early tomorrow, and after that I expect to be no more than another five or six days in Switzerland.

Your

Felix.

FROM A LETTER TO EDWARD DEVRIENT

Lucerne, August 27, 1831.

I quite feel that any opera I were to write now, would not be nearly so good as any second one I might compose afterwards; and that I must first try the new path I have decided to pursue, and follow it for some little time, in order to discover whither it will lead, and how far it will go, whereas in instrumental music I already begin to see clearly what I really want to do. Having worked so much in this field, I feel much more certain and tranquil with regard to it; in short, it urges me onwards. Besides, I have been made very humble lately by a chance occurrence that still dwells in my mind.

In the valley of Engelberg I found Schiller's "Wilhelm Tell", and on reading it over again, I was enchanted and fascinated anew by such a glorious work of art, and by all the passion, fire, and fervour it displays. An expression of Goethe's suddenly recurred to my mind. In the course of a long conversation about Schiller, he said that Schiller had been able to supply two great tragedies every year, besides other poems. This business-like term supply struck me as the more remarkable on reading this fresh, vigorous work; and such energy seemed to me so wonderfully grand that I felt as if, in the course of my life, I had not yet produced anything of importance; all my works seem so isolated. I feel as if I, too, must one day supply something. Pray do not think this presumptuous; but rather believe that I only say so because I know what ought to be, and what is not. Where I am to find the opportunity—or even catch a glimpse of one—is so far a complete mystery. If, however, it by my mission, I firmly believe that the opportunity will be granted, and if I do not profit by it, another will; but in that case I cannot divine why I feel such an impulse to press onwards. If you could manage not to think about singers, decorations, and situations, but feel absorbed only in representing men, nature and life, I am convinced that you, yourself, would write the best libretto of anyone living; for no one as familiar with the stage as you are could possibly write anything undramatic, and I really do not know what you could wish to change in your poetry. If one has an innate feeling for nature and melody, the verses cannot fail to be musical, even though they sound rather lame in the libretto; but so far as I am concerned, you may write prose if you like, I will compose music for it. But when one form is to be moulded into another, when the verses are to be made to sound musical, but are not felt musically, when fine words have to be substitutes for an utter deficiency of fine feeling . . . there you are right, that is a dilemma from which no man can extricate himself. For as surely as pure meter, happy thoughts, and classical language cannot make a good poem without a certain spark of poetical inspiration pervading the whole, so an opera can only become thoroughly musical—and thereby thoroughly dramatic—when a vivid feeling of life is diffused through all the characters.

There is a passage on this subject in Beaumarchais, who is censured because he makes his people utter so few fine thoughts, and has put so few poetical phrases into their mouths. He answers, that that is not his fault. He tells that during the whole time he was writing the piece, he was engaged in the liveliest conversations with his dramatis personae: that while seated at his writing table he was exclaiming, "Figaro, prends garde, le Comte sait tout!—Ah! Comtesse, quelle imprudence! vite, sauve-toi, petit page!" and then he wrote down their answers, whatever they chanced to be—nothing more. This strikes me as being both charming and true.

The sketch of the opera, introducing an Italian Carnival, and ending in Switzerland, I already knew, but was not aware that it was yours. Be so good however as to describe Switzerland with great vigour and immense spirit. If you are to depict an effeminate Switzerland, with yodeling and languishing, such as I saw here in the theatre last night in the "Swiss Family", when the very mountains and Alpine horns became sentimental, I shall lose all patience, and criticise you severely in Spener's paper. I beg you will make it full of animation, and write to me again on the subject.

TO WILHELM TAUBERT

Lucerne, August 27, 1831.

Should I wish to offer you my thanks, I really would not know where to begin; should I start with the pleasure your songs gave me in Milan, or with your kind letter which I received yesterday? Both, however, are closely connected, and so I think we have already become acquainted. It is quite as fitting that people should be presented to each other through the medium of music-paper as by a third person in society; indeed, I think that in the former case they feel even more intimate and confidential. Moreover, people who introduce anyone often pronounce the name so indistinctly that you seldom know who is standing before you; and as to whether the man is gay and friendly or sad and gloomy you are never told. So we are better off. Your songs have pronounced your name clearly and plainly; they also disclose what you think and what you are; that you love music, and wish to make progress; thus I perhaps know you better than if we had met frequently.

What a source of pleasure it is, and how cheering, to know there is another musician in the world who has the same purposes and aspirations, and who follows the same path as one's self. Perhaps you cannot feel this as strongly as I do at the moment, having just come from a country where music no longer exists among the people. Never before could I have believed this of any nation, and least of all of Italy, with its rich and luxuriant nature, and such inspiring antecedents. But alas! the things I latterly witnessed there fully proved to me that even more than music is dead; it would indeed be marvellous if any music could exist where there is no fixed principle. At last I was really bewildered, and thought that I must have become a hypochondriac, for all the buffoonery I saw was most distasteful to me, and yet a vast number of serious people and sedate citizens acquiesced in it. When they played me anything of their own, and afterwards praised and extolled my pieces, I cannot tell you how repugnant it was to me; I felt disposed to become a hermit, with beard and cowl; the whole world was at a discount with me. It is in Italy that you first learn to value a true musician, that is, one whose thoughts are absorbed in music, and not in money, or decorations, or ladies, or fame; it is doubly delightful when you find that, unaware, your own ideas exist and are being developed elsewhere. Your songs therefore gave me especial pleasure, because I could gather from them that you must be a genuine musician; and so let us mutually stretch out our hands across the mountains.

I beg that you will also look on me in the light of a friend, and not write so formally as to my "counsel" and "teaching". This portion of your letter makes me feel almost nervous, and I do not know what to say. The most agreeable part however is your promise to send me something to Munich, and to write to me again. I will then tell you frankly and freely my honest opinion, and you shall do the same with regard to my new compositions, and thus I think we shall give each other good counsel. I am very eager to see those recent works that you have promised me, for I do not doubt that I shall be much gratified by them, and many things which are only foreshadowed in the former songs will probably become manifest and distinct in them. I can therefore say nothing today of the impression your songs have made on me, because possibly any suggestion or question will already be answered in what you are about to send. I earnestly entreat you to write to me fully, and in detail, about yourself, in order that we may become better acquainted. I can then write to you what I purpose and what I think, and thus we shall continue in close connection.

Let me know what you have recently composed and are now composing; your mode of life in Berlin, and your plans for the future; in short, all that concerns your musical life, which will be of the greatest interest to me. Probably this will be obvious in the music you have so kindly promised, but fortunately both may be combined. Have you hitherto composed nothing on a larger scale? Some wild symphony? or opera? or something of the kind? I, for my part, feel at this moment the most urgent desire to write an opera, and yet I scarcely have the leisure to commence even any smaller work; but I do believe that if the libretto were to be given me today, the opera would be written by tomorrow, so strong is my impulse towards it. Formerly the bare idea of a symphony was so exciting, that I could think of nothing else when one was in my head; the sound of instruments has such a solemn and heavenly effect; and yet for some time past I have laid aside a symphony that I had begun in order to work on a cantata of Goethe's, merely because it also included voices and a chorus. I intend, of course, to complete the symphony, but there is nothing I so strongly covet as a real opera.

Where the libretto is to come from, I know less than ever since last night, when for the first time for over a year, I saw a German aesthetic paper. The German Parnassus seems in as disorganised a condition as European politics. God help us! I was obliged to swallow the supercilious Menzel, who presumed modestly to depreciate Goethe, and the supercilious Grabbe, who modestly depreciates Shakespeare, and the philosophers who proclaim Schiller to be rather trivial! Is this new, arrogant, overbearing spirit, this perverse cynicism, as odious to you as it is to me? And are you of the same opinion as myself, that the first and most indispensable quality of any artist is to feel respect for great men, and to bow down in spirit before them; to recognise their merits, and not to endeavour to extinguish their great flame, in order that his own feeble rushlight may burn a little brighter? If a person is incapable of feeling true greatness, I should like to know how he intends to make me feel it? And as all these people, with their airs of contempt, succeed at last only in producing imitations of this or that particular form, without any suspicion of free, fresh, creative power that is unfettered by individual opinion, or aesthetics, or criticism, or anything else in the world, do they not deserve to be abused? I do abuse them. Pray do not take this amiss; perhaps I have gone too far. But it was long since I had read anything of the kind, and it vexes me to see that such folly still goes on, and that the philosopher who maintained that art is dead, still persists in declaring it so; as if art could ever really die.

These are truly strange, wild, and troubled times; and let those who feel that art is no more, allow it, for heaven's sake, to rest in peace. But however wildly the storm may rage without, it cannot *so quickly succeed in sweeping away the dwellings, and he who works on quietly within, fixing his thoughts on his own capabilities and purposes and not on those of others, will see the hurricane blow over, and afterwards find it difficult to realise that it ever was as violent as it appeared at the time. I have resolved to act thus as long as I can, and to pursue my path quietly, for no one will deny that music still exists, and that is the chief thing.*

How cheering it is to meet with a person who has chosen the same object and the same means, and how gratifying each new confirmation of this kind! I would like to tell you of it, but I do not know how! You must imagine it for yourself, and your own thoughts must supply any deficiencies; so farewell! Let me hear from you soon, and frequently. I beg to send my kindest wishes to our dear friend Berger; I have long wanted to write to him, but have not yet accomplished it. But I shall do so one of these days. Forgive this long, dry letter; next time it shall be more interesting; and now once more farewell.

Yours,

Felix Mendelssohn Bartholdy.

TO GOETHE

Lucerne, August 28, 1831

Your Excellency,

Although on this tramp across the mountains it is not possible for me to write to you as I ought, and to give you an account of things that might interest you even for a single moment, I cannot refrain from writing because I have always been so happy on this particular date and I have been used to celebrating it each year.[1] So I want to tell you how much I appreciated, on this same day, living in these times and being born a German. And this is why I use your gracious permission to approach you again. Even while trying my utmost, I am unable to express what a happy day this is for all of us.

However, as I was told to report to you about the chief events of my journey . . . I could not leave out Switzerland which has always been my favourite country. I shall never forget the time that I have just spent roaming about the mountains on foot, all alone, without knowing a soul, and thinking of nothing but the new and wonderful things that burst upon me every moment.

I came from the land of bright skies and warmth; but Switzerland gave me a very different reception: I found rain and storm and mist, and on the mountains often had to go through snowstorms. But somehow or other, I rather like it; and occasionally, when the great, black, rocky peaks emerge from the clouds, or a whole stretch of country seems to burst into sunshine out of the midst of the fog, it is glorious. No amount of bad weather could stop me from climbing about as much as possible. Sometimes the guide refused to go with me, often I could not see anything at all, but still I did what I could, and when a fine day came at last, it was twice as pleasant. Here, nature seems to make an even grander impression on me than elsewhere, for she surrounds me more completely, and the whole country and people depend entirely and solely upon her.

You must have heard of the terrible inundations and storms in the Bernese Oberland; I was there just at that time, and it was awful to see how everything connected with human beings, even the most durable things—streets, bridges, meadows and houses—could so easily disappear in a moment, without leaving a trace—as if they had never existed. Three days afterward, nature was all calm and smiling again, as if nothing had happened, and the people were

1. *Goethe's last birthday.*

at work to restore order as far as possible. I was just on my way to the Lake of Thun, without a guide and quite alone. Since the day that you told me about your observations on the weather and on clouds, I have taken a special interest in the subject and paid more attention to what was happening above me. I could see distinctly the gradual way in which the storm came on. The clouds had been gathering for two days, and at last, on the evening of the seventh, a great thunderstorm burst forth and lasted the whole night with incessant rain. In the morning it looked as if clouds were coming down instead of rain. I never saw clouds lie so low before; they had stationed themselves all round about the bases of the mountains, far down into the valleys, quite thick and white, with nothing overhead but black mist. It did not rain at all for a little while, not until the lower clouds began to float up and down, and then the rain went on again for that whole day and night; but the serious masses of clouds and mist only collected on the third morning—the ninth—and then the whole breadth of the horizon and the sky were completely filled with them. Storms generally come up with a clear sky; but in this case the masses of clouds piled themselves one upon the other and were driven across country from the plains in the northwest right into the mountains in the northeast. It was impossible to distinguish the opposite side of the lake. In the intervals, when one layer of clouds had passed, it stopped raining; but in another minute it began pouring down out of the next one with indescribable fury. The footpaths were soon under water, streams were running across the roads in every direction and the mountain-torrents came rushing down like mad, quite dark-brown, so that they looked as if earth were boiling up out of the river-bed, and being dashed into the lake; you could see the dark streams far out upon the clear water. The smaller bridges had all been carried off in the morning, the piers and arches of the large stone ones were also torn away and one forest stream brought a quantity of furniture and household goods into the lake without anybody's knowing what houses had been demolished. Some days afterward, when the rain had ceased and I had come into the valley of Lauterbrunnen, the broad high-road had completely vanished, and the ground where it had been was nothing but a heap of shingle and sand and great blocks of stone, for fully a mile. The same damage had been done on that day almost all over the country, on the St. Gotthard, at Unterwalden, Glarus, etc. Sometimes it was difficult to get along and one had to go over the mountains because the water left no room in the valleys—but that only made it all the finer.

I spent last week at Engelberg, in an Unterwald monastery several thousand feet above the sea, perfectly secluded, where I found a good organ and pleasant monks. They had never heard of Sebastian Bach, so a few of his fugues on the organ were a complete novelty to them; but still they were pleased, and on the saint's day (St. Bartholomew's) I had to play the organ for them, accompany the Mass and make the Responses. It was the first time on this journey that I got my hands on a decent organ, for in Italy I did not find a single one in good order. Besides this, the monks had a good library; and as neither politics, strangers, nor newspapers ever enter the valley, I had a pleasant time of it there.

At last the weather cleared up again, and today it is as if Nature herself wanted to celebrate this great occasion. The sky is of the brightest blue, the mountains have decked themselves in their most brilliant colours, the landscape looks gay and festive—everything seems to know what an important day it is.

I have just come from the theatre, the only one in all Switzerland—and have been hearing Schiller's "Wilhelm Tell". This being the time of the Diet, the Swiss depart from their custom of preferring no theatre to a bad one. And as it is the only one in the country, you must allow me to say a few words about so national a performance. The whole troupe numbers about ten persons, and the stage is the size and height of a small room; but still they wanted to give the crowd scenes. So two men in pointed hats represented Gessler's army, two others in round hats the Swiss country people, and the subordinate parts were done away with. Even when there was something important to say, they omitted it without compunction and coolly went on with the next words in their parts without any connection, and occasionally with the most comical effect. Some of the actors had only learned the drift of their parts and made their own verses on the spot; Gessler's envoy, with the first beat, knocked the drum out of his button-hole onto the ground and could not fasten it on again, to the great delight of the liberty-loving public who laughed heartily at the tyrant's slave; but it was impossible to kill the piece entirely and even with all this, it was effective. When the familiar names and places occurred, which one had seen the day before, the people were in raptures, nudging one another and pointing to the pasteboard lake, which they could see far better in reality by walking out of their houses.

But it was Gessler who provided the greatest delight because he behaved so uproariously and ranted and raged in such a furious style; his dishevelled beard, red nose and cap all awry, made him look just like a drunken workman; the whole thing was quite Arcadian and primitive, like the infancy of the drama. And when I remembered an opera of Spontini [1] where everything is imitated in such a very careful and realistic way, where four hundred people sang to represent a huge army, where the anvils were tuned in key, in order to make the forge of the Cyclops visible, where the decorations were changed every moment and each was more glittering than the last—then, after all, the theatre in Lucerne with its bumpy wooden waves seemed to give me more illusion, because here the imagination can have free play and create its own illusions, while there it is oppressed and has its wings clipped. And this makes me feel so uneasy and childish.

Your Excellency will pardon me for daring to write to you about trifles of this kind. But should I venture to tell you how I really feel

1. *The opera "Alcidor", presented for the first time at a court festival May 28, 1825, in Berlin.*

today, it would be the same thing you have heard so many times from the best and greatest men, and my own words would just seem the more insignificant; so I prefer to remain silent.

I wrote you from Rome that I had been bold enough to compose your "First Walpurgis Night".[1] I completed the work in Milan; it is a kind of cantata for chorus and orchestra, longer and more enlarged than I had planned it originally, because the more I was occupied with the task, the more important it seemed to me. Allow me to thank you for the heavenly words; when the old Druid offers up his sacrifice and the scene grows to immeasurable heights and solemnity, there is no need of inventing music; it is there already; everything sounds clear, and I started to sing the verses to myself before even thinking of the composition. In case I should find a good choir and an opportunity in Munich—whence I depart tomorrow and where I plan to stay until the end of September—I intend to perform the work. The only thing I hope for, is that my music should be able to express how deeply I was moved myself by the beauty of the words.

May I ask you kindly to remember me, and give my best wishes, to Ottilie and Ulrike? Apologising once more for this letter, I remain in boundless reverence

Your Excellency's most devoted

F. M. B.

1. *Mendelssohn had completed the score in Milan, July 15, 1831; the overture was added in Paris, 1832, and the whole work was rewritten in 1842 and published as "Ballade" op. 60, in 1843. Some words from Goethe's letter written as an answer to this on September 9, 1831, are quoted in the preface to the score.*

TO HIS FAMILY

Munich, October 6, 1831.

It is a glorious feeling to waken in the morning and to know that you are going to write the score of a grand allegro with all sorts of instruments, and various oboes and trumpets, whilst bright weather holds out the hope of a cheering, long walk in the afternoon. This is what I have enjoyed for a whole week past, so the favourable impression that Munich made on me during my first visit, is now very much enhanced. I scarcely know a place where I feel as comfortable and domesticated as here. Above all it is very pleasant to be surrounded by cheerful faces, and to know your own is the same, and to be acquainted with everyone you meet in the streets.

I am now preparing for my concert, so my hands are pretty full; every moment my acquaintances interrupt me in my work, the lovely weather tempts me to go out, and the copyists, in turn, force me to stay at home. All this makes up the most agreeable and exciting life. My concert had to be postponed on account of the October festival, which begins next Sunday, and lasts all the week. Every evening there is to be a performance at the theatre and a ball, so all idea of an orchestra or a concert hall is out of the question. On Monday evening, however, the 17th, at half-past six, think of me, for then we dash off with thirty violins and two sets of wind instruments. The first part begins with the symphony in C minor, the second with the "Midsummer Night's Dream". The first part closes with my new concerto in G minor, and at the end of the second I have unwillingly agreed to extemporise. Believe me, I do not like to do it, but the people insist upon it. Every morning I have to write, correct and score till one o'clock, when I go to

Scheidel's coffee-house in the Kaufinger Gasse and where I know each face by heart, and find the same people every day in the same position: two playing chess, three looking on, five reading the newspapers, six eating their dinner, and I am the seventh. After dinner Baermann usually comes to fetch me and we make arrangements about the concert, or after a walk we have cheese and beer, and then I return home and set to work again.

This time I have declined all invitations for the evening; but there are so many agreeable houses to which I may go uninvited, that a light is seldom to be seen in my room on the ground floor till after eight o'clock. You must know that I lodge on a level with the street, in a room which was once a shop, so that if I unbar the shutters of my glass door, one step brings me into the middle of the street and anyone passing along can put his head in at the window, and say good morning. Next to me lodges a Greek, who is learning the piano, and he is truly odious; but to make up for that, my landlord's daughter, who wears a round silver cap and is very slender, looks all the prettier.

I have music in my rooms at four o'clock in the afternoon, three times every week.

Last Wednesday we had capital fun; several wagers had been won, and it was agreed that we should enjoy the fruits of them all together; and after various suggestions, we at last decided on having a musical soirée in my room, and inviting all the dignitaries. So a list of about thirty people was made out; several also came uninvited, who were presented to us by mutual friends. There was a great lack of space—at first we tried to seat several people on my bed—but a number of patient sheep managed to cram into my small room. The whole affair was extremely lively and successful. First I played my old quartet in B minor; then Breiting sang "Adelaide"; Mr. S played variations on the violin (doing himself no credit); Baermann performed Beethoven's first quartet (in F major), which we had arranged for two clarinets, corno di bassetto, and bassoon; an air from "Euryanthe" followed, which was furi-

ously encored, and as a finale I extemporised—I did not want to—but they made such a tremendous uproar that nolens I was forced to comply though I had nothing in my head but wine-glasses, benches, cold cuts, and ham.

The Cornelius ladies were next door with my landlord and his family, to listen to me; the Schauroths were making a visit on the first floor for the same purpose, and even in the hall and in the street people were standing; in addition to all this there was the heat of the crowded room, the deafening noise and the gay audience. When at last the time for eating and drinking arrived, everybody went crazy; we fraternised, glass in hand, and gave toasts; the more formal guests, with their grave faces, sat in the midst of the jovial throng, apparently quite contented, and we did not separate till half-past one in the morning.

The following evening formed a striking contrast. I was summoned to play before the Queen and the Court; there all was proper and polite, and polished, and every time you moved your elbow, you nudged an Excellency; the smoothest and most complimentary phrases circulated in the room, and I, the roturier, stood in the midst of them, with my citizen heart, and my aching head! I managed however to get on pretty well, and at the end, I was commanded to extemporise on royal themes, which I did, and was mightily commended. What I liked best was that, when I had finished my extempore playing, the Queen said to me that she found it strange, the power I possessed of carrying away my audience, for during such music no one could think of anything else; on which I begged to apologise for carrying away Her Majesty, etc.

You see this is how I pass my time in Munich. I forgot, however, to say that every day at twelve o'clock I give little Mademoiselle L an hour's instruction in double counterpoint, and four-part composition, etc., which makes me realise more than ever the stupidity and confusion of most masters and books on the subject; for nothing can be clearer than the whole thing when properly explained.

She is one of the sweetest creatures I ever saw. Imagine a small, delicate-looking, pale girl, with noble but not pretty features, so singular and interesting that it is difficult to turn your eyes from her; while her every gesture and word are full of talent. She has the gift for composing songs, and singing them in a way I never heard before, causing me the most unalloyed musical delight I ever experienced. When she is seated at the piano and begins one of the songs the sounds are unique; the music floats strangely to and fro, and every note expresses the most profound and delicate feeling. When she sings the first note in her tender tones, every one present subsides into a quiet and thoughtful mood, and each, in his own way, is deeply affected. If you could but hear her voice! so innocent, so unconsciously lovely, emanating from her inmost soul, and yet so tranquil! Last year the disposition was all there; she had written no song that did not contain some bright flash of talent; and then M and I sounded forth her praises to the musical world; still no one seemed to believe us. Since that time she has made the most remarkable progress. Those who are not affected by her present singing, have no feeling at all. Unluckily it is now the fashion to beg the little girl to sing her songs and to remove the lights from the piano, in order that the society may enjoy her melancholy.

This forms an unpleasant contrast, and repeatedly, when I was requested to play something after her, I was quite unable to, and declined. It is possible that she may one day be spoiled by all this nonsense, because she has no one to understand or to guide her, and because, strangely enough, she completely lacks musical culture; she knows very little, and can scarcely distinguish good music from bad; in fact, except for her own pieces, she thinks everything is wonderfully fine. If she were to become satisfied, as it were, with herself, it would all be over with her. I have, for my part, done what I could, and implored her parents and herself in the most urgent manner, to avoid society, and not to allow such divine talent to be wasted. Heaven grant that I may be successful! I may, perhaps, dear sisters, soon send you some of her songs that she has copied out for me, in token of her gratitude for my teaching her what she already knows from nature, and because I have led her a little way towards good and solid music.

I also play on the organ every day for an hour, but unfortunately I cannot practice properly, as the pedal is short of five upper notes, so that one cannot play any of Sebastian Bach's passages on it. But the stops, with which you can vary chorales, are wonderfully beautiful; so I edify myself with the celestial, flowing tone of the instrument. Moreover, Fanny, I have discovered here the particular stops which have to be used in Sebastian Bach's "Schmuecke dich, O liebe Seele". They seem actually made for this melody, and sound so touching, that a feeling of awe invariably comes over me when I begin to play it. For the flowing parts I have a flute stop of eight feet, and also a very soft one of four feet, which continually floats above the chorale. You know this from Berlin. But there is a keyboard for the chorale with nothing but reed stops, so I use a mellow oboe and a soft clarion (four feet) and a viola. These give the chorale in subdued and touching tones, like distant human voices, singing from the depths of the heart.

Sunday, Monday, and Tuesday—by the time you have received this letter, I shall be on the "Theresien Wiese",[1] with eighty thousand other people, so think of me there, and farewell.

Felix.

1. *A vast square, for popular festivities, such as the famous* "Oktoberfest".

TO HIS FATHER

Paris, December 19, 1831.

Dear Father,

Receive my hearty thanks for your letter of the 7th. Though I do not quite comprehend your meaning on some points, or may differ from you, still I hope that everything will come all right when we talk things over more, together, and you permit me, as you have always done hitherto, to express my opinion in a straightforward manner. I allude chiefly to your suggestion that I should procure a libretto for an opera from some French poet, and then have it translated, and compose the music for the Munich stage.[1]

Above all, I must tell you how sincerely I regret that you have only now made known to me your views on this subject. I went to Duesseldorf, as you know, expressly to consult with Immermann on the point. He was ready and willing, accepted the proposal and promised to send me the poem by the end of May at the latest, so I do not see how it is possible for me now to withdraw; indeed I do not wish it, as I have complete confidence in him. It was impossible for me even to suspect what you allude to in your last letter about Immermann and his incapacity for writing an opera. Although I by no means agree with you in this opinion, still it would have been my duty to settle nothing without your express sanction, and I could have arranged the affair by letter from here etc. I believed, however, that I was acting entirely to your satisfaction when I made him my offer. In addition to this, some new poems that he read me convinced me more than ever that he was a true poet; and

1. *Felix Mendelssohn, during his stay in Munich, received a commission from the director of the theatre, to write an opera for Munich.*

supposing that I had another choice of equal merit, I would always decide in favour of a German, rather than a French libretto; and lastly, he has fixed on a subject which has been long in my thoughts, and which, if I am not mistaken, my mother wished to see made into an opera, I refer to Shakespeare's "Tempest". I was therefore particularly pleased, so I should doubly regret it if you do not approve of what I have done. In any event, however, I entreat that you will neither be displeased with me, nor—especially—be distrustful with regard to the work, nor cease to take any interest in it.

From what I know of Immermann, I feel assured I may expect a first-rate libretto. What I said about his solitary life merely referred to his inward feelings and doings, for in other respects he is well acquainted with what is going on in the world, what people like, and what to give them. But above all he is a genuine artist, which is the chief thing. I am sure I need not say that I will not compose music for any words I do not consider really good, and which do not inspire me. For this purpose it is essential that I should have your approval. I shall reflect deeply on the poem before I begin the music. The dramatic interest or, in the best sense, the theatrical part, I shall of course immediately communicate to you, in short, regard the affair as seriously as it deserves. The first step, however, is taken, and I cannot tell you how deeply I should regret your not being pleased.

There is one thing, though, which consoles me, and it is that if I were to rely on my own judgment, I would again act precisely as I have done now, though I have had an opportunity of becoming acquainted with a great deal of French poetry, and seeing it in the most favourable light. Pardon me for saying exactly what I think. To compose for the translation of a French libretto, seems to me for various reasons impracticable. I have an idea that you are in favour of it more on account of the success which it is likely to enjoy than for its own intrinsic merit. Moreover I well remember how much you disliked the subject of the "Muette de Portici", a muette, too, who had gone astray, and of "William Tell", which the author seems almost purposely to have rendered tedious, etc. The success, however, that these enjoy all over Germany assuredly does not depend on the work itself being either good or dramatic (for "Tell" is neither) but on their coming from Paris, and having succeeded there. Certainly there is one sure road to fame in Germany, and that goes via Paris and London; still it is not the only one. This is proved not only by all Weber's works, but also by those of Spohr, whose "Faust" is here considered classical music, and which is to be given at the Grand Opera House in London next season. Besides, I could not possibly take that course, as my grand opera has been commissioned for Munich, and I have accepted. I am resolved therefore to make the attempt in Germany, and to remain and work there as long as I can and make my living there, for that I consider my first duty. If I find that I cannot do this, then I must leave it for London or Paris, where it is easier to get on. If I must, I shall know at least that one is better remunerated and more honoured and lives more gaily and at ease there than in Germany, where a man must press forward, and toil, and take no rest. Still, I prefer the latter.

None of the new libretti here would, in my opinion, be attended with any success if brought out for the first time on a German stage. One of the distinctive characteristics of all of them is precisely of a nature that I should resolutely oppose, although the taste of the present day may demand it, and I truly admit that it may, in general, be more prudent to go with the current than to struggle against it. I allude to that of immorality. In "Robert le Diable" the nuns come one after the other to seduce the hero, till at last the abbess suceeds. The same hero is conveyed by magic into the apartment of the one he loves and casts her from him in an attitude which the public here applauds, and probably all Germany will do the same; she then implores his mercy in a grand aria. In another opera a young girl divests herself of her garments, and sings a song to the effect that next day at this time she will be married; all this produces effect, but I have no music for it. I consider it *ignoble, and if the present epoch demands this style and considers it indispensable, then I will write oratorios.*

Another strong reason why it would prove impracticable is that no French poet would undertake to furnish me with a poem. It is no easy matter to procure one from them for the theatre here, for all the best authors are overwhelmed with commissions. I think it quite possible that I might succeed in getting one; but it never would occur to any of them to write a libretto for a German theatre. In the first place it would be much more feasible to give the opera here, and more rational too; in the second place, they would decline writing for any other stage than the French because they cannot realise any other. Above all it would be impossible to procure a sum equivalent to what they receive here from the theatres, and what they draw as their share from the part d'auteur.

I know you will forgive me for having told you my opinion without reserve. You always allowed me to do so in conversation, so I hope you will not put a wrong construction on what I have written, and I beg you will amend my views by communicating your own.

Your

Felix.

FROM A LETTER TO KARL KLINGEMANN

Paris, December 10, 1831.

I wish I were already in London, because yesterday, when I read in the newspapers that the progress of the cholera had already extended to Newcastle, I became somewhat anxious that it might also reach the city, and that my father, who anyway seems rather worried about it in these circumstances, would not consent to my trip. I would have preferred to have this incident happen in

France; that would have made me seek refuge with you, and I would thus avoid having to stay here the whole winter. I feel most uncomfortable here to this day. These ways and doings seem to me to smack of the devil; if a man does not pull himself together, he may as well hand over his soul (I mean his musical soul!) to that gentleman in comfort and pleasure. The superficialities are so tempting, people enjoy honours and money and decorations and cheers and orchestras, and lack absolutely nothing—if only they were not such execrably bad musicians! This is what struck me so unpleasantly in Paris; in all kinds of small places in Germany I have met better and greater musicians, but nowhere can they make so much ado about themselves and make people believe everything to the letter. Perhaps this is the point: they never can relax in our country, they have to worry all their lives long and are never appreciated—and yet, they produce WORKS. Here it is just the contrary, and I do not know what to make of it. One day, when I have written a number of important compositions, I shall come and have myself admired to my heart's content; but until that day I want to live in Germany—and that is my impression of Paris this time. One easily comes to look upon oneself as very distinguished and much greater than anybody else; one dons an intellectual dressing-gown and assumes the part of an intellectual burgomaster—but it is not good. Therefore, I also want to do my best to persuade Hiller, who would like to settle down here, to return to Germany. He feels that those other gentlemen are unable to appreciate his ideas and work, and so he takes to writing down whatever flits through his mind; then again he feels that he does better than others, and thus is on his way to becoming mannered, unless he soon gets out of all this and finds his place among musicians who really know about music and understand the great masters and who will praise and criticise and stimulate him. For he is gifted and a pleasant, bright fellow and it would really be a great pity if he were to be engulfed in the nonsense of Parisian melancholy and the école allemande. He has written an overture to "Faust", which is as horribly weak as anything that could have been done by a Frenchman aping the German school, and on the other hand, a symphony which contains some of the most charming things imaginable. But people just praise and blame everything alike, without discrimination, and how can one avoid becoming confused?

Anyway, today and all this last week I have gone through one of those dark moods of dissatisfaction with myself. This nearly always occurs when I have done no serious work for some time; in fact, I wanted to compose here, and now I am not able to sit down to work owing to the distractions and dissipations of the life around. I really do not see how I can change it. Either I must retire into complete seclusion and leave all these people alone, or I must look forward to a most disagreeable winter. If only you could be with me, everything would go better. We would have a thousand topics to discuss and could collaborate on some music. With all this I cannot deny that whenever I do not know what to do with myself and have no big work in mind or in hand, I have great fun with those musicians. But when things are different, I would just about like to kill them, with their well-fed faces and their weary two-penny melancholy . . .

A symphony of mine will probably be performed in the Concerts du Conservatoire, and when the last chord has died away I will probably already have one foot in the stage-coach, the other in Calais, the third in Dover, and all and everything in Bury Street with my dear old chum. There is one good thing here in Paris. You think I mean "La Liberté"? O no, it is the Taglioni. I heard that you were raving about her dancing; well, I am raving about herself altogether. She is a real artist and dances with amiable innocence. Do you think I ought to meet her? She seems to be the only genuine musician in Paris, but who knows but what I will be disappointed in her, with all my lovely ideas, because in the end she will marry some count and leave the theatre and become une grande dame, or the devil knows what. She is perfection itself, and so is her dancing. Up to now I have only seen her in "Robert le Diable". She acts a ghostly nun who wants to seduce the fat Nourrit. It is a most touching affair, because she is ever so much more candid than either the fat fellow or the entire audience. Afterwards he is coaxed into kissing and hugging her, much to the delight of the public. Then there are other nuns who would love to do some seducing too, but compared to the sweet young child they look like pugdogs and tomcats, and last of all, one would just like to do away with all the music and take the place of Nourrit who is having such a good time. The opera itself is having great success although it is just one of thousands which are exactly like the other thousands; the libretto is wretched, muddled, and just as cold-blooded, crazy and fantastic as you would expect from a jeune Français; the music is not bad at all. Effects are well calculated, there is no lack of suspense, the right pungencies are fitted into the right places; there is melody to be hummed, harmony for the educated listeners, instrumentation for the Germans, contredances for the French, in fact, something for everybody—but there is no heart! Such a work is as different from art as decorating is from painting; decorating produces more effect, but if you take a good look at it, you see that it is painting done with the feet. As I said before: it is neither music nor poetry; the rest is inimitably beautiful . . .

TO KARL IMMERMANN

Paris, January 11, 1832.

You permitted me to give you occasional tidings of myself, and since I arrived, I have daily intended to do so; the perpetual restlessness here, however, is such that up to today I have not been able to write. When I contrast this constant whirl and commotion and the thousand distractions among a foreign people, with your house in the garden and your warm winter room, your wish to exchange with me and to come here in my place, often recurs to me, and I almost wish I had taken you at your word.

I rejoice at the prospect of my return to Germany; everything there is indeed on a small scale, and paltry, if you will, but men live there; men who know what art really is, who do not admire, nor praise, in fact who do not criticise, but create. You do not admit this, but it is only because you are yourself among the number.

I beg you will not, however, think that I am like one of those German youths with long hair, that wander about, filled with nostalgia, and call the French superficial and Paris frivolous. I only say all this because I thoroughly enjoy and admire Paris, and am becoming better acquainted with it, and I say it because I am writing to you in Duesseldorf. I have, on the contrary, plunged myself headlong into the vortex, and do nothing the whole day but see new things, the Chambers of Peers and Deputies, pictures and theatres, dio- neo- cosmo- and panoramas, society, etc. Moreover, the musicians here are as numerous as the sands of the sea—all hating each other. So each must be visited individually, and wary diplomacy is advisable, for they are all gossips, and what one says to another, the whole corps knows next morning.

The days have thus flown as if they were only half their length, and as yet I have not been able to compose a single bar; in a few days, however, this exotic life will cease. My head is now dizzy from all I have seen and wondered at; but I intend to collect my thoughts and set to work, and then I shall once more feel happy and domesticated.

My chief pleasure in the evening is going to the little theatres, because they mirror the whole of French life and the people; for instance, I like the "Gymnase Dramatique" where nothing is given but small vaudevilles. It is extraordinary how one finds now, in all these little comedies, such extreme bitterness and deep disgust, and although they are cloaked by the prettiest phrases and the liveliest acting, they become only the more conspicuous. Politics everywhere play the chief part, which might have sufficed to make me dislike these theatres, for we have enough of that elsewhere; but the politics of the "Gymnase" take a light and ironical turn—referring to the occurrences of the day, and to the newspapers, in order to excite laughter and applause, and at last you can't help laughing and applauding with the rest. Politics and sensuality are the two great subjects of interest round which everything revolves; and none of the many pieces I have seen have omitted an attack on the Ministry and a scene of seduction.

The whole style of the vaudeville is thoroughly French and introduces certain conventional music at the end of the scene in every piece, when the actors partly sing and partly declaim some couplets with a witty point. We could never learn this, nor in fact wish to do so, for this mode of connecting the wit of the day with an established refrain does not exist in our conversation, nor in our ideas. I cannot imagine anything more striking and effective, nor yet more prosaic . . .

I cannot say how it may be at the French Opéra, for that is bankrupt, so there has been no acting there since I came. In the Académie Royale, however, Meyerbeer's "Robert le Diable" is played every night with great success; the house is always crowded, and the music has given general satisfaction. There is an expenditure of all possible means of producing stage effects that I never saw equalled. All who can sing, dance, or act in Paris, sing, dance, and act on this occasion. The sujet is romantic; that is, the devil appears in the piece (this is quite sufficient romance and imagination for the Parisians). It is very bad, however; and were it not for two brilliant scenes of seduction it would produce no effect whatever.

I seldom see Heine, because he is entirely absorbed in liberal ideas and in politics. He has recently published sixty "Fruehlings Lieder". Very few of them seem to me either genuine or truthful, but these few are indeed wonderful. Have you read them? They appeared in the second volume of the "Reisebilder". Boerne intends to publish some new volumes of letters: he and I are full of enthusiasm for Malibran and Taglioni; all these gentlemen are abusing and reviling Germany and all that is German, and yet they cannot speak even tolerable French; I cannot quite swallow this.

Yours,

Felix Mendelssohn-Bartholdy

TO CARL FRIEDRICH ZELTER

Paris, February 15, 1832.

Dear Professor Zelter,

Had I wished to write you about nothing more than the outstanding events of my journey, I should really have written from Germany. Because now, after having enjoyed the beauties of Italy and Switzerland, after all the wonderful sights and experiences in those countries, I came back to Germany; and while visiting Stuttgart, Heidelberg, Frankfort and the Rhine valley down to Duesseldorf, I realised that here was the climax of my journey. Here I became aware that I am a German, and I knew that I want to live in Germany as long as I can. It is true that there is not such beauty to be enjoyed there, nor so many wonderful things to be experienced; but there I am at home. It is not that any single place particularly appeals to me, or that there is one where I particularly want to live—it is the country as a whole, the people—whose character, language and customs I need not to learn in order to understand them—who just make me feel at home, without having to *think about it. And so I hope to find in Berlin, too, what I need for my life and my career, and that there, close to you, my family and my friends, I shall feel no less at home than in all the other German places. If one day people do not want me any more in Germany, I can still go abroad where life is easier for the foreigner; but I hope it will never prove necessary. And so I cannot begin to tell you how much I am looking forward to seeing you again.*

I was struck to see how widely-spread the feeling for music and art has become in Germany and how it continues to spread, while elsewhere (for instance here) it tends to become more and more concentrated. This perhaps accounts for the fact that with us this sense does not shoot upward so fast, but neither is it cultivated to the extreme, and moreover, for the fact that we are able to send out our musicians to other countries and yet remain sufficiently rich ourselves. I have thought this all out for myself while having to listen so often to politics and sometimes even having had to talk politics; and also when I heard how people, mostly Germans, chided Germany or pitied it because it has no centre, no leader, and no concentration, and when they believe that all this will surely come soon. It will surely not come, and I also believe that that is a good thing. What must and will come, however, is the end of our exaggerated modesty which makes us accept everything that comes from others as good, and which keeps us from appreciating our own until it has first been recognised by others. Let us hope that the Germans will soon stop their grumbling about their lack of unity, thus themselves becoming the first disintegrating factor; and let us hope too that one day they will begin to imitate the unity of others which is the best quality those others have. Nevertheless, I am not going to give them up, even though they should not unite soon enough—I shall just go on with my composing, as long as something keeps coming into my mind. But I always regret that we do not appreciate the things in which we are superior.

I went to Stuttgart and enjoyed again its excellent orchestra

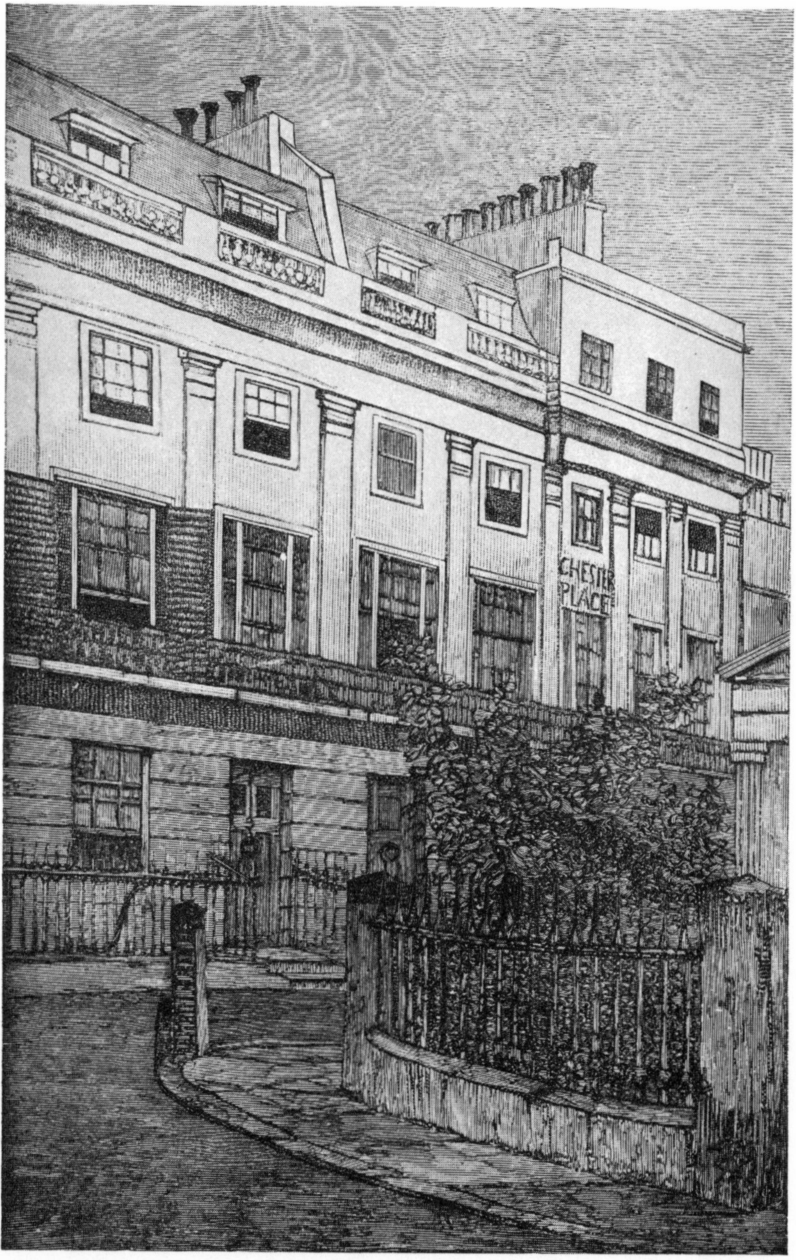

3 Chester Place, London, residence of the Moscheles family.
Drawing by Mendelssohn, 1835.

Frankfort-on-the-Main. View from the window of his fiancée.
Drawing by Mendelssohn, 1836.

. . . They were just about to start the first of their subscription concerts during which they perform the great symphonies every year. I was asked to play and to give some compositions; but I was in a hurry and could not wait long enough. So I promised to stay for a while on my return journey. During the summer there is but little to do. When there are no rehearsals for a few days, the conductor, together with his wife, some underwear and a tobacco-pipe, sets out for a cross-country walk and comes home again after several days by way of the hill-side vineyards. The main thing is that everybody grumbles and yet nobody would leave at any price. I have really gained perfect insight into the musical life of a small German provincial town. In Frankfort things are done in a more distinguished, businesslike and metropolitan way, but it is not nearly so much fun. On the other hand there is the St. Cecilia Society which alone would make it worth while to be in Frankfort. The singers work with such enthusiasm and precision that it is sheer delight to listen to them. It meets once a week and has two hundred members. Besides that, Schelble has a small group of about thirty voices who meet at his place every Friday evening and he works with them at the piano; little by little they prepare his favourite compositions which he does not dare to give directly to his big chorus. I have heard a great deal of lovely music there, several of Bach's "Sunday Services", his Magnificat and the great Mass. Just as in your own Academy, the female singers are always the more eager; the males sometimes leave something to be desired; their heads are full of their business affairs. I believe it is the same everywhere; women are more community-minded than men. In the big Society I heard, among other music, the motet, "Gottes Zeit ist die allerbeste Zeit", which we used to sing at your Friday nights. The part "Es ist der alte Bund", sung by the large choir with its lovely, soft sopranos, sounded heavenly. One can hardly believe how much a single person, who has the will, can accomplish with others. Schelble works entirely by himself. The sense for serious music is certainly not outstandingly well de-

veloped in Frankfort, and yet it is astonishing how well young lady amateurs play the "Wohltemperiertes Clavier", the "Inventions" and all of Beethoven. They know everything by heart, they check every false note, and they possess a genuine musical culture. Schelble has created for himself an important field of activity, and has educated his public in the real sense of the word. Then, there is Philipp Veit, painting quietly at his canvases, which are so pure, and lovely and devout that I have seen their like only among the old masters. There is no mannerism and no affectation, such as can be found with the "Teutons" in Rome; there is nothing but the sincerity of an artist's soul.

And then one goes to Duesseldorf where Schadow is to be found, with his students, toiling and striving with all his might, in order to create something; where Lessing so very occasionally sketches his designs and works them out when he gets an order. And there again they have their small orchestra and their Beethoven symphonies. I do not know why I write you all this, for you know it better than I; but it came into my mind while I was thinking about all the people, scattered in every city, and of whom the country is composed.

This, however, is France, and that is why no German city can be compared to Paris. For all outstanding elements to be found in France flow together in this spot, while in Germany they become disseminated. Germany is made up of so and so many cities, but as far as music is concerned—and I believe that is true of all the arts—Paris is France. Here is their Conservatoire where people are educated and where a school is growing up; where all the talents from the provinces must be sent if they wish, in any degree, to complete their educations. For outside of Paris, in the whole of France there is hardly an orchestra worthy the name, and no outstanding musicians whatever. While here we have 1800 piano teachers—and still not enough—there is practically no music at all in the other cities. When an entire country is concentrated in a single city before one's eyes, when one is surrounded by the élite of a whole population, the surge of activity and the way in which everything is multiplied a thousandfold, is all more than I can describe. That is why everything and everybody here is immediately divided into compartments. Everyone seeks and finds his place. As for me, I hold to what you and my parents have taught me to love and have therefore been allotted to the école allemande (German school). I will not write about fashionable music; that is the same as I knew it seven years ago. What is most important and outstanding that I had not yet heard, is the Conservatoire Orchestra. Naturally it is the best that can be heard in France because it is the Paris Conservatoire that gives the concerts; but it is also the best that can be heard anywhere. They combined the best musicians in Paris and also took young violinists from the classes; they put one of the directors—a capable and enthusiastic musician—in charge and the orchestra then rehearsed for two years, until they were genuinely a unit and there was no longer any possibility of errors before they risked a performance. Actually, every orchestra should be like this, errors in rhythm and notes should never occur. But as such, unfortunately, is not the case, this is the best I have ever heard. Baillot's, Rode's and Kreutzer's schools supply the violinists; it is a joy to see that mass of young people in the orchestra, and how they start with exactly the same bowing, the same style, the same deliberation and ardour. Last Sunday there were fourteen on each side and Habeneck conducted with his bow . . . One can hear how each player completely fills his place, masters his instrument, knows his part and everything it requires, from memory; in short, that this orchestra is not made up of individual musicians but is a community. Also the outward conditions are very practically and intelligently treated. The concerts are not frequent (only once a fortnight) and take place on Sunday at two o'clock, so the occasion is a holiday in every respect, and the people afterward do nothing but go home for dinner; the impres-

sion remains with them because there is no opera on that night. The hall is small, so in the first place the music is doubly impressive and every detail is doubly clear; in the second place, the public is small, very distinguished and like a large social gathering. The musicians themselves really enjoy the great Beethoven symphonies, they are thoroughly familiar with them and take pleasure in having mastered them. Some people, for instance Habeneck himself, are certainly sincere in their love of Beethoven. But of the others, and especially the greatest shouters and enthusiasts, I do not believe one word; for now they make a point of disdaining the other masters; they speak of Haydn as of an old wig and of Mozart as of a good fellow, and such narrow-minded ecstasy cannot possibly be genuine. If they really appreciate what Beethoven had in mind, they must also know what Haydn was and feel very small. But they do not, and go briskly ahead with their judgments. The public at these concerts also loves Beethoven devotedly because it believes one has to be a connoisseur in order to love him; but only the fewest can take genuine pleasure in him, and I simply cannot bear to listen to people depreciating Haydn and Mozart; it makes me wild. The Beethoven symphonies to them are a kind of exotic plant, people sniff at their perfume but look upon them as curiosities, and if anybody goes far enough to count the stamens, and finds that they really belong to a familiar species, he is satisfied and lets the matter drop. There are already complaints about the coldness of the public this season and last, and several violin quartets scored for full string orchestra, with twenty-eight violins, etc. and double basses, without winds, will be given in order to present something new of his. I was even asked to do some instrumentation of this kind and to arrange the Sonate Pathétique for the Orchestre du Conservatoire, but I gave them a good lecture, and so it is going to be omitted; it will be given without wind instruments. But they must present one new composition, and this is my own gain, because my overture to the Midsummer Night's Dream will thus be played next Sunday . . .

FROM A LETTER TO HIS FATHER

Paris, February 21, 1832.

It is now high time, dear father, to write you a few words with regard to my travelling plans, and on this occasion in a more serious strain than usual, for many reasons. I must first, in taking the past in review, refer to what you designed to be the chief object of my journey; desiring me strictly to adhere to it. I was to examine the various countries closely, and to fix on the one where I wished to live and to work. I was, further, to make my name and capabilities known in order that the people, among whom I decided to settle, should receive me well, and not be wholly ignorant of my career. Finally, I was to take advantage of my own good fortune, and your kindness, to push forward in my subsequent efforts. It makes me feel happy to be able to say that I believe this has been done.

Always excepting those mistakes which are not discovered till too late, I think I have fulfilled your appointed object. People now know that I exist, and that I have a purpose; and any talent that I display, they are ready to approve and to accept. They have made advances to me here, and asked for my music, which they seldom do; as all the others, even Onslow, have been obliged to offer their compositions. The London Philharmonic has invited me to perform something new of my own there on the 10th of March. I also got the commission from Munich without taking any step whatever to obtain it, and they even did not wait till after my concert. It is my intention to give a concert here (if possible) and certainly in London in April, if the cholera does not prevent my going there; this is on my own account, in order to make money; also in order to try out such an affair before I return to you. Therefore, I may say that I have also fulfilled this part of your wish—that I should make myself known to the public.

Your injunction, too, to make a choice of the country that I preferred to live in, I have carried out just as completely; at least in a general way. That country is Germany. This is a point on which I have now quite made up my mind. I cannot yet, however, decide on the particular city; for the most important one of all, which for various reasons has so many attractions for me, I do not yet know well enough from this angle—I allude to Berlin. On my return, therefore, I must ascertain whether I shall be able to remain and establish myself there according to my views and wishes, after having seen and enjoyed other places.

This is also why I am not endeavouring to get a commission for an opera here. If I compose really good music, which in these days is indispensable, it will both be understood and valued in Germany. (This has been the case with all the good operas there). If I compose indifferent music, it will be quickly forgotten in Germany, but here it would often be performed and extolled, and sent to Germany, and given there on the authority of Paris, as we see daily. But I do not want this; and if I am not capable of composing good music, I have no wish to be praised for it. So I shall first try Germany; and if things go so badly that I can no longer live there, the foreign countries will still be left. Besides, few German theatres are so bad or in so dilapidated a condition as the Opéra Comique here, where one bankruptcy succeeds another. When Cherubini is asked why he does not allow his operas to be given there, he replies, "Je ne sais pas donner des opéras, sans choeur, sans orchestre, sans chanteurs, et sans décorations" ("I do not know how to give operas without a chorus, without an orchestra, without singers and without scenery"). The Grand Opéra has bespoken operas for years to come, so there is no chance of anything being accepted by it for the next three or four years.

In the meantime, therefore, I intend to return to you to write my "Tempest", and to see how it succeeds. The plan, therefore, dear father, that I wish to lay before you is this—to remain here till the end of March, or the beginning of April, (the invitation to the Philharmonic for the 10th of March, I have of course declined—taking an option) then to go to London for a couple of months. If the Rhenish Music Festival takes place, to which I am summoned, I shall go to Duesseldorf; and if not, I shall return direct to you by the shortest road, and be by your side in the garden soon after Whitsunday. Farewell!

Felix.

TO HIS FATHER

[*England*], *May 18, 1832.*

Dear Father,

I have received your letter of the 9th; God grant that Zelter may by this time be safe, and out of danger! You say that he already is so—but I shall anxiously expect your next letter, to see the news of his recovery confirmed. I have dreaded this ever since Goethe's death, but when it actually occurs, it is a very different thing. May heaven avert it!

Pray tell me also what you mean by saying "there is no doubt that Zelter both wishes, and needs, to have you with him, because, at all events for the present, it is quite impossible for him to carry on the Academy, whence it is evident that if you do not undertake it, another must, etc." Has Zelter expressed this wish to you, or do you only imagine that he might wish it? If the former were the case, I would instantly, on receiving your reply, write to Zelter, and offer him every service in my power—of every kind—and try to relieve him of all his labours, for as long a period as he desired; and this it certainly would be my duty to do.

I intended to have written to Lichtenstein before my return, about the proposal formerly made to me,[1] but of course I have given up all thoughts of doing so at present; for on no account would I assume that Zelter could not resume his duties, and even in that event, I could not reconcile myself to discuss the matter with any one but him. Every other mode of proceeding I should consider unfair towards him. If, however, he requires my services, I am ready, and shall rejoice if I can be of any use to him; and all the more, if he does not need me, and is entirely recovered. I beg you will write me a few words on this subject.

I must now inform you of my plans and engagements up to my departure. Yesterday I finished the "Rondeau brillant", and I am to play it this day a week at Mori's evening concert. The day after, I rehearse my Munich concerto at the Philharmonic, and play it on Monday the 28th at their concert; on the 1st of June is Moscheles' concert, where, with him, I play a concerto of Mozart's for two pianos, and conduct my two overtures, "The Hebrides" and "The Midsummer Night's Dream". Finally, the last Philharmonic is on the 11th, where I am to conduct some pieces. I must finish the arrangement for Cramer, and some "Lieder" for the piano, also some songs with English words, besides some German ones for myself; for after all it is spring, and the lilacs are in bloom. Last Monday "The Hebrides" was given for the first time in the Philharmonic; it went admirably, and sounded very quaint among a variety of Rossini pieces. The audience received both me and my work with extreme kindness. This evening is Mr. Vaughan's concert; but I am sure you must be quite sick of hearing of so many concerts, so I conclude.

---

1. *In reference to a situation in the Singakademie.*

Norwood, Surrey, May 25.

These are hard times, which obliterate much.[1] May God preserve you all to me, and grant us a joyful meeting! You will receive this letter from the same villa whence I wrote you three years ago last November, just before my return.

I have now come out here for a few days to rest, and to collect my thoughts, just as I did at that time, on account of my health. Nothing is changed, my room is precisely the same; even the music in the old cupboard stands in exactly the same spot; the people are quite as considerate, and quiet, and attentive as formerly, and the three years have passed over both them and their house as peacefully as if half the world had not been uprooted during that period. It is pleasant to see; the only difference is, that we now have gay spring and apple-blossoms and lilacs and all kinds of flowers, whereas at that time we had autumn, with its fogs and blazing fires. But how much is now gone for ever that we then still had; this gives much food for thought. Just as at that time I wrote to you saying little, save "farewell till we meet"; so must it be today. It will be a graver meeting, and I bring no "Liederspiel" with me, composed in this room, as the former one was, but God grant I may only find you all well.

You write, dear Fanny, that I ought especially to hurry back now—at double speed—in order that I may possibly get the position at the Singakademie. But I am not going to do it. I will return as soon as I can, because Father wrote me that he wished me to do so. But for no other reason than that; in fact the other motive would rather tend to keep me here, if any motive could do so; for I will in no manner solicit the situation. When I reminded my father formerly of the director's proposal, the reason which he then advanced against it seemed to me perfectly just. He said that he regarded the place rather as a sinecure for more advanced years,

1. *He had received the news of Zelter's death.*

"when the Academy might be resorted to as a harbour of refuge". For the next few years I aspire as little to this as to any other situation; my purpose is to live by what I compose, just as I do here, and I want to be independent. Considering the peculiar position of the Academy, the small salary they give, and the great influence they might exercise, the position of director seems to me only an honorary post, which I have no desire to sue for. If they were to offer it to me, I would accept it, because I promised formerly to do so; but only for a certain length of time and on certain conditions; and if they do not intend to offer it, then my presence can be of no possible use. I certainly do not need to convince them of my ability to fill the office; and I neither will, nor can, intrigue. Besides, for the reasons I mentioned in a previous letter, I cannot leave England till after the 11th, and the affair will no doubt be decided before then.

I wish, therefore, that no step of any kind may be taken on my behalf, except that which my father mentioned concerning my immediate return; but nothing in the smallest degree approaching to solicitation; and when they do make their choice, I only hope that they may find a man, who will perform his duties with as much zeal as old Zelter.

I received the intelligence in the morning just as I was going to write to him; then came a rehearsal of my new piece for the piano, with its wild gaiety, and when the musicians were applauding and complimenting me, I could not help feeling strongly that I was indeed in a foreign land. Then I came here, where I found both men and places unchanged; but Hauser unexpectedly arrived, and we fell into each other's arms, and recalled the happy days we had enjoyed together in South Germany the previous autumn, and all that has passed away for ever during the last six months. Your mournful news was always present in its sad reality —so this is the manner in which I have spent the last few days here. Forgive me for not being able to write properly today. I go to town this evening to play, and also tomorrow, Sunday, and Monday.

I now have a favour to ask of you, dear Father, in reference to the cantatas of Sebastian Bach, which Zelter possessed. If you can possibly prevent their being disposed of before my return, do so, for I am anxious at any price at least to see the entire collection before it is dispersed.

I might have told you of many agreeable things that have occurred to me during the last few weeks, for every day brings me fresh proofs that the people like me, and are glad to associate with me. It is gratifying, and makes my life here easy and pleasant, but today I really cannot. Perhaps in my next letter my spirits may be sufficiently restored to return to my usual narrative vein.

Many remembrances from the Moscheleses; they are excellent people, and after so long an interval, it is very cheering once more to meet an artist who is not a victim of envy, jealousy, or miserable egotism. He makes continued and steady progress in his art.

The warm sun is shining out-of-doors, so I shall now go down into the garden to perform some gymnastics there and to smell the lilacs; this will show you that I am well.

London, June 1.

On the day that I received the news of Zelter's death, I thought that I would have a serious illness; and indeed during the whole of the ensuing week I could not shake off this feeling. My manifold engagements, however, have now diverted my thoughts and brought me to myself, or rather out of myself. I am well again, and very busy.

First of all I must thank you, dear Father, for your kind letter. It is in a great measure already answered by my previous one, but I will now repeat why I decline to send any application to the committee. In the first place, I quite agree with your former opinion, that this situation in the Academy is not desirable at the outset of my career; indeed I could only accept it for a certain time, and under particular conditions, and even then, solely to keep my previous promise. If I solicit it, I am bound to accept the position as they choose to give it, and to comply with their conditions as to salary, duties, etc. without knowing them.

In the second place, the reason they gave you why I should write, seems to me neither a true nor a straightforward one. They say they wish to be certain I would accept and that for this reason I should enroll myself among the candidates. But they offered it to me three years ago, and Lichtenstein said they did so to ascertain whether I would take it, and begged me to give a definite answer. At that time I said yes, that I was willing to carry it on, along with Rungenhagen. I am not sure that I should think the same now; but as I said so then, I can no longer draw back, and must keep my word. It is not necessary to repeat my assent, for as I once gave it, so it must remain; it is even less possible to apply when that means that I should have to offer myself to them for the post they once offered to me. If they were disposed to adhere to their former offer, they would not require me to take a step which they took themselves three years ago; on the contrary, they would remember the assent I then gave, for they must know that I am incapable of breaking such a promise.

A confirmation of my former promise is therefore unnecessary, and if they intend to appoint another to the situation, my letter would not prevent their doing so. I must further refer to my letter from Paris, in which I told you that I wished to return to Berlin in the spring, as it was the only city in Germany with which I was still unacquainted.

This is my well-considered purpose; I do not know how I shall get on in Berlin, or whether I shall be able to remain there—that is, whether I shall be able to enjoy the same facilities for work and progress, that are available to me in other places. The only house that I know in Berlin is our own, and I feel certain I shall again be happy there. But I must also be active and I shall discover how when I return. I hope that all will come to pass as I wish, for of course the spot where you live must always be dearest to me. But till I know this for a certainty, I do not wish to fetter myself by any fixed position.

I conclude, because I have a vast deal to do to enable me to leave after the next Philharmonic. I must publish several pieces before I go; I receive numbers of commissions on all sides, and some so gratifying that I exceedingly regret not being able to accept them.

I received a note this morning, among others, from a publisher, who wishes to bring out the scores of two grand pieces of sacred music, for morning and evening service. You can imagine how much I am pleased with this proposal, and immediately on my arrival in the Leipziger Strasse I intend to begin them.

"The Hebrides" I mean to reserve for a time for myself, before arranging it as a duet; but my new rondo is in hand, and I must finish those everlasting "Lieder" for the piano, as well as various other arrangements, and probably the concerto. I played it last Monday in the Philharmonic, and I think I never in my life had such success. The audience went wild with delight and declared it was my best work. I am now going to Moscheles' concert, to conduct there and to play Mozart's concerto, in which I have inserted two long cadenzas for each of us.

Felix.

FROM LETTERS TO KARL KLINGEMANN

Berlin, July 4, 1832.

. . . Today, for the first time, I begin to feel that I want to stay here for no more than a year. My room is in order, the pictures are hung, Sebastian Bach over the piano, . . . and Rebecca's portrait side by side with Beethoven and a couple of Raphaels—so the walls are rather a medley. I also have a toilet table and on it stands a bottle of Eau de Cologne in its basket, which is particularly admired by all my aunts and my cousins, my three little travel-diaries, . . . several wallets, my sketch-books, . . . and my old paintbox with a couple of half-finished coloured landscapes, on which I should like to work now. On the other side of the room is my old wretched piano without strings which you certainly remember. I have just played my new song on it, "Sie wandelt im Blumengarten". Then there is a chest with old letters in which I found one that you sent me to Hamburg in April 1829, and which begins with, "it is a great and good thing that you are coming!"; and many potted plants, books, tables, several chairs and a lot of dust on the floor. And if by now you do not know what my place is like, it is not my fault.

There is not much news; my family is well and happy and we cannot understand how we managed to live apart for two whole years. The first real work I shall do here will probably be on my Scottish Symphony, although I would so much like to write the songs before that. All my clothes still smell strongly of coal and half of me is really still over there. Yesterday I visited the Singakademie for the first time; you cannot imagine how sad the hall looked to me without old Zelter and without Rietz. Its foundation was gone; but all the drawbacks have remained and stood out glaringly; there was nothing to cover them up; it was a mournful impression. I declared that I would never ask nor apply for the position of director; if they want to have me, let them make their offer, and I might accept it or not, but probably nothing will happen. The main conditions I would have to make would be a yearly leave of several months and the possibility of quitting whenever I choose, but I do not believe they can consent to such terms. However, my family also believes that the main object of my life now is to write six songs and a Symphony and many other works, and I am glad that they agree with me on this point . . .

Berlin, July 25, 1832.

. . . . *Time has not yet adjusted itself properly. I am still hanging between the present and the past; the recollections of my journey are still too vivid and every step I take in these streets or in the garden evokes dim images which I do not know where to place. This makes me feel restless and undecided, more than ever in my life, and since I have been here not one single note has come into my mind. Moreover Fanny is constantly ailing, my father had a heavy, feverish cold for some time, my own stomach rebels again in a most disagreeable manner, and above all, the weather is the most horrible I can remember; it pours the whole day long and is bitterly cold. The advent of cholera is announced again today, and I am led to believe that it is very serious in London; write me about it and reassure me about yourselves. I must also attend to the formalities concerning my year of service, and must—at last—write that sweet little letter to Immermann saying that I am unable to set his libretto to music; where should I find an inspiration for music and tone?* . . .

Berlin, August 4, 1832.

. . . *My life here begins slowly to take on a regular routine, but I still cannot get down to work. The morning and evening service for Novello which I have started does not count; that is just a daily chore—every morning one hour, and double canons to my heart's content—in other words, depending on my boredom. So I lie fallow and wait for better times, which, God willing, may come soon. I decided that your songs should get me into my stride again—when I begin to compose once more, I shall not stop again. And so I am awaiting them with twofold impatience; it would be nice if it turned out that they should be the first to set me going again.*

Moreover I made several unfortunate attempts to find the

brighter side of Berlin life, but it proved a dead failure. I went to a "musicale" at Jagor's, a meeting at the Academy of Arts, and a popular festival. The musicale was tame and lame, until Mr. Rex struck up the "integer vitae" and Bernhard Klein began to crack his bad jokes. At the Academy I witnessed a genuine blossoming of philistinism: a public report was scheduled and the treasurer announced that since the proceeds had not amounted to more than so-and-so-much, it had not been deemed appropriate to render a statement of the expenses. And finally there was not one single fresh face or pretty girl to be seen at the festival; so, out of sheer exasperation, I bought a ticket for eight groschen for the "Elysium", where in honour of the king's birthday they had set up a multicoloured arch over the entrance with "Love and Reverence", and had fireworks, and illuminations, and rope dancers, but not one decent person to look at—well, after all, my spirit of adventure became overwrought, and I swore never again to set eyes on festival, Academy or Elysium in this city . . .

TO VINCENT NOVELLO

Berlin, August 22, 1832.

My dear Sir,

I have to beg your pardon that the first letter I write to you is to be a letter of business, but if it were not for that, I should not venture to give you the trouble of reading so bad an English as mine is. I do not try to repeat you the thanks for all your kindness because I am not able to express it as I wish to do and as I feel it.

I want to ask you today whether you still remember your writing to me on that you wished me to compose an evening and morning

Mendelssohn's wife, Cécile Jeanrenaud.
Painting by Edouard Magnus, 1836.

Mendelssohn, 1836.

service for publication in your country? I could not then fix the time when I was to do it as it was the first thing in that style I was to compose. But as soon as I got quiet here I tried to begin the Te Deum in the style of your cathedral music, and it is now finished. Although it is not entirely as I wish it to be, and although I hope the following pieces will be better, I do not think it unworth being published and I accordingly want to ask you whether you are still of the same opinion which you expressed then to me in your kind note, and whether I am to go on with the composition of the service and to send it to you when it is finished. You asked me also for my terms; but I am really at a loss to fix them, as I never published any composition of the kind in your country. You would oblige me particularly if you would tell me your opinion on this subject, or if you do not like this let me know how you use to pay other compositions in that style, that I may fix my terms accordingly.

I hope if you answer to this you will write me at large how you and your family is going on, I want to know which painting your son is working at, what progresses the charming talent of your daughter has made, pray, let me know everything that concerns you and your family. It is now so long since I did not hear from you, and you know how glad I shall be to have news of you and all my friends there. I have still to thank you for your kindness you showed me in having my pianoforte melodies sold at your house; I think they must now be published already and I am excessively obliged to you for your kind and friendly behaviour. Adieu, my dear Sir, excuse this letter and let me soon have a great from you. Believe me to remain

Yours very truly

F. M. B.

FROM LETTERS TO KARL KLINGEMANN

Berlin, September 5, 1832.

. . . Since your last letter, old boy, my face has again visibly lengthened and my cheer shortened, because in the last few weeks I have felt so indescribably downhearted and depressed. Where this mood comes from hardly matters, though there are reasons enough. I would have preferred to conceal it from you, and not write at all for a long time, had I not decided once and for all to tell you everything I experience, pleasant or unpleasant, just as it happens. Of course I often tell you days later and by that time it may be all over. But as, at this moment, I am particularly despondent and because writing to you cheers me and eases my mind I know you will gladly grant me this pleasure although I also know how dreadful it is to receive such letters. The greatest contributing cause is the loss of beloved friends; with the death of lovely Miss Robert a goodly bit of my own youth has passed away. Moreover, I have been in ill health; I suffered from a terrible pain in the ear and later on from headache, but these things always go together. Then there is the present great quiet and monotony following upon the earlier period of excitement; the stagnation of Berlin, the negotiations about the Academy with which they annoy me more than necessary, and in the end will appoint their Rungenhagen to the post, or God knows whom else; and then there is my dull head which repels any cheerful thought—the devil take such a time! I have never lived through a more miserable period. Please write to me often; I have not much else to look forward to, and forgive me if I have nothing more to say today, except "I am down", and on these words I would like to write a canon . . .
I would also like to have you write me, first, whether Erard is in

Paris or in London because I have to dun him about my piano . . . Neukomm behaves here just as you would expect; he is just the right man for spinsters, for he really is a spinster himself. His extraordinary gentility in contrast to the Berliners, produces an exotic effect, and would be completely wasted if I did not make occasional notes about it in my memory and in my diary. Recently he read me a beautiful lecture on morale; I was admonished to be gay and happy, he had had his black days too and done this and that about them—I just listened patiently, so that when I get to be an old man I will know how to be like Neukomm; but all the time I wished him at the bottom of the sea; he is too boring.

Yesterday we practised his "Ten Commandments" [1] *in the Singakademie; the chorus "Thou shalt not commit adultery" sounded excellent. The girls do not understand what they are singing about, and the married women do not care. To me the work seems terribly dry; but that does not matter for nothing pleases me now. Apart from this, everything is going well; it will be performed in the Garnisonskirche for charity; Spontini and the Army are providing the brass. "Thou shalt not steal" roars and rolls like thunder, and the composer can be sure of a medal for Art and Science, or some other decoration of the kind. How all this disgusts me—when a chap keeps steering for such goals while pretending he is a philosopher with the highest standards.*

Give my love to my dear ones at Kensington,[2] *there is more poetry in them than Neukomm could dream of, although he is very fond of them too; but that is not difficult. And give my special greetings to the three charming, beautiful young girls; I feel definitely better when I think of them, and also when I think of you, and thus this letter has done me good, so let it go at that, even if you feel cross . . . We will meet again in spring!*

Your Felix.

1. *One of Neukomm's oratorios.*
2. *The Horsley family at whose country place in Kensington Mendelssohn and his friends spent many happy days.*

TO THE SECRETARY OF THE PHILHARMONIC SOCIETY OF LONDON

Berlin, November 28, 1832.

Dear Sir,

I am very much obliged to you for transmitting to me the resolution passed on the 5th November at the meeting of The Philharmonic Society. I beg you will be so kind as to express my sincerest acknowledgements and my warmest thanks for the gratifying manner in which the Society has been pleased to remember me. I feel highly honoured by the offer the Society has made, and I shall compose, according to the request, a Symphony, an Overture, and a vocal piece under the conditions mentioned in the resolution.

TO IGNAZ MOSCHELES

Berlin, February 27, 1833.

Dear Moscheles,

Here they are, wind instruments and fiddles, for the heir and son must not be kept waiting till I come [1]—he must have a cradle song with drums and trumpets and janissary music; fiddles alone are

1. *Birth of Moscheles' first son whose godfather Mendelssohn was.*

not nearly lively enough. May every happiness and joy and blessing attend the little stranger; may he be prosperous, may he do well whatever he does, and may it fare well with him in the world!

So he is to be called Felix, is he? How nice and kind of you to make him my godchild in forma! The first present his godfather

makes him is the above entire orchestra; it is to accompany him through life, the trumpets when he wishes to become famous, the flutes when he falls in love, the cymbals [1] when he grows a beard; the piano explains itself; and should people ever play him false, as will happen to the best of us, there stand the kettledrums and the big drum in the background.

Dear me! I am so very happy when I think of your happiness, and of the time when I shall have my full share in it. By the end of April at the latest, I intend to be in London, and then we will duly name the boy and introduce him to the world at large. It will be grand!

To your septet I look forward with no small pleasure. Klinge-

1. *The German word "Becken" has the double meaning of "cymbals" and "basin".*

mann has written out eleven notes of it for me, and those I like very much indeed:

I can quite imagine what a bright and lively finale they would make. He also gave me a good description and analysis of the andante in B-flat; but after all it will be better to hear it. Do not expect too much of the compositions I shall bring with me. You will be sure to find frequent traces of moodiness, which I can shake off only slowly and by dint of an effort. I often feel as if I had never composed at all, and had to learn everything over again; now, however, I have got into better trim, and my last things will sound better.

My sister and I make a great deal of music, every Sunday morning with accompaniment; and I have just received from the bookbinders a big grass-green volume of "Moscheles", and next time we are going to play your trio. Farewell, and remain happy!

Yours

F. M. B.

FROM LETTERS TO PASTOR BAUER

Berlin, March 4, 1833.

. . . Since I have begun my work again I am in such good spirits that I am anxious to cling to it as closely as possible and make it monopolise every moment that I do not spend with my family. The fact of a period like this last half year having already passed, makes me feel doubly grateful. The sensation is like that of going out for the first time after an illness; and in fact, such a term of

uncertainty, doubt and suspense really amounted to a malady, and one of the worst kind, too. Now, however, I am entirely cured; so, think of me as of a joyous musician who is doing many things, who is resolved to do many more, and who would like to accomplish all that can be done.

If I understand correctly the meaning of your last question and discussion, and if I were forced to give you an answer, it would be better to give up the ghost at once. Universality and everything bordering on aesthetics immediately render me dumb and dejected. Is it for me to tell you how you ought to feel? You strive to discriminate between an excess of sensibility and genuine good taste, and you say that a plant, too, may bloom itself to death.

But there is no such thing as an excess of sensibility, and what is called a "too-much" is always rather a "too-little". The soaring, elevated emotions inspired by music—so welcome to the listeners—are no excess; let him, who is capable of emotions, feel them to the utmost of his capacity—and more so, if possible. If he dies of it, it will not be a death in sin, for nothing is certain but what is felt, or believed, or whatever term you may choose to employ. Moreover, the blooming of a plant never causes it to perish; except when the blooming is forced, and forced to the utmost. And such sickness is no more a blossom than sentimentality is sentiment.

I am not acquainted with Mr. W., nor have I read his book; but it can only be deplored when anyone but a genuine artist attempts to purify and restore the public taste. On such a subject words are only pernicious; deeds alone are effective. Even if people really feel this antipathy for the present, they can give nothing of themselves to replace it and therefore had better leave it alone. Palestrina effected a reform during his lifetime; he could not do so at the present time any more than Sebastian Bach or Luther. The men are yet to come who will advance along the straight road—and it is they who will lead the others forward—or back to the ancient and correct path, which ought in fact to be termed the forward path; but they will write no books on the subject . . .

Berlin, April 6, 1833.

. . . My work,[1] which had given me many doubts recently, is finished; and now when I look it over it gives me satisfaction, contrary to my expectation. I believe it is a good composition, and, be that as it may, I feel that it shows progress, and that is the main point. As long as I feel thus, I can enjoy life and be happy; the period of last fall, when I had doubts of myself, was the most bitter I can think of, and that I have ever endured. Would that this mood of happy satisfaction could be hoarded and stored up! But this much is bad, namely my certainty that when similar unhappy days occur again, I shall have forgotten all about this; and I know of no cure, and even you will not be able to help me! Since at this moment, however, a whole mass of music is buzzing in my head, I trust that it will not, please God, pass away quickly.

Strange that all this should happen at a time which otherwise is so imbued with deep fervour and earnestness. I shall leave this place feeling more solitary than when I came. I have found only my nearest relatives unchanged, my parents, my brother and sisters, and this is a happiness for which I certainly cannot be sufficiently grateful to God. Now that I am—as they call it—independent, I have learned to love and to honour my parents even more than before and with better understanding. But otherwise I see, branching off to the right and to the left, many of those whom I hoped to have going along with me, and yet I cannot follow them on their path, even if I would try to do so . . .

1. *St. Paul.*

TO JULIUS SCHUBRING

Coblenz, September 6, 1833.

Dear Schubring,

Just as I was beginning to arrange the sheets of my oratorio[1] and was meditating on the music that I intend to write for it this winter, your letter enclosing your extracts came into my hands. All of it seemed to me to be so good, that I copied the whole text as far as it has gone, and now return it to you with the same request as at first: that you will kindly send me your remarks and additions. You will notice various annotations on the margin as to what I miss and as to what passages I would like to have from the Bible or the Hymn Book. Above all, I am anxious to have your opinion:

1) As to the form of the whole, especially the narrative part, and whether you think that the general arrangement may be retained—the blending of the narrative and the dramatic representation. I dare not adopt the Bach form along with this personified recital; so this combination seems to me the most natural, and not very difficult, except in such passages, for example, as that of Ananias, owing to the length of the continuous narration.

2) Whether you are of the opinion that any of the principal features in the history of the acts, and also in the character and teaching of St. Paul, have been either omitted or falsified.

3) Where you would mark the divisions of the first and the second part.

4) Whether you approve of my using chorales. From this I have

1. *St. Paul.*

been strongly dissuaded by various people and yet I cannot decide to give them up entirely, for I think they must be in character in any oratorio founded on the New Testament. If this be also your opinion, then you ought to supply me with all the hymns and passages. You see I require much from you, but I wish first to enter fully into the spirit of the words, and then the music will follow; and I know the interest you take in the work.

If you will do all this for me, write me a few lines immediately to Berlin, for I am obliged to go there for three or four days with my father, who went to England with me, and fell dangerously ill there. Thank God, he is now quite restored to health, but I was under such dreadful apprehension the whole time that I shall leave nothing undone on my part to see him once more safe at home. After that I must return forthwith and proceed to Duesseldorf. You are probably aware that I directed the Music Festival there and subsequently decided to take up my abode there for two or three years—nominally in order to direct church music and the Vocal Association, and probably also a new theatre which is now being built—but in reality for the purpose of securing quiet and leisure for composition. The country and the people suit me admirably, and this winter "St. Paul" is to be given. I brought out my new symphony in England, and people liked it; and now the "Hebrides" is about to be published and also the symphony. This is all very gratifying; but I hope the things of real value are yet to come. I trust it may be so. It is not fair of me to have written to you such a half-dry and wholly serious letter, but such has been the character of this recent period, and so, to a certain degree, I have grown like it.

TO REBECCA

Duesseldorf, October 26, 1833.

My dear little Sister,

The history of my life during the last few weeks is long and pleasant. Sunday I had my first Mass; the choir was crammed with singers, male and female, and the whole church decorated with green branches and tapestry. The organist flourished away tremendously, up and down. Haydn's Mass was scandalously gay, but the whole thing quite tolerable. Afterwards came a procession, playing my solemn march in E-flat, the bass performers repeating the first part, while those in the treble went straight on; but this was of no consequence in the open air; and when I encountered them later in the day, they had played the march over so often that it went famously; and I consider it a high honour that these itinerant musicians have asked me for a new march for the next fair.

Previous to that Sunday, however, there was rather a touching scene. I must tell you that no really appropriate epithet exists for the music which has hitherto been given here. The chaplain came and complained to me of his dilemma; the Mayor had said that though his predecessor was evangelical and perfectly satisfied with the music, he himself intended to form part of the procession, and insisted that the music should be of a better class. A very peevish old musician, in a threadbare coat, was summoned. Hitherto it had been his office to beat time. When he came and they attacked him, he declared that he neither could nor would have better music; that if we wanted to have it, we should look for somebody else; that he knew perfectly well what vast pretensions some people had nowadays; everything was expected to sound so beautiful; this had not been the case in his day, and he played just as well now as formerly. I was really very reluctant to take the affair out of his hands, though there could be no doubt that others would do infinitely better; and I could not help thinking how I should feel myself were I to be summoned some fifty years hence to a town hall, and have to speak in this way, and a young greenhorn snubbed me, and my coat was shabby, and I had not the remotest idea why the music should sound better—and I felt rather uncomfortable.

Unluckily I could not find among all the music here even one single, tolerable solemn Mass; not a single one of the old Italian masters; nothing but modern stuff. I took a fancy to travel through my domains in search of good music; so, after the Choral Association on Wednesday, I got into a carriage and drove off to Elberfeld, where I hunted out Palestrina's "Improperia", and the Misereres of Allegri and Baini, and also the score and the vocal parts of "Alexander's Feast", which I carried off forthwith, and went on to Bonn. There I rummaged through the whole library alone, for poor Breidenstein is so ill that he is hardly expected to recover. But he gave me the key and lent me whatever I chose. I found some splendid things and took away with me six Masses of Palestrina, one of Lotti and one of Pergolesi, and Psalms by Leo and Lotti, etc., etc. At last, in Cologne, I succeeded in finding the best Italian pieces which I have known so far, particularly two motets of Orlando Lasso, which are wonderfully fine, and even deeper and broader than the two "Crucifixus" of Lotti. One of these, "Populus meus", we are to sing in church next Friday.

The following day was Sunday, so the steamboat did not come, and knowing that my presence was necessary in Duesseldorf, I hired a carriage and drove here. People were crowding into the chaussée from every direction; a number of triumphal arches had been erected and the houses were all adorned with lamps. I arrived with my huge package, but nobody would look at it; there was only the "Crown Prince", the "Crown Prince", again and again. He arrived safely at the Jaegerhof on Sunday evening, passing under all the triumphal arches—during the illumination and amid the pealing of bells and firing of cannon—with an escort of burgher guards, between lines of soldiers and to the sound of martial music. Next day he gave a dinner to which he invited me, and I amused myself famously, because I was very jovial at a small table with Lessing, Huebner, and a few others. Besides, the Crown Prince was as gracious as possible and shook hands with me, saying that he really was quite angry at my forsaking both him and Berlin for so long a time, listened to what I had to say and called me out from my corner as "Dear Mendelssohn". In short, you see, I am thought infinitely more precious when I am a little way from home.

I must now describe to you the fête that was given in his honour, and for which I suggested the use of some old transparencies, to be connected—by appropriate verses from "Israel in Egypt"—with tableaux vivants. They took place in the great hall of the Academy, where a stage was erected. In front was the double chorus (about ninety voices altogether), standing in two semicircles round my English piano; and in the room were seats for four hundred spectators. R. in medieval costume, interpreted the whole affair, and contrived very cleverly, in iambics, to combine the different objects, in spite of their disparity. He exhibited three transparencies: first "Melancholy", after Duerer, a motet of Lotti's being sung by men's voices in the distance; then the Raphael, with the Virgin appearing to him in a vision, to which the "O Sanctissima" was sung (a well-known song, but which always makes people cry); thirdly St. Jerome in his tent, with a song of Weber's "Hoer' uns, Wahrheit". This was the first part. Now came the best of all. We began from the very beginning of "Israel in Egypt". Of course, you know the first recitative and how the chorus gradually swells in tone; first the voices of the alti are heard alone, then more voices join in until the loud passage comes with single chords: "They sighed", etc. (in G minor). Then the curtain rose and displayed the first tableau, "The Children of Israel in Bondage", designed and arranged by Bendemann. In the foreground was Moses, gazing dreamily into the distance in sorrowful apathy, beside him an old man sinking to the ground under the weight of a beam, while his son makes an effort to relieve him of it; in the background some beautiful figures with uplifted arms, a few weeping children in the foreground, the whole scene closely crowded together like a mass of fugitives. This remained visible till the close of the first chorus; and when it ended in C minor, the curtain at the same moment dropped over the bright picture. A finer effect I have hardly ever seen.

The chorus then sang the plagues, hail, darkness and the first-born, without any tableau; but at the chorus, "He led them through like sheep", the curtain rose again, and Moses was seen in the foreground with raised staff, and behind him, in gay tumult, the same figures, who in the first tableau were mourning, now all pressing onwards, laden with gold and silver vessels. One young girl was especially lovely; with her pilgrim's staff, she seemed to be advancing from the wings and was about to cross the stage. Then came the choruses again, without tableau: "But the waters", "He rebuked the Red Sea", "Thy right hand, O Lord", and the recitative, "And Miriam the Prophetess", at the close of which the solo soprano appeared. At the same moment the last tableau was discovered: Miriam, with a silver timbrel, sounding praises to the Lord, and other maidens with harps and zithers, and in the background four men with trombones, pointing in different directions. The soprano solo was sung behind the scene, as if proceeding from the picture; and when the chorus came in forte, real trombones and trumpets, and kettledrums, were brought on the stage and burst in like a thunder-clap. Haendel evidently intended this effect, for after the commencement he makes them pause till they come in again in C major, when the other instruments in turn appear and disappear. And thus we concluded the second part.

This last tableau was by Huebner, and pleased me exceedingly. The effect of the whole was wonderfully fine. Much might possibly be said against it had it been a pretentious affair, but its character was entirely social and not public, and I think it would hardly have been possible to devise a more charming fête. The next that followed was a tableau vivant, designed and arranged by Schadow, namely "Lorenzo di Medici, surrounded by the Geniuses of Poetry, Sculpture and Painting, leading to him Dante, Raphael, Michelangelo and Bramante", with a fine complimentary allusion to the Crown Prince, and a final chorus. The second division consisted of the comic scenes from the "Midsummer Night's Dream", represented by the painters here; but I did not care so much for it, having been so absorbed by the previous one.

Do you attend to my advice about piano playing and singing? If you want any songs, as Christmas is drawing near, you can get them from me if you wish. Send for the "Hebrides" arranged as a duet; it is no doubt published by this time. I think, however, that the overture to "Melusine" will be the best thing I have yet done; as soon as it is finished I will send it to you. Adieu!

Felix.

FROM A LETTER TO KARL KLINGEMANN

Berlin, December 26, 1833.

. . . This is not just an ordinary day: it is the 28th anniversary of my parents wedding, and at the same time, the third anniversary of the performance of a "Liederspiel" in A major. Do not tell me about the peculiar depressions of those blessed with good fortune; it has nothing to do with me, for I know how thankful I am for the happiness that is vouchsafed me. But if my mind is sometimes troubled, I feel it very deeply, and I do not like to hide it from you.

Things are no longer what they were at the time of the "Liederspiel", and although I really have completely overcome all feelings of depression at the change, it was no easy task and I still have a very strange sensation when I compare conditions. Only my parents are completely unchanged, or rather, even kinder and less reserved; when I am with them, I miss nothing, and the same thing with my sisters. But outside of our home every step reminds me how the city has stopped dead, and therefore gone backward. Music suffers, people have grown more narrow-minded than ever, the best of them have passed away, others who once nursed fine plans are now happy philistines and sometimes remember the days of their youth . . .

FROM A LETTER TO IGNAZ MOSCHELES

Duesseldorf, February 7, 1834.

My dear friend,

Pardon my long silence; I know how guilty I am, but I reckon on your indulgence. I am so deeply buried in my work and papers that even now I doubt if I would have emerged from them, were it not that a special circumstance obliges me to write to you. So let me pass over the last four months and all my excuses into the bargain, remembering what a dear old friend you are and how ready to forgive.

Thus encouraged, I fancy myself in Chester Place and wish you "Good evening". What I have to say is this: I have ventured to dedicate to you, without asking your permission, a piece [1] which is to appear at Simrock's, and of which I am very fond. But that is not what I was going to say. I had thought how nice it would be if you met with it during one of your trips to Germany; but now my Rondo Brillant [2] is just finished, and I have the very greatest desire to dedicate that to you, as well; but I do not venture to do it without your special permission, for I am well aware that it is not the correct thing to ask leave to dedicate two pieces at once; and perhaps you will think it rather an odd proceeding on my part. But I cannot help it, I have set my heart upon it. Write me a line on the subject, as the Rondo is to appear in Leipzig too; and once you have written a line, you may feel inclined to add another, or

1. *Fantasie in F-Sharp minor, op. 28.*
2. *Rondo E-Flat major, op. 29.*

perhaps a few more, as you did in your last kind letter, for which I have not even thanked you yet.

The last of your compositions of which I heard was the Impromptu for Mary Alexander, and since then I am sure you have produced all kinds of delightful things. My own poverty in shaping new forms for the piano struck me again more forcibly while I was writing the Rondo. It is there that I got into difficulties and had to toil and labour, and I am afraid you will notice it. Still, there are things in it which, I believe, are not bad, and some parts that I really like; but how I am to start writing a calm and quiet piece (as you advised me last spring) I really do not know. All that passes through my head in the shape of piano music is about as calm and quiet as Cheapside; and when I sit down to the piano and compel myself to start improvising very quietly, it is of no use—by degrees I fall back into the old ways.

My new "Scena",[3] however, which I am writing for the Philharmonic, will, I am afraid, be only too tame. But so much self-criticism is not good; so I stick to my work, and that means in plain language that I am well and happy.

I feel particularly comfortable in this place, having just as much official occupation as I want and like, and plenty of time for myself. When I do not feel inclined to compose, there is conducting and rehearsing, and it is quite a pleasure to see how well and brightly things go. And then the place is so charmingly diminutive that you can always fancy yourself in your own room, and yet it is complete in its way. There is an opera, a choral society, an orchestra, church-music, a public, and even a small opposition; it is simply delightful. I have joined a society formed for the improvement of our theatre and we are now rehearsing the "Wasserträger". It is quite touching to see how eagerly and hungrily the singers pounce upon every hint, and what trouble they will take if anyone will trouble to teach them; how they strain every nerve

3. *"Infelice", concert air for soprano and orchestra, op. 94.*

and really make our performance as perfect as can be imagined, considering the means at our disposal. Last December I gave "Don Juan" (it was the first time I had conducted an opera in public) and, I can assure you, many things went better and with more precision than at performances I have heard at some of the large and famous theatres; because from first to last everyone concerned threw himself into it heart and soul. Well, we had twenty rehearsals. The lessee of the theatre had, however, thought fit to raise the prices on account of the heavy expenses; and when the curtain rose on the first performance the malcontent section of the public called wildly for Signor Derossi and made a tremendous disturbance. After five minutes, order was restored and we began, going through the first act splendidly, constantly accompanied by applause. But lo and behold! as the curtain rose on the second act, the uproar broke out afresh with redoubled vigour and persistence. Well, I felt inclined to hand the whole concern over to the devil; never did I conduct under such trying circumstances. I cancelled the opera which was announced for the next night, and declared I would have nothing more to do with the whole theatre. Four days later I allowed myself to be talked over, gave a second performance of "Don Juan", was received with hurrahs and a threefold flourish of trumpets, and now the "Wassertraeger" is to follow. The opposition consists mainly of beerhouse-keepers and waiters; in fact, by four P.M. half Duesseldorf is drunk. Anybody wanting to see me must call between eight and nine in the morning; it is quite useless attempting to do any kind of business in the afternoon.

Now what do you think of such a discreditable state of affairs, and can you have anything more to say to such boors as we are?

Can you not send me one or the other of your new works, a copy, or whatever you like? I hear from my mother that the "Gipsies' March", or rather the "April Variations" are out. Is that the case? I hope you have done a good deal of patching and polishing to my part—you know, I am thinking of those restless passages of mine. The whole of the last number needs repairing or lining with a warm melody; it was too thin. The first variation too, I hope, you have turned inside-out and padded . . .

But I must really take courage and another little sheet of paper and write to your wife, for I haven't half finished. Good-by—till we meet again on the next page!

Dear Mrs. Moscheles,

It is only after having spent two hours in writing to Moscheles that I venture on the letter to you . . . I am sorry to say I shall not be going to England this spring. I mean to have a good spell of work and have something to show for it before I stir from here. You can hardly imagine how much better and brighter I feel for the last two months' work, and how much more easily I get on with it. So I must keep it up and get into full swing. My birthday came just in time to remind me how necessary this was . . .

By the way, you are rather opposed to Goethe in some things; so I recommend that you read a newly published correspondence between him and Zelter, in which you will find plenty to confirm your opinion; and yet I should vigorously oppose you and stand up for my old favourite as before. Do you know the chorus on Lord Byron, which occurs in the second part of "Faust" and begins with "Nicht allein"? Should you not know it, pray read it at once, for I believe it will please you.

Ever your

F. M. B.

TO HIS FATHER

Duesseldorf, March 28, 1834.

Dear Father,

A thousand thanks for your kind letter on my mother's birthday. I received it in the midst of a dress rehearsal for the "Wassertraeger", otherwise I should have answered and thanked you for it the same day. Pray write to me thus often. More than anything I feel grateful to you for your admonitions about industry and my own work. Believe me, I intend to profit by your advice; still I do assure you that I have not had an atom of that philosophy which would counsel me to give way to indolence, or even in any degree to condone it. During the last few weeks, it is true, I have been incessantly engaged in active business, but exclusively of a nature to teach me much that was important, and calculated to improve me in my profession; and thus I never lost sight of my work.

My having composed beforehand the pieces bespoken by the Philharmonic and the English publishers, was owing not only to having received the commission, but also to my own inward impulse, because it is really very long since I have written—or worked at—anything steadily, for which a certain mood is indispensable. But all this leads to the same point, so I certainly do not believe that these recreations will dispose me to become either more careless or more indolent. And, as I said before, they really are not mere amusements but positive work, and often pleasant work, too. A good performance in the Duesseldorf theatre does not find its way into the world at large—indeed, scarcely perhaps beyond the Duesseldorfers themselves. But if I succeed in thoroughly delighting and exciting both my own feelings and those of all in the house who are in favour of good music, that is worth something, too!

The week before the "Wassertraeger" was given was most fatiguing; every day two long rehearsals—that often averaged from nine to ten hours—besides the preparations for the church music this week; and I was obliged to oversee everything,—the acting, the scenery, and the dialogue—or it would all have gone wrong. On Friday, therefore, I came to my desk feeling rather weary; we had been obliged to have a complete dress rehearsal in the forenoon, and my right arm was quite stiff. The audience, too, who had neither seen nor heard of the "Wassertraeger" for the last fifteen or twenty years, were under the impression that it was some old forgotten opera, which the committee wished to revive, and all those on the stage felt very nervous. This, however, gave exactly the right tone to the first act; such tremor, excitement, and emotion pervaded it all that at the second piece of music the Duesseldorf opposition kindled into enthusiasm, and they all applauded and shouted and wept by turns.

It is long since I have had such a delightful evening in the theatre, for I took part in the performance like one of the spectators, and laughed, and applauded, and shouted "bravo", and yet conducting with spirit the whole time; the choruses in the second act sounded as precise as if fired from a pistol. The stage was crowded between the acts, every one pleased, and congratulating the singers. The orchestra played with precision, except some plaguey fellows who, in spite of all my threats and warnings, could not be prevailed upon to take their eyes off the stage during the performance, and to look at their notes. On Sunday it was given again and did not go half as well; but I had my full share of enjoyment the first time, though the house, on this second occasion, was far more crowded, and the effect the same. I write you all these details, dear Father, for I know that you are interested in this opera, and in our provincial doings. We really have as much music, and as good music, as could be expected during my first winter here. Tomorrow evening (Good Friday) we are to sing in church the "Last Seven Words" of Palestrina, which I found in Cologne, and a composition of Lasso, and on Sunday we give Cherubini's Mass in C major.

The Government order prohibiting the celebration of the Music Festival on Whitsunday is a bad business; the news came yesterday, and has inflicted such a blow on the festival that we have no idea here how it can be arranged; for on no other day can we reckon on so much support from strangers. The first meeting of the Theatrical Association took place recently; the matter has been very sensibly begun, and may turn out well; but I keep out of the way, because, in spite of the pleasure that the opera, for instance, has given me lately, I can feel no sympathy for actual theatrical life, or the squabbles of the actors and the incessant striving after effect; it also estranges me too much from my own chief purpose in Duesseldorf, which is to work for myself. I am the chief superintendent of the musical performances, the arrangements of the orchestra, and the engaging of the singers, and about every month I have an opera to conduct (but even this is to depend on my own convenience). Of course I still have my three months' vacation. In short, I wish to be entirely independent of the theatre and to be considered only as a friend, but with no official duties; on this account I have given up all claim to any salary which is to be transferred to a second conductor, on whom the chief trouble will devolve.

Last week I had a great treat, for Seydelmann from Stuttgart was here and enchanted us all. As "Nathan" he could not be excelled. I thought of you, and wished you were here a hundred times at least. When he told the story of the rings it was just as if you saw a broad tranquil stream gliding past, so rapid and flowing, and yet so smooth and unruffled; the words of the discreet judge were most exciting. It is indeed a splendid piece! It is good to know that there is such clearness in the world. It offends many, however, and when we were on the Grafenberg next day we had a war to the knife, because Schadow was so irritable on the subject, and a gentleman from Berlin declared that "viewed from a dramatic aspect . . ." I did not argue the point at all, for where there is such a total difference of opinion on any subject, even about first principles, there is nothing to be done.

I must now ask your advice on a particular subject. I have long wished to ride here, and when Lessing recently bought a horse he advised me strongly to do the same. I think the regular exercise would do me good—this is in favour of the scheme; but against it there is the possibility of its becoming an inconvenient and even tyrannical custom, as I should think it rather my duty to ride, if possible, every day. Then I also wished to ask you whether you don't think it rather too genteel for me, at my years, to have a horse of my own. In short, I am undecided, and beg now, as I have often done before, to hear your opinion, by which mine will be regulated. Farewell, dear Father.

Your

Felix.

FROM LETTERS TO IGNAZ AND CHARLOTTE MOSCHELES

Duesseldorf, April, 1834.

Dear Moscheles,

I cannot tell you how happy those letters from you and your wife made me. Such kind and friendly words as you wrote about my overture[1] give me greater pleasure than anything that I could possibly hear after completing a composition. This I know for a

1. Moscheles had been studying and rehearsing Mendelssohn's "Melusina" overture to prepare its first performance in England.

certainty: you might have sent me three of the finest Russian orders or titles for the overture without giving me one hour of such happiness as I have had from your letters . . .

It is quite a painful feeling to have a piece performed and not be present, not to know what succeeded and what went wrong. But when you are conducting I really feel less nervous than if I were there myself, for no one can take more interest in his own works than you do in those of others; and then you hear and take note of a hundred things that the composer, preoccupied as he is, has neither time nor mind for. After reading your letter I took up the score and played it straight through from beginning to end, and felt that I liked it better than before.

By the way, you complain of difficulty in getting the piani observed, and as I was playing the piece over again, it struck me that that was really my fault. The whole thing is due, I believe, to the marks of expression; if you have those altered in the parts, it will be set right at once. First, everything ought to be marked one degree weaker; that is, where there is a p in the wind instruments, it should be a pp; instead of mf, piano; instead of f, mf. The pp alone might remain, as I particularly dislike ppp. The sf's, however, should be struck out everywhere as they really are quite wrong; it is not an abrupt accent that is intended, but a gradual swelling of the tone, which is sufficiently indicated by the

The same is true again wherever the

etc. recurs; in all such passages the sf's should be done away with; and in the strings as well. For instance at the very opening, and where the trumpets first come in, it should be pp; the f's should simply disappear. Klingemann would, I am sure, make these alterations in the score, a copyist could transfer them to the parts, and then the whole thing would sound twice as mermaidish.

What you say of Berlioz's overture,[1] I thoroughly agree with. It is a chaotic, prosaic piece, and yet more humanly conceived than some of his others. I always felt inclined to say with Faust:

> *"He ran about, he ran about,*
> *His thirst in puddles laving;*
> *He gnawed and scratched the house throughout,*
> *But nothing cured his raving;*
> *And driven at last, in open day,*
> *He ran into the kitchen."*

For his orchestration is such a frightful muddle, such an incongruous mess, that one ought to wash one's hands after handling one of his scores. Besides, it is really a shame to set nothing but murder, misery and wailing to music; even if it were well done, it would simply give us a record of atrocities. At first he made me quite melancholy, because his judgments on others are so clever, so cool and so correct, he seems so thoroughly sensible, and yet he does not perceive that his own works are such nonsensical rubbish . . .

And so, dear Mrs. Moscheles, the people at the Philharmonic did not like my "Melusine"? Never mind; that won't kill me. I felt sorry when you told me, and at once played the overture through, to see if I too should dislike it; but it pleased me, and so there is no great harm done. Or do you think it would make you receive me less amiably on my next visit? That would be a pity, and I should much regret it; but I hope that won't be the case. And perhaps it will be liked somewhere else, or I can write another which will have more success. The first desideratum is to see a thing take shape and form on paper; and if, besides, I am fortunate enough to get such kind words about it as those I had from you and Moscheles, it has been well received and I may go on quietly doing more work . . .

1. *Overture "Les Francs Juges".*

. . . I am taking regular lessons in water colours now with one of our artists, working most enthusiastically for several hours every Sunday morning. Shall I send you a sketch? And what country should it represent? Switzerland or Italy? In the foreground I shall introduce a girl with a green apron and a carnation, to ingratiate myself with Serena.[1] I only wish I had more leisure, but just now all my time is taken up by the rehearsals of the "Wassertraeger".[2]

By-the-by, do you know a book by Thomas Moore on religion? [3] It appeared recently, is said to have gone through at least seventy editions, and to have extinguished all Protestants, Dissenters, nations and nationality. It is read here by all the orthodox Catholics, and praised highly.

I have lately read Shakespeare's "King John" for the first time. I do assure you, it is downright heavenly, like everything else of his. But now I must end at once, or I shall begin talking about Goethe's and Zelter's letters, which I did not much like. You are of a different opinion, so my letter might become not only too long, but also tedious, which it is already; besides, the paper obliges me to conclude . . . Let me have a few lines, telling me that Chester Place is flourishing. Once more thanks and farewell!

F. M. B.

TO HIS MOTHER

Duesseldorf, May 23, 1834.

A week ago yesterday I drove to Aix-la-Chapelle, as a ministerial order was issued, only five days before the Festival, sanctioning the celebration of Whitsunday . . . The diligence was eleven

1. *Eldest daughter of the Moscheles'.*
2. *Opera of Cherubini.*
3. *"Travels of an Irish Gentleman in Search of a Religion".*

hours on the journey and I was shamefully impatient and downright cross when it arrived. We went straight to the rehearsal and, seated in the pit, I heard a movement or two from "Deborah"; whereupon I said: "I positively will write to Hiller from here for the first time in two years, because he has performed his office so well". For really his work was unpretentious and harmonious, and subordinated to Haendel, from which he had cut out nothing. So I was rejoiced to see that others are of my opinion, and act accordingly. In the first tier a man with a moustache was seated, reading the score; and when, after the rehearsal, he went downstairs just as I was coming up, we met in the passage, and who should stumble right into my arms, but Ferdinand Hiller who almost hugged me to death for joy. He had come from Paris to hear the oratorio, and Chopin had left his scholars in the lurch and come with him, and thus we met again. I now had my full share of delight in the Musical Festival, for we three lived together and got a private box in the theatre (where the oratorio is performed), and of course next morning we betook ourselves to the piano where I had the greatest enjoyment. They have both much improved in execution, and, as a pianist, Chopin is now one of the very first of all. He produces new effects like Paganini on his violin, and achieves wonderful passages, such as no one could formerly have thought practicable. Hiller, too, is an admirable player—vigorous and yet light. Both, however, rather toil in the Parisian spasmodic and impassioned style, too, often losing sight of time and sobriety and of true music; I, on the other hand, do so perhaps too little,—thus we all three mutually learn and improve each other, while I feel rather like a schoolmaster, and they a little like mirliflores or incroyables. After the festival we travelled together to Duesseldorf and passed a most agreeable day there, playing and discussing music; then I accompanied them yesterday to Cologne. Early this morning they went off to Coblenz per steamer,—I in the other direction,—and the pleasant episode was over . . .

TO KARL KLINGEMANN

Duesseldorf, June 28, 1834.

Here you have a fanfare for the commencement of the opera. Have you really begun it? Send me immediately at least the first line—and at best, everything that is finished. Seriously, my dear boy, I am very grateful to you and I beg you to stick to it now, so that for once in my life I shall have an opportunity to write an opera. Will you kindly send me by return of post a copy of the approximate outline, as far as you have made it. I have a number of ideas for the last act but cannot arrange them until I know—if only in the most general outline—how you want to start the plot;

but those ideas might prove useful if I could cultivate them now. Let me know what you have retained from your and my notes and plans and what you have dropped so that I can finish my part. I had several suggestions for the first act, in two different styles each, and in order to go on with the third, I have to know which of them you would like to adopt. The third act will be the most difficult, but if I am not mistaken, the newest and most appealing of the whole work. Our favourite idea—the "closing of the circle"—can be completely realised.

Thanks, thanks, old boy! Tell me! what kind of overture ought I write to the opera? One of the fairy-kind, or otherwise fantastic? And in what key? I believe that if you let me have the libretto this year, I can bring the completed score to England next spring. Because I know I shall get into the stride!

I also would like to write for next spring a new overture for the Philharmonic Society. Probably "Macbeth". Do you like the idea? Or would you prefer another of Shakespeare's?

So, God willing, we shall meet early next year, play over our opera, have a happy, happy time again and enjoy life. Keep in good health, work hard and let me soon hear from you, see, read, and compose you. In fact, let us form a double-alliance, as they call it now. Actually we could give Talleyrand the model for one.

F. M. B.

FROM A LETTER TO PASTOR BAUER

Duesseldorf, January 12, 1835.

. . . What I do not understand is the purport—musical, dramatic, oratorical, or whatever you choose to call it—that you have in view. What you say regarding that—the time before John, and then

John himself, till the appearance of Christ—is to my mind equally conveyed by the word "Advent", or the birth of Christ. You are aware, however, that the music must represent one particular moment, or a succession of moments, and you do not write what your conception is of this point. Real church music, that is, music for the Evangelical Church Service, which could be introduced in the celebration of the service proper, seems to me impossible; and this not merely because I cannot see into which part of the public worship music could be introduced, but because on the whole I cannot imagine that such a part even exists. Perhaps you have something to say that may give me further enlightenment on the subject, but actually I do not know—even setting aside the Prussian Liturgy which excludes everything of the sort, and which probably will neither remain as it is, nor go further—how one could arrange to make music form an integral part of our service instead of becoming a mere concert which more or less evokes a devotional mood. This was the case with Bach's "Passion"; it was sung in church as an independent piece of music, for edification. As for actual church music, or if you like to call it so, music for public worship, I know none but the old Italian compositions for the Papal Chapel, where, however, music is a mere accompaniment, subordinate to the sacred functions, co-operating with the wax candles, the incense, etc. If it be this style of church music that you mean, then, as I said before, I am unable to find a connecting link which would enable one to employ it. For an oratorio, one principal theme must be adopted, the progressive history of particular persons, else the object would seem too vague; for if it is all to be only contemplative, with reference to the coming of Christ, then this task has already been more grandly and beautifully accomplished in Haendel's "Messiah", where he begins with Isaiah and, taking the Birth as a focal point, closes with the Resurrection.

When you say, however, "our poor Church", I want to tell you that to my great astonishment I have discovered that the Catholics, who have had music in their churches for several centuries and sing a musical Mass every Sunday if possible, to this day have not a single one which can be considered even tolerably good, or, in fact, one which is not downright annoying and operatic. This applies from Pergolesi and Durante, who introduce the most ridiculous little shakes into their "Gloria", down to the opera finales of the present day. Were I a Catholic, I would set to work at a Mass this same evening, and whatever the result, it would at all events be the only Mass written with constant attention to its sacred purpose. But for the present I do not intend to do it—perhaps some time in years to come, when I am older . . .

FROM A LETTER TO IGNAZ MOSCHELES

Duesseldorf, February 7, 1835.

. . . Recently I was asked to edit a musical review. I should have liked to call down the firm that made the request; for nothing seems more unsatisfactory or distasteful to me than a concern of that kind, in which you undertake to suit other people's pleasure and keep all the annoyance to yourself. The other day a local composer sent me some songs with guitar accompaniment and asked for my opinion. The first began thus:

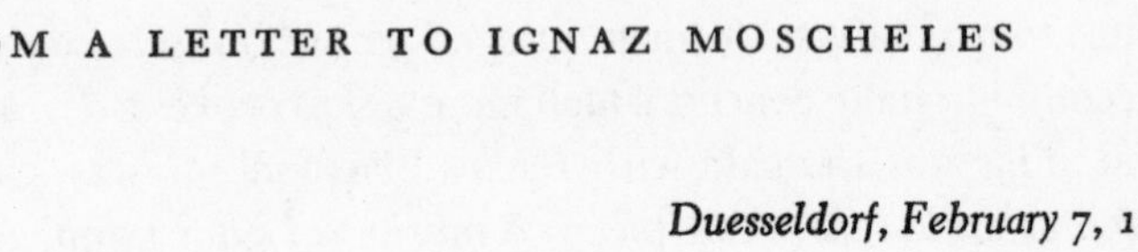

whereupon the voice comes in, and towards the end of the letter the man asks me whether in my judgment Haendel was really the great man he is usually taken to be. Now, wouldn't he do for the editor? What better qualification for the post than that song and that question? . . . Among the new music you are constantly looking through, have you come across anything good? I have not seen anything that I quite like. A book of Mazurkas by Chopin and a few new pieces of his are so mannered that they are hard to stand. Hiller, too, has written two books of songs that he had better left unwritten. I so wish I could admire it all; but it is really so little to my taste, that I cannot. There are also a few things by some Berliners and Leipzigers, who would like to begin where Beethoven left off. They can "clear their throats" as he does, and "cough his cough", and that is just all. To me it is like riding across fields after a rain; on horseback they can dash along splendidly, even if they get splashed, but when they try to walk, they get stuck fast in the mud. I have heard "Gustave III" by Auber; in that kind of opera the music is fast becoming of secondary importance—a good thing, too . . . But I dare say you know all that, as well as the good news that the "Oeuvres complètes de Moscheles" are about to appear at Schlesinger's . . .

TO LOUIS SPOHR

Duesseldorf, March 8, 1835.

Respected Capellmeister,

I thank you very much for your friendly communication. The intelligence from Vienna was most interesting to me; I had heard nothing of it. It strongly revived my feeling as to the utter impossibility of my ever composing anything with a view to competing for a prize. I should never be able even to make a beginning; and if I were obliged to undergo an examination as a musician, I am convinced that I should be refused at once for I should not do half as well as I could. The thoughts of a prize, or a judgment would distract my thoughts; and I still cannot rise so superior to this feeling as entirely to forget it. But if you find that you are in the mood for such a thing, you should not fail to compose a symphony by that time and to present it, for I know no man living who could dispute the prize with you (this is the second reason), and then we would have another symphony of yours (first reason). With regard to the members of the Judicial Committee in Vienna, I have my own thoughts, which are not very legitimate, but, on the contrary, somewhat rebellious. Were I one of the judges, not a single member of the Committee would obtain a prize if he competed for one.

You wish me to write to you on the subject of my works, and I cordially thank you for asking about them. I began an oratorio about a year ago, which I expect to finish next month, the subject of which is St. Paul. Some friends have compiled the words for me from the Bible, and I think that both the subject and the compilation are well adapted to music and very solemn. If the music only proves to be as good as I wish! At all events, I have enjoyed the most intense delight while engaged in writing it. Some time ago I also composed a new overture to "Lovely Melusina", and have another in my head at this moment. How gladly would I write an opera! but near and far I can find no libretto and no poet. Those who have the genius of poetry abhor music, or know nothing of the theatre; others are neither acquainted with poetry, nor with mankind, only with the boards and lights and wings and canvas. Thus I never succeed in finding the opera which I have so eagerly, yet vainly striven to procure. I regret this more every day, but I hope at last to meet with the kind of man I desire. I have also written several pieces of instrumental music recently, chiefly for *the piano, but also others; perhaps you will permit me to send you some of these as soon as I have an opportunity to do so. I am, with the highest esteem and consideration,*

Your devoted

F. M. B.

LETTER TO FELIX MENDELSSOHN-BARTHOLDY FROM HIS FATHER[1]

Berlin, March 10, 1835.

This is the third letter I have written to you this week, and, if it goes on, reading my letters will become a permanent item in the distribution of your time budget; but you must blame yourself for this, as you spoil me by your praise.

I will pass at once to the musical portion of your last letter. Your aphorism, that every room in which Sebastian Bach is sung is transformed into a church, I consider peculiarly appropriate; and when I once heard the last movement of the piece in question, it made a similar impression on me, otherwise I confess that I cannot overcome my dislike for figured chorales in general, because I cannot understand the fundamental idea on which they are based, especially where the contending voices maintain constant balance of power. For example, in the first chorus of the "Passion"—where the chorale forms only a more important and consistent part of the basis; or where, as in the above mentioned movement of the cantata (if I remember it rightly, having only heard it once) the chorale represents the principal building, and the individual parts only the ornaments—I can better figure the purpose and the

1. *This letter from Mendelssohn's father throws so clear a light on the intellectual relations between father and son that a place may appropriately be found for it here.*

conception, but definitely not where the passage in a particular manner carries out variations on the theme. Assuredly no liberties should ever be taken with a chorale. Its highest purpose is that the congregation should sing it in all its purity to the accompaniment of the organ; all else seems to me idle and inappropriate for a church.

At Fanny's last morning's musical the motet of Bach, "Gottes Zeit ist die allerbeste Zeit", and your "Ave Maria" were sung by selected voices. A long passage in the middle of the latter, as well as the end, appeared to me too learned and intricate to accord with the simple and pious, although certainly genuine Catholic spirit, which pervades the music. Rebecca's remark that there was some confusion in the execution of those very passages which I considered too intricate only proves that I am an ignoramus, but not that the end is not too abstrusely modulated. With regard to Bach, the composition in question seems to me worthy of the highest admiration. It is long since I have been so struck or surprised by anything as by the Introduction which Fanny played most beautifully; and I could not help thinking of Bach's solitude, of his isolation among his associates and his contemporaries, of his pure, mild, and vast power, and the transparency of its depths. The particular pieces which at the time were forever engraved on my memory were: "Bestelle Dein Haus", and "Es ist der alte Bund". I cared less for the bass aria, or the alto solos. What his "Passion" first made quite clear to me, namely that Bach is the musical prototype of Protestantism, becomes either negatively or positively more apparent every time that I hear a new piece of his. It happened thus with a Mass that I heard recently in the Academy, and which seemed to me most decidedly anti-Catholic; and consequently, it was as impossible even for all its great beauties to reconcile the inner contradictions as for a Protestant clergyman to read Mass in a Protestant Church. Moreover, I felt more strongly than ever how great a merit is was on Zelter's part to restore Bach to the Germans; for, between Forkel's days and his, very little was ever said about Bach, and that little was principally with regard to his "Wohltemperiertes Clavier". Zelter was the first person on whom the light of Bach clearly dawned, thanks to his acquisition of Bach's other works with which—as a collector of music—he became acquainted, and of which—as a genuine artist—he imparted his knowledge to others. His musical performances on Fridays were a proof that no work begun in earnest and followed up with quiet perseverance, can ultimately fail to command success. There is no doubt, that without Zelter, your own musical tendencies would have been of a totally different nature.

Your intention to restore Haendel to his original form has led me to some reflections on his later style of instrumentation. A question is not unfrequently raised as to whether Haendel, if he had written in our day, would have made use of all the existing musical facilities in composing his oratorios—which in fact only means: would the wonted artistic form to which we give the name of Haendel assume the same shape now that it did a hundred years ago; and the answer to this presents itself at once. The question, however, ought to be put in a different form: not whether Haendel would have composed his oratorios now as he did a century ago, but, rather, whether he would have composed oratorios at all. Hardly—if they had to be written in the style of those of today.

From my saying this to you, you may gather with what eager anticipation and confidence I look forward to your own oratorio, which will, I trust, solve the problem of combining ancient conceptions with modern means. Otherwise the result would be as great a failure as that of the painters of the nineteenth century, who only make themselves ridiculous by attempting to revive the religious content of the fifteenth, with its long arms and legs and topsy-turvy perspective. These new resources seem to me, like everything else in the world, to have been developed just at the right time for animating the inner impulses which were daily becoming more feeble. The heights of religious feeling on which Bach, Haendel, and their contemporaries stood, were such that they required no large orchestras for their oratorios; and I well remember from my earliest years that the "Messiah", "Judas" and "Alexander's Feast", were given exactly as Haendel wrote them, without even an organ, and yet to the delight and edification of everyone.

But how is this matter to be stopped nowadays, when vacuity of thought and noise in music are gradually being developed in inverse ratio to each other? The orchestra is now established and is likely to maintain its present form without any essential modification, for a long time to come. Wealth is a fault only when we do not know how to use it. How, then, is the wealth of the orchestra to be applied? What guidance can the poet give for this, and in what regions? Or is music to be entirely severed from poetry, and work its own independent way? I do not believe it can accomplish the latter; at least, only to a very limited extent, and—in general—not authentically. To effect the former, an object must be found for music—just as for painting—which by its fervour, its universal sufficiency and perspicuity may take the place of the pious emotions of former days. It seems to me that also from this point of view both the oratorios of Haydn are very remarkable phenomena. The poems of both, as poems, are weak, but they have happily substituted the old positive and almost metaphysical religious impulses with those which nature, as a visible emanation of the Godhead, in her universality and her thousandfold individualities, instils in every susceptible heart. Hence the profound depth, but also the cheerful efficiency, and certainly genuine religious influence of these two works, which hitherto stand by themselves. Hence the combined effect of the playful and detached passages with the most noble and sincere feelings of gratitude produced by the whole; hence it is, also, that I, individually, would like as little to be deprived—in the "Creation" and in "The Seasons"—of the crowing of the cock, the singing of the lark, the lowing of the cattle, and the rustic glee of the peasants, as in nature herself. In other words, the "Creation" and "The Seasons" are founded on nature and on the visible service of God; and are no new materials for music to be found there?

The publication of "Goethe's Correspondence with a Child" I consider a most provoking and pernicious abuse of the press, through which, more and more rapidly, all illusions will be destroyed, without which life is only death. You, I trust, will never lose your illusions, and ever preserve your filial attachment to your father.

TO HIS FATHER

Duesseldorf, March 23, 1835.

Dear Father,

I have still to thank you for your last letter and my "Ave". I often cannot understand how it is possible to have so acute a judgment as regards music, without being yourself technically musical; and if I could express what I assuredly feel, with as much clearness and intuitive perception as you do, as soon as you enter upon the subject, I never would make another obscure speech all my life long. I thank you a thousand times for this, and also for your words on Bach. I ought to feel rather provoked that you discovered after only one very imperfect hearing of my composition what I found out after long familiarity; but then, again, it makes me happy that you have such a definite sense of music; for the deficiencies in the middle movement and at the end consist of such minute faults—which might have been remedied by a very few notes, mainly cancellations—that neither I nor any other musician would have been aware of them without hearing the piece repeatedly because as a rule we seek the cause much deeper. The simplicity of the har-

mony, which I rather like at the beginning, is spoiled; and though I believe that these faults would be less perceptible if it were perfectly performed—especially with a numerous choir—something will always remain. Another time I shall do better. I should like you, however, to hear the Bach again, because there is a part of it which you extol less but which pleases me best of all. I mean the alto and bass arias; only the chorale must be given by a great number of alto voices, and the bass very well sung. However admirable the arias "Bestelle Dein Haus" and "Es ist der alte Bund" may be, still there is something very sublime and profound in the plan of the ensuing movements, the way the alto begins and the bass interrupts it with fresh and new spirit, and continues with the same words while the chorale joins in as the third, the bass closing exultantly, whereas the chorale goes on for some time, soft and solemn. There is something peculiar in this music; its date must be placed either very early or very late, for it differs entirely from his usual style of writing in middle age. The first chorale movements and the final chorus are of a kind that I should never have attributed to Sebastian Bach, but to some other composer of his day, whereas no other man in the world could have written a single bar of the middle movements. Now farewell, dear Father. I beg you will soon let me hear from you again. Your

Felix.

TO IGNAZ MOSCHELES

Duesseldorf, March 25, 1835.

. . . What you say about Berlioz's Symphony is literally true, I am sure; only I must add that the whole thing seems to me so dreadfully slow; and what could be worse? Music may be a piece of uncouth, crazy, barefaced impudence, and still have some "go" about it and be amusing; but this is simply insipid and altogether lifeless . . . What you say of Liszt's harmonies is depressing. I had seen the work before, and put it away with indifference because it simply seemed very stupid to me; but if that sort of stuff is noticed and even admired, it is really provoking. But is that the case? I cannot believe that impartial people can take pleasure in discords or be in any way interested in them: whether a few writers puff the piece or not, matters little; their articles will leave no more trace than the composition. What annoys me is, that there is so little to throw into the other side of the balance; for what our Reissiger & Co. compose, though different, is just as shallow; and what Heller and Berlioz write is not music either, and even old Cherubini's "Ali Baba" is dreadfully poor and borders on Auber. It is very sad.

But what is the use of grumbling about bad music? As if it could ever take the lead, even if all the world were to sing it; as if there were no good music left! All such things, however, make me conscious of an obligation to work hard and to exert myself to shape to the best of my abilities that which I fancy to be music. I do feel sometimes as if I should never succeed; and today I am quite dissatisfied with my work, and should just like to write my oratorio [1] over again from beginning to end. But I have quite decided to bring it out at Frankfort next winter, and at the Duesseldorf Musical Festival at Whitsuntide; so I must finish it now. Besides, I think I have worked too long at it; at least I am quite impatient to get to other things, so it is evidently high time to end . . .

1. *St. Paul.*

TO HIS FAMILY

Leipzig, October 6, 1835.

. . . The day I accompanied the Hensels to Delitzsch, Chopin came; he intended to remain only one day, so we spent this entirely together and made music. I cannot deny, dear Fanny, that I have lately found that you are not doing him sufficient justice in your judgement; perhaps he was not in the right humour for playing when you heard him, which can often be the case with him. But, as for myself, his playing has enchanted me afresh, and I am persuaded that if you, and Father also, had heard him play some of his better pieces as he played them to me, you would say the same. There is something entirely original in his piano playing, and it is at the same time so masterly, that he may be called a perfect virtuoso; and as, in music, I like and rejoice in every style of perfection, that day was most agreeable to me. It was so pleasant to be once more with a thorough musician, and not with those semi-virtuosi and semi-classicists, who would gladly combine in music les honneurs de la vertu et les plaisirs du vice, (the honours of virtue and the pleasures of vice) but with one who has his own perfect and well-defined way; however far asunder we may be in our different spheres, I can still get on famously with such a person—but not with those semi-demi people. Sunday evening was really very remarkable, when Chopin made me play over my oratorio to him, and when, between the first and second part, he dashed into his new Etudes and a new Concerto, to the amazement of the Leipzigers, and then I resumed my "St. Paul"; it was just as if a Cherokee and a Kaffir had met to converse. He has also one, just too lovely, new notturno, a considerable part of which I learnt by ear. So we got on most pleasantly together; and he promised faithfully to return in the course of the winter if I ventured to compose a new symphony and to perform it in honour of him. We took an oath on this in the presence of three witnesses, and we shall see whether we both adhere to our word. My collection of Haendel's works arrived before Chopin's departure and were a source of quite childish delight to him; they really are so beautiful that I am charmed with them, thirty-two great folios, bound in thick green leather, in the usual distinguished English fashion, and on the back, in big gold letters, the title and contents of each volume; and in the first volume, besides, there are the following words, "To Director F. M. B., from the Committee of the Cologne Music Festival, 1835". The books were accompanied by a very friendly letter with the signatures of all the members, and on picking up "Samson" at random, just at the very beginning I found a grand aria for Samson which is quite unknown and which yields in beauty to none of Haendel's; so you see what pleasure is in store for me in all the thirty-two volumes . . .

TO JULIUS SCHUBRING

Leipzig, December 6, 1835.

Dear Schubring,

No doubt you have heard of the crushing blow that has fallen on my happy life and on those dear to me.[1] It is the greatest misfortune that could have befallen me, and a trial under which I must either strive to bear up or go down utterly. I say this to myself after the lapse of three weeks, without the acute anguish of the first

1. *Death of his father.*

days, but I feel it more deeply; a new life must begin for me, or everything must be at an end; the old life is now severed. For our consolation and example, our mother bears her loss with the most wonderful composure and firmness; she comforts herself with her children and grandchildren and thus strives to hide the chasm that can never be closed. My brother and sisters try the more to fulfil their duties better than ever, the more difficult they have become. I was ten days in Berlin, so that my mother might at least have all of us around her; but I need hardly tell you what those days were: you know it well, and no doubt you thought of me in that dark time. I do not know whether you are aware that, especially for some years past, my father was so good to me, so thoroughly my friend, that I was devoted to him with my whole soul, and during my long absences scarcely ever passed an hour without thinking of him; but as you knew him in his own home with us, in all his kindliness, you can well realise my state of mind. The only thing that now remains is to do one's duty, and this I strive with all my strength to accomplish, for he would wish it to be so if he were still here, and I shall never cease to endeavour to gain his approval as before, though I can no longer enjoy it.

When I delayed answering your letter I little thought that I should have to answer it thus. Let me thank you for it now and for all your kindness. One passage for "St. Paul" was excellent, "Der Du der rechte Vater bist". A chorus for it came forthwith into my head, which I shall very soon write down. I shall now work with doubled zeal at the completion of "St. Paul", for my father urged me to it in the very last letter he wrote to me, and he looked forward very impatiently to the completion of my work. I feel as if I must exert all my energies to finish it and to make it as good as possible, and then think that he takes an interest in it. When it is done, God will direct what is to come next . . .

LETTERS OF THE MAN

1836–1847

Early in 1836 Mendelssohn was compensated for the partial frustration of his affections by meeting, in Frankfort, Cécile Jeanrenaud, whom he married after an engagement of ten happy months. The reason for the scanty traces left in his correspondence by his unclouded matrimonial bliss has already been mentioned.

In this period also, the letters to his family in general became shorter and scarcer. An extensive, professionally oriented exchange of opinions with his musician friends prevails, and discussions of publishing, editing, performing and organising, occupy most of the time devoted to letter-writing. The decade 1837-1847 is highlighted by the conception and production of the two great oratorios, "St. Paul" and "Elijah", by the ever-augmenting enthusiasm of the English public headed by the charming Royal hosts at Buckingham Palace, and the whole-hearted respect accorded him by musical Germany as, for the time being, the leading authority in the realm of his art. The highest honours are bestowed upon the composer, who creates without interruption one important masterpiece after the other, among them the violin concerto, the second piano concerto, the Scotch Symphony, the "Antigone" music, the music to "Ruy Blas",[1] the "Variations sérieuses".

A circle of devoted friends and enthusiastic admirers surrounds the man, who, at the age of thirty, is described by the English music critic, Henry Fothergill Chorley, in his autobiography, as follows: "He is very handsome, with a particularly sweet laugh, and a slight cloud (not to

1. *See facsimile on page 282.*

call it a thickness) upon his utterance which seemed like the voice of an old friend . . . No one could be kinder than he . . ."

Nevertheless, the spirit of many of the later letters seems to become subdued by the encroaching shadows of overwork, of excessive strain and fatigue, of too-much-of-everything. From the year 1841 on, Mendelssohn was irritated by unpleasant divergencies of opinion about his activities at the Prussian Court, by unrewarding duties which he had to shoulder under the pressure of King Friedrich Wilhelm IV and his counsellors, by the failure of his cherished plans for the organisation of an Academy of Music at Berlin in accordance with his own ideas. This failure resulted, subsequently, in the final decision to shift his residence from the Prussian capital back again to Leipzig. All this sapped, slowly but relentlessly, the physical strength of a delicate organism which had been mercilessly overtaxed since early childhood. He frequently complained of being tired, and even the last trips to England, where his participation in the great choral festivals whipped up his fame as a composer and conductor to its zenith, left him exhausted to the point of wishing for nothing but quiet, and more quiet, in the company of his gentle wife.

The exact nature of the illness that felled Mendelssohn has not been clearly established. From the time of Fanny's death, six months before his own, he was a broken man. He shared with her the boon of a painless and peaceful departure. The profile of him on his death-bed, sketched by his brother-in-law, Wilhelm Hensel, reveals the gentleness of his passing.

Sketches by Mendelssohn, made on his honeymoon, 1837.

Sketch by Mendelssohn, made on his honeymoon, 1837.

FROM A LETTER TO PASTOR BAUER

Leipzig, December 9, 1835.

I received your kind letter here—on the day when the christening in your family was to take place—when I returned from Berlin where I had gone in the hope of alleviating my mother's grief, during the first days after the loss of my father. So I received the intelligence of your happiness, whilst once more crossing the threshold of my empty room and when I felt for the first time in my inmost being what it is to suffer the most painful and bitter anguish. The wish which of all others recurred to my mind every night was that I might not survive my loss (because I so entirely clung to my father), a sorrow which of all others from my childhood I always thought the most acute. The loss was also that of my only perfect friend during the last few years, and my master in art and in life.

It was strange to read your letter, which breathed only joy and satisfaction; calling on me to rejoice with you on your future prospects, at the very moment when I felt that my past was lost and gone for ever. I thank you for wishing me, though so distant, to be your guest at the christening; and though my name may make a graver impression now than you could have thought, I trust that impression will only be a grave and not a painful one to you and your wife. When some time, in later years, you tell your child of those whom you invited to his baptism, do not omit my name from your guests, but say to him that one of them on that day recommenced his life afresh, too, though in another sense, with new purposes and wishes, and with new prayers to God.

My mother is well, and bears her sorrow with such composure and dignity that we can all only wonder and admire, and ascribe it to her love for her children and her wish for their happiness . . .

TO HIS SISTER FANNY

Leipzig, January 30, 1836.

Dear Fanny,

Today at length I can reply to your charming letters, and give you a terrible scolding for saying in your first letter that it was long since you have been able to please me with your music, and asking me why? I totally deny the whole fact, and assure you that all you compose pleases me. If two or three works in succession did not satisfy me as thoroughly as others of yours, I think the reason lay no deeper than this, that you have written less than in former days when one or two songs that did not exactly suit my taste were so rapidly composed and replaced so quickly by others, that neither of us considered much why it was that they seemed less attractive; we only laughed together about them, and there was an end of it.

I may quote here, "Die Schoenheit nicht, O Maedchen", and many others in the "prima maniera of our master", which we heartily abused. Then came beautiful songs in their turn; and so it is at present; only they cannot follow each other in such quick succession, because now you must often have other things to occupy your thoughts besides composing pretty songs, and that is a great blessing. But if you suppose that your more recent compositions seem to me inferior to your earlier ones, you are entirely mistaken, for I know no better song of yours than the English one in G minor, or the close of the "Liederkreis", and many others of later date: besides, you are aware that formerly there were entire books of your compositions for which I cared less than for others, because it always was my nature to be a screech-owl, and to belong to the savage type of brothers. But you know well how much I love all your productions, and some are especially dear to my heart; so you must write to me forthwith that you have done me injustice by considering me a man devoid of taste, and that you will never do so again.

And then, neither in this letter nor in your former one, do you say one word about "St. Paul" or "Melusina", as one colleague should write to another—that is, remarks on fifths, rhythm and motion of the parts, on conception, counterpoint, et coetera animalia. You ought to have done so, however, and should do so still, for you know the value I attach to it, and as "St. Paul" is shortly to be sent to the publisher, a few strictures from you would come just at the right moment. I write to you this way today solely in the hope of soon receiving an answer, for I am very weary and exhausted from yesterday's concert, where, in addition to conducting three times, I was obliged to play Mozart's D minor concerto. In the first movement I made a cadenza, which succeeded wonderfully and caused a tremendous sensation among the Leipzigers. I must write down the end for you. You remember the theme, of course? Towards the close of the cadence, arpeggios come in pianissimo in D minor, thus:

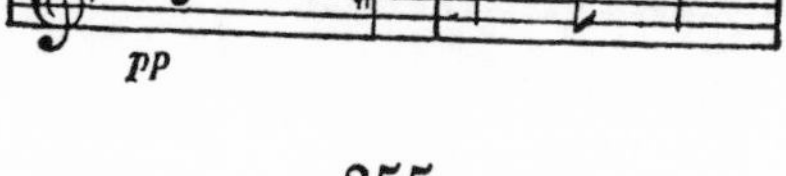

Then again G minor arpeggios; then:

then: 

arpeggios, and:

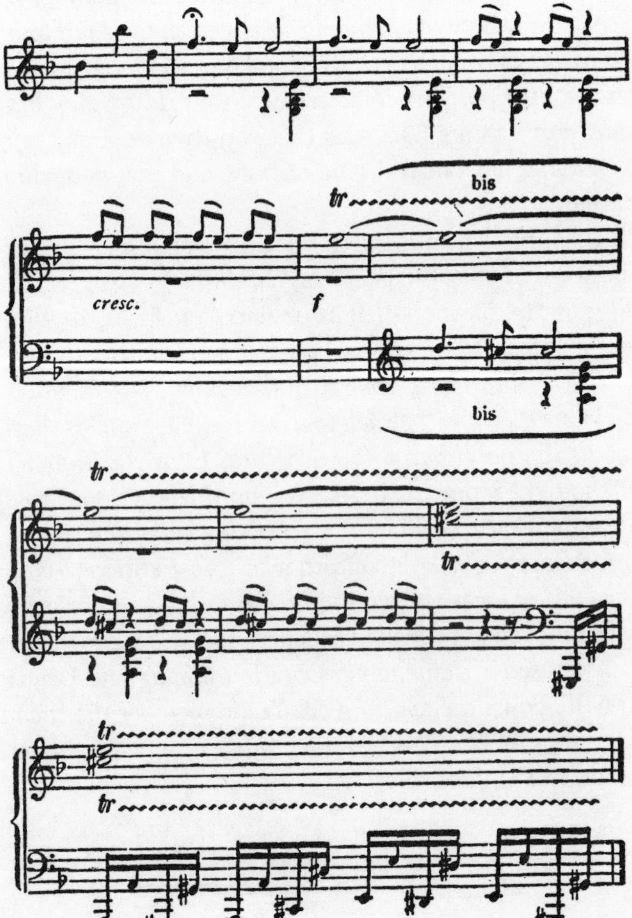

etc., to the close in D minor. Our second violin player, an old musician, said to me afterwards, when he met me in the passage, that he had heard it played in the same hall by Mozart himself, but since that day he had heard no one introduce such good cadenzas as I did yesterday—which gave me very great pleasure.

Do you know Haendel's "Coronation Anthem"? It is most singular. The beginning is one of the finest which not only Haendel, but any man ever composed; and all the remainder, after the first short movement, is horribly dry and commonplace. The performers could not master it, but are certainly far too busy to grieve much about that.

Many persons here consider "Melusina" to be my best overture; at all events, it is the most deeply felt; but as to the fabulous nonsense of the musical papers, about red coral and green sea-monsters, and magic palaces, and deep seas, this is stupid stuff and fills me with amazement. But now I take my leave of water for some time to come, and must see how things are going on elsewhere.[1] I received today a letter from Duesseldorf with the news of the musical doings there, and a request to send "St. Paul" soon for the Music Festival. I cannot deny that when I read the description of their concerts and some concert bills which were enclosed, and realised the state of the musical world there, I had a pleasant sensation at my change of position. One cannot well compare them, for while everybody there is engaged in perpetual quarrelling and strife and petty criticism, here, on the contrary, during the course of this whole winter, my situation has not caused me to pass one disagreeable day, scarcely to hear one annoying expression, whilst I have enjoyed much pleasure and gratification. The whole orchestra, which includes very able men, strive to guess my

1. *This refers to the circumstance of Mendelssohn's father having advised him to "put on a shelf" the elfin and spirit life with which, for a certain period, Mendelssohn had chiefly occupied himself in his compositions, and to proceed to graver works.*

wishes at a glance; they have made the most extraordinary progress in finish and refinement, and are so devoted to me that I often feel quite moved by it.

Would that I were less sad and depressed, for sometimes I do not know what to do, and can only hope that the approaching spring and the warm weather may cheer me.

I trust you and yours may all continue well and happy and sometimes think of me.

Your

Felix.

TO HIS MOTHER AND SISTER REBECCA

Frankfort, July 14, 1836.

Dear Mother and dear Rebecca,

I have just received your affectionate letters, and must answer them right away. I had been expecting them for several days past, during which I have done nothing but lie on the sofa and read Eckermann's "Conversations with Goethe", and long for letters from home which I could answer. I am as much delighted with Eckermann as you are, my dear ones! I feel just as if I heard the old gentleman speaking again, for many things are introduced into the work which are the very same words I have heard him use, and I know his tone and gestures by heart. I must say that Eckermann seems not to be sufficiently independent. He is always rejoicing over "this important phrase, which pray mark well". But it must be admitted that it was a difficult position to face the old man, and we ought to be grateful to him for his faithful notices—also for his delicacy, in contrast to Riemer.[1]

Here I am, seated in the well-known corner room with the beautiful view, in Schelble's house, he and his wife having gone to visit his property in Swabia, and they will not return as long as I am in Frankfort. There is no one living in the house but Schelble's mother-in-law with a maid-servant on one side, and myself, with two travelling-bags and a hatbox, on the other. A very kind reception, an excellent grand piano, plenty of music, complete rest, and undisturbed tranquillity are all things which are nowhere to be found in an inn. I came here with plans for great industry, but for nearly a week I have done little else every forenoon but admire the view and sun myself. I must go on in the same way for a couple of days more—idleness is so pleasant, and agrees with me so well. My last days in Duesseldorf and my first days here were just too crammed; now I have to recover my balance gradually. The very day of my arrival I had to direct the St. Cecilia Association; then came my numerous acquaintances, old and new, and the arrangements for the next few weeks had to be made. I was obliged to take a rest after all this, or at least so I said to myself, to palliate, and furnish a pretext for, my love of idleness. My life assumes a most agreeable form here. I would never have thought that I could become such a lion in the musical world through my overtures and songs. The "Melusina" and the "Hebrides" are as familiar to everybody here as they are to us at home, (I mean, Nr. 3., Leipziger Strasse) and the dilettanti discuss my intentions warmly.

Then Hiller is here, at all times a delightful sight to me, and we always have much to discuss that is interesting to both of us. Only he seems to me—what shall I call it?—not sufficiently one-sided. By nature he loves Bach and Beethoven above all others, and would, therefore, prefer wholly adopting the graver style of music. On the other hand he also likes Rossini, Auber, Bellini, etc., and

1. *Friedrich Wilhelm Riemer (1774-1845) Librarian in Weimar who published a volume, "Mitteilungen ueber Goethe" in 1841.*

with such a catholicity no man can make real progress. This is the topic of all our conversations, and thus I am twice as pleased to spend some time with him just now, and if possible, exert some influence on him by my own mode of thinking.

Early yesterday I went to see him, and whom should I find sitting there? Rossini, big, fat, and in the sunniest disposition of mind. I really know few men who can be so amusing and witty as he, when he chooses; he kept us laughing the whole time. I promised that the Cecilia Association would sing the B minor Mass for him and several other works of Sebastian Bach. It will be quite too much fun to see Rossini obliged to admire Sebastian Bach. He thinks, however, "different countries, different customs", and is resolved to howl with the wolves. He says he is fascinated by Germany, and when he once gets the list of wines at the Rhine Hotel in the evening, the waiter is obliged to show him the way to his room, or he could never manage to find it. He tells the most laughable and amusing tales about Paris and all the musicians there, as well as about himself and his compositions, and how he entertains the deepest respect for all the men of the present day—so that you might really believe him, if you had no eyes to see his clever face. Intellect, animation and wit sparkle in all his features and in every word, and whoever does not consider him a genius ought to hear him expatiating in this way, in order to change his opinion.

The scenery around Frankfort pleases me this time beyond everything—such fruitfulness, richness of verdure, gardens and fields, and the beautiful blue hills as a background! And there is a forest on the other side; to ramble in the evening under the splendid beech-trees, among the innumerable herbs and flowers and blackberries and strawberries—it is a true delight for one's heart.

I could not prevail upon myself to go to the Rothschilds in spite of their very flattering invitations. I am not in the vein or humour at present for balls or other festivities, and "like should draw to like". It is only peculiar that those people should cause me real pleasure; their splendour and luxury, and the way they compel the philistines to regard them with the utmost respect (though these would gladly give them a sound thrashing if they were let loose!) is a source of exultation to me, because they owe all this entirely to their own industry, good fortune and abilities. Actually, the 15th has dawned!—this is a regular chatter-and-gossip-letter!

Your

Felix.

TO IGNAZ MOSCHELES

Frankfort, July 20, 1836.

My dear friend,

It is an age since I wrote to you last; but it was a monotonous age, and I was not in a mood to write about it or anything else . . . I have not yet thanked you for that good, kind letter of yours which reached me through Klingemann at the Music Festival, with your congratulations on its success. How the oratorio went off you heard long ago. There was much that pleased me at the performance, and much that dissatisfied me; and even now I am at work on certain parts of the piano arrangement—which is to appear shortly—and on the orchestral score; so much is there that completely fails to express my idea, in fact, does not even come near it. You have often advised me not to alter so much, and I am quite aware of the disadvantages of doing so; but if, on the one hand, I have been fortunate enough to express my idea in some parts of my work, and have no desire to change those, I cannot help striving, on the other hand, to express my idea in other parts, and, if possible, throughout. But the task begins to weigh heavily upon me, as I am gradually more and more attracted by other work, and I wish I could look back upon the oratorio as finally completed.

I wish I could finish a few symphonies and that sort of thing in the course of the year, and more still, I long to write an opera; but of that, I am afraid, there is not the least prospect. I am looking in vain throughout Germany and elsewhere for someone to help me realise this and other musical plans, and I despair of finding him. It is really absurd to think that in all Germany one should not be able to meet a man who knows the stage and writes tolerable verses; and yet I positively believe there is none to be found. Altogether this is a queer country. Much as I love it, I hate it in certain respects. Look at the musical men of this place, for instance; their doings are quite shameful. Considering the size and importance of the town, there is really a fine muster of excellent musicians, men of reputation and talent, who might do good work, and who, one would think, would do it willingly. So far that is the good side of Germany. But the fact is, they do nothing, and it were better if they did not live together, and grumble, or brood over their grievances till it is enough to give one the blues . . . All that is bad, and the German Diet should interfere; for where so many musicians congregate in one place, they ought to be forced by the authorities to give us the benefit of a little music, and not only their philosophical views about it . . .

FROM A LETTER TO HIS SISTER REBECCA

Frankfort, July 24, 1836.

Although I am a bad correspondent just now, I must write you a line to Franzensbad before I start for the seaside, for I will not have it said that at any period of my life I did not write to you.

The present period is a very strange one, for I am more desperately in love than I ever was in my life before, and I do not know what to do. I leave Frankfort the day after tomorrow, but I feel as if it would cost me my life. At any rate I intend to return here and see this charming girl once more before I go back to Leipzig. But I have not an idea whether she likes me or not, and I do not know what to do to make her like me, as I have already said. But one thing is certain, that to her I owe the first real happiness I have enjoyed this year, and now I feel fresh and hopeful again for the first time. When I am away from her, though, I am always sad—now you see, I have let you into a secret, which nobody else knows anything about; but in order that you may set the world an example of discretion, I will tell you nothing more. If you want further information, write to me at the Hague, poste restante, for the day after tomorrow I am going to the detestable seaside. O Rebecca! What shall I do?

FROM A LETTER TO HIS SISTER REBECCA

Frankfort, August 2, 1836.

. . . Such is my mood now the whole day; I can neither compose nor write letters, nor play the piano; the utmost I can do is to sketch a little. But I must thank you for your kind expressions about "St. Paul"; such words from you are the dearest and best that I can ever hear, and what you and Fanny say on the subject is what the public says. I know . . . no other. I only wish you would write to me several times more about it, and very minutely about my other music. The whole time I have been here I have worked at "St. Paul", because I wish to publish it in as perfect a form as possible; and moreover, I am quite convinced that the

beginning of the first and the end of the second part are now nearly three times as good as they were—thus it was my duty. In many points, especially subordinate ones in so large a work, I only succeed by degrees in realising my thoughts more closely and in expressing them clearly; in the principal movements and melodies I can no longer make any alteration, because they occur suddenly to my mind just as they are; but I am not yet sufficiently advanced to say this of the whole. I have now, however, been working for rather more than two years at this one oratorio; it is certainly a very long time, and I am looking forward to the moment when I shall have done the proofreading and can begin something else.

I must tell you of the real delight with which I have here read the first books of Goethe's "Wahrheit und Dichtung". I had not taken up the book since my boyhood, because I did not like it then; but I cannot express how much it now pleases me, and how much additional pleasure I take in it, from knowing all the localities. One of its pages makes me forget all the misères in literature and art of the present day . . .

FROM A LETTER TO HIS MOTHER

The Hague, August 9, 1836.

. . . I received your kind letter the day before yesterday and thank you for it from my heart. But you really see more in my last letter than I intended to say, and when you speak of my betrothal, my happiness, and the coming change in my prospects, I can only say that as yet all is very uncertain. But I thank you for the dear, kind words you wrote about the mere possibility, and feel inclined to consider them as your permission to take this step, so necessary for my happiness. In any case I should like to have your consent, that I may no longer be tormented by doubts, on this head at any rate. Indeed, my special object in writing is to ask you for it. If you tell me that you are ready once more to trust me entirely and offer me again the full liberty I have enjoyed in former years, you will make me very happy. You may rest assured that I will not abuse your confidence, and perhaps I have done something to deserve it. Please, tell me so, dear mother.

With all this, however, bear in mind what I wrote in the beginning. All I ask is that you will give me your consent; for, though I suppose my age makes it no longer legally necessary, I will not act without it. But whether I shall be able to avail myself of it on my return to Frankfort, that, as I said before, is a perfect mystery. All depends on the state in which I find matters there, for I really feel completely ignorant now. On one point, however, I am quite clear, and that is that I would gladly send Holland, its Dutchmen, seabaths, bathingcars, Kursaal and visitors to the devil, and wish I were back in Frankfort. When I have seen this charming girl again, I hope the suspense will soon be over, and I shall know whether we are to be anything—or rather everything—to each other, or not; at present I really know very little of her, and she of me, so I cannot answer all your questions about her. This much I can tell you, that she made my stay at Frankfort very happy, just when I needed a little happiness and did not expect to get it; also that her father, Pastor Jeanrenaud, is dead, and that she has been educated at home with the utmost care and tenderness by her mother (a Souchay), that her Christian name is Cécile, and that I love her very much.

Dear mother, there is one thing more I wish to ask, and that is, that you will not allow yourself to be agitated about me. I perceive from your letter that you are very anxious, and that will make me anxious too, whereas I wish to be calm and collected, and go through this affair with the coolness I have always managed to preserve hitherto when taking an important step in life. I beg you also not to speak about the matter to any one, especially not to any one in Frankfort, as it may destroy my whole chance. Dear mother, please answer this immediately.

FROM A LETTER TO HIS SISTER FANNY[1]

Freiburg i/Br., April 10, 1837.

. . . You will remember the time when we went through the pouring rain to the cathedral, and how we admired it and its dark, stained glass windows; but we could not then see the situation of the town, which is more beautiful than anything which I either remember or can imagine. It is all so peaceful and fertile, the pretty valleys, the hills in every direction, the villages fading away in the distance, the people so good-looking and so neatly dressed, the splashing mountain-streams, and over all the first green of spring in the valleys below and the last snow of winter on the hills above. You may fancy how lovely it all is, and that, as we saunter about the whole afternoon in the warm sunshine, standing still now and then to look around and talk over the past and the future, I may well say with true thankfulness that I am a happy man.

I intend to work very hard and bring out a great many new works, and make real progress; but before I do that it is necessary to complete all the accumulation of unfinished music. This shall be my task for the summer when I mean to carry out many old projects which I think you will like; a book of songs without words is nearly ready for printing, but I do not mean to publish any more of these just now, as I would rather write bigger things. I have almost finished a string quartet, and shall soon begin another. I am in the right vein for working now . . .

1. *Mendelssohn had married Cécile Jeanrenaud in March 1837, and was spending his honeymoon in Freiburg i/Breisgau.*

FROM A LETTER TO HIS MOTHER

Frankfort, June 2, 1837.

. . . You write to me about Fanny's new compositions, and say that I ought to persuade her to publish them. Your praise of those works is, however, quite unnecessary to make me heartily rejoice in them or think them charming and admirable; for I know by whom they are written. No need to say that if she does resolve to publish anything, I will do everything in my power to obtain every facility for her and to relieve her as far as I can from any trouble which she can possibly be spared. But I cannot persuade her to publish, because this would be contrary to my views and to my convictions. We have often discussed the subject and my opinion still remains exactly the same. I consider the publication of a work a serious matter (at least it ought to be one!) for I maintain that no one should publish unless he is resolved to appear as an author for the rest of his life. For this purpose however a succession of works is indispensable. Nothing but annoyance can be expected from publishing where one or two works alone are in question; or it becomes what is called a "manuscript for private circulation", which I also dislike; and from my knowledge of Fanny I should say she has neither the inclination nor the vocation for authorship. She is too much of a woman for this. She manages her home and neither thinks of the public, nor of the musical world, nor even of music at all, until her first duties are fulfilled. Publishing would only disturb her carrying them on, and I cannot say that I would approve of it. I will not, therefore, persuade her to take this step; forgive me for saying so. If she decides to publish, either from her own impulse, or to please Hensel, I am, as I said before, ready to assist her; but I cannot encourage her to do what I do not deem right myself . . .

TO JULIUS SCHUBRING

Bingen a/Rh., July 14, 1837.

Dear Schubring,

I wish to ask your advice in a matter which is important to me, and will therefore not be indifferent to you; of this I feel sure, after having received so many proofs from you of the contrary. It concerns the selection of a subject for an oratorio which I want to begin next winter. I am most anxious to have your counsel, as the best suggestions and contributions for the text of my "St. Paul" came from you.

There are many obvious reasons in favour of choosing St. Peter as the subject; especially the fact that it is destined for the Duesseldorf Music Festival at Whitsuntide, and the prominent position the feast of Whitsunday would occupy in this subject. In addition to these external grounds, I may add my desire (in connection with a greater plan for a subsequent oratorio) to bring the two chief apostles and pillars of the Christian Church side by side in oratorios, so that I should have my "St. Peter" as well as my "St. Paul". I need not tell you that there are sufficient inner motives to make me prize the subject, chief among them being the outpouring of the Holy Ghost, which must form the central point, or chief object. The question therefore is (and this you can decide far better than I, because you possess the knowledge in which I am deficient) whether the place that Peter assumes in the Bible, apart from the dignity which he enjoys in the Catholic or Protestant Churches as a martyr, or the first Pope, etc., etc., whether what is said of him in the Bible is alone and in itself sufficiently important to form the basis of a symbolical oratorio. For, accord-

Thomasschule in Leipzig.
Drawing by Mendelssohn, about 1840.

Mendelssohn.
Sketch by Carl Mueller, 1842.

ing to my feeling, this subject should not be treated historically, indispensable as this was in the case of "St. Paul". In a historic treatment, Christ would have to appear in the earlier part of St. Peter's career, and where He appears, St. Peter could not lay claim to the chief interest. I think, therefore, it must be symbolical, though all the historical points might eventually be introduced—the betrayal and repentance, the keys of heaven handed to him by Christ, his preaching at Pentecost—all this not in an historical, but a prophetic light in the broader sense, if I may so express myself.

My question then is, whether you think this possible, or at least so far possible that it may become something important and personal for every member of the community? Also whether it is your opinion, that, even if actually feasible, it should be carried out entirely by means of scriptural passages, and what particular parts of the Bible you would especially recommend for the purpose? Lastly, if in this event you will hereafter, as you previously did, make a selection of certain passages out of the Bible, and send them to me?

The chief thing, however, is the first point, for I am still in the dark about it; in fact, about the possibility of the whole undertaking. Write me as soon as you can on the subject. My first idea was that the subject ought to be divided into two parts: the first, from the moment of forsaking the fishermen's nets down to the "Tu es Petrus" with which it must close; the second to consist of the Feast of Pentecost only—from the misery after the death of Christ and the repentance of Peter, to the outpouring of the Holy Ghost.[1] Forgive me for assailing you so suddenly with all this.

I cannot tell you what a great and happy change has taken place in my life in the few months since we met.[2]

I hope you will come and stay with us next winter, and pass some

---

1. *This project was never realised, but the letter is inserted as it shows the deep earnestness with which Mendelssohn treated such subjects.*
2. *Mendelssohn's marriage.*

days here; then you will see for yourself in a short time what I really could not describe even at any length. I intend to be in Leipzig again, the end of September, and till then shall remain principally here on the Rhine, or at Frankfort. Pray answer me soon, if only with a few lines.

Your

F. M. B.

FROM A LETTER TO FERDINAND HILLER

London, September 1, 1837.

Dear Ferdinand,

Here I sit–in the fog–very cross–without my wife–writing to you, because your letter of the day before yesterday requires it; otherwise I should hardly do so, for I am much too cross and melancholy today. It is nine days since I parted from Cécile at Duesseldorf; the first few were quite bearable, though very wearisome; but now I have got into the whirl of London–great distances–too many people–my head crammed with business and accounts and money matters and arrangements–and it is becoming unbearable, and I wish I were sitting with Cécile, and had let Birmingham be Birmingham, and could enjoy my life more than I do today. D--n it! You know what that means, don't you? and I have three more weeks of it before me, and have to play the organ at B. on the 22d and be in Leipzig again on the 30th–in a word, I wish I were rid of the whole business. I must be a little fond of my wife, because I find that England and the fog and beef and porter have such a horribly bitter taste this time–and I used to like them so much . . .

I have heard nothing from my people in Berlin for so long (more than five weeks) that I am beginning to be anxious—and that adds greatly to my unhappiness. I composed a great deal whilst we were on the Rhine, but I do not mean to do anything here, but swear and long for my Cécile. What is the good of all the double counterpoint in the world, when she is not with me? I must leave off my complaints and my letter, or you will be laughing at me in Innsbruck in the sunshine. Address me in Leipzig—again—I wish I were there. It seems that Chopin came over here quite suddenly a fortnight ago, paid no visits and saw nobody, played very beautifully at Broadwood's one evening, and then took himself off again. They say he is still very ill and miserable . . . Farewell, dear Ferdinand, and forgive me this horribly stupid letter, it is exactly what I am myself.

Your

Felix M. B.

FROM A LETTER TO HIS BROTHER

Leipzig, October 29, 1837.

. . . You mention in your letter of yesterday that your quiet, settled, and uneventful position sometimes makes you almost uneasy—but I cannot see that you have a right to feel as you do, any more than I could were you to complain of the contrary. Why should it not be enough for a man to know how to merit and to enjoy happiness? I cannot acknowledge that it is indispensable to earn peace of mind by anticipating worries and misfortune; in my opinion heartfelt and grateful appreciation is the Polycrates-ring, and certainly in these days it is something of a problem to acknowledge one's good fortune and other blessings in such a manner as *to share them with others, thus rendering them cheerful and happy too, or making them feel that it is a long way from such rejoicing to idle arrogance. It seems strange that I, in my position, should complain of what is just the opposite of your troubles. The more I find in my vocation of what is termed encouragement and recognition, the more restless and unsettled they become in my hands, and I cannot deny that I often long for some of that rest you complain of. Very little remains of performances and festivals, and of all that personal stuff; people shout and applaud, but it passes so quickly, without leaving a trace; and yet it absorbs as much of one's life and strength as the better aims—or even more. The evil side of the affair is that once one has gone in, it is impossible to get out half way; either one has to do it completely or not at all. I dare not even withdraw, lest the cause for which I stand should suffer. But how much I would prefer to see that the cause is not mine alone, but rather a common, a universal one! But this is the very point where people are needed to follow the same path—not an approving public, for that is an indifferent matter—but fellow-workers in art; these are indispensable. And it is in this sense that I long for a less busy life, in order to be able to devote myself more to what is my real mission: to compose music, and to leave the task of performing it to others. It seems, however, that this may not be granted to me; and I would be ungrateful were I dissatisfied with life as it is . . .*

FROM LETTERS TO FERDINAND HILLER

Leipzig, December 10, 1837.

My dear Ferdinand,

. . . I feel that it might be doubly interesting and good for us both to hear about each other, now that we have become so desperately divided, and yet just for that reason all the closer. At least I find that whenever I think of Milan and Liszt and Rossini, it gives me a curious feeling to remember that you are in the midst of it all; and it is perhaps the same with you in the plains of Lombardy when you think of me and Leipzig. But next time you must write me a long detailed letter, full of particulars; you cannot imagine how they interest me. You must tell me where you live, what you are writing, and everything you can about Liszt and Pixis and Rossini, about the white dome, about the Corso—I do so love that enchanting country, and it is a double pleasure to hear from you there—you really must not use half sheets. Above all, tell me if you enjoy it and revel in it as thoroughly as I did. Mind you do, and mind you drink in the air with as much ecstasy, and idle away the days as systematically as I did—but why should I say all this, you will do it anyway. Only please write me a great deal about it.

You want to know whether I am satisfied here? Just tell me yourself whether I ought not to be satisfied, living here with Cécile in a nice, comfortable house with an open view over gardens and fields and the city towers, and feeling as serenely happy, as calmly joyful, as I have not felt since I left my parents' house. Here I am able to command good things and good-will on all sides. I am decidedly of the opinion: either this place or none at all . . . However there are many days when I think no post could be the best. Two months of such constant conducting takes more out of me than two years of composing all day long; in the winter I hardly get to it at all here. At the end of the greatest turmoil, if I ask myself what I have actually accomplished, it is after all hardly worth mentioning. At least it does not interest me particularly, whether or not all the recognised good works are given once more or given better. I am interested now only in the new things, and of these there are few enough. I often think I should like to retire completely and never conduct any more, but only write; but then again there is a certain charm in an organised musical system like this, and in having the directing of it. But what will you care about this in Milan? Still I must tell you, if you ask me how I like being here. I felt the same thing in Birmingham; I have never before achieved such a decided effect with my music as there, and have never seen the public so entirely taken up with me alone. And yet there is something about it—what shall I call it—something flighty and evanescent, which depresses and frightens rather than encourages me . . .

The finest of the new things was Beethoven's "Glorreicher Augenblick", a long cantata (three-quarters of an hour, choruses, solos, etc.) in honour of the three monarchs who met at the Vienna Congress. There are splendid things in it, among others a cavatina, a prayer, quite in Beethoven's grand style but with wretchedly stupid words, where "heller Glanz" is made to rhyme with "Kaiser Franz", followed by a great flourish of trumpets. And now Haslinger has actually put other words to it, and calls it the "Praise of Music", and these are even more wretched, for "poesy" is made to rhyme with "noble harmony", and the flourish of the trumpets comes in—still more stupidly. And so we spend our days in Germany . . . Give Liszt many greetings from me, and tell him how *often and with what pleasure I think of him. Remember me to Rossini, if he likes to be remembered by me. And above all, stay fond of me yourself.*

Your

Felix.

Leipzig, January 20, 1838.

. . . I should have written to you at New Year's and thanked you for your dear good wishes, and given you mine, but I was prevented in the most tiresome way by an indisposition, or illness, which attacked me in the last week of the year and, I am sorry to say, has not yet subsided. This has put me in bad spirits, and at times made me so desperate that even today I write only because I see that it is no use waiting till I am better. I am suffering, as I did four years ago, from complete deafness of one ear, with occasional pains in the head and neck, etc.; the weakness in the ear keeps on without any interruption, and as I have to conduct and play in spite of it (I have kept to my room for a fortnight) you may imagine my agony, not being able properly to hear either the orchestra or my own playing on the piano! Last time it went off after six weeks, and God grant that it may do the same this time; but though I summon up all my courage, I cannot quite help being anxious as, till now, in spite of all remedies, there is no change, and often I do not even hear people speaking in the room . . .

Berlin, July 15, 1838.

Dear Ferdinand,

. . . You will have to answer this as a man of business, for I am writing on business, to ask about the overture which you promised us for the concerts. What has become of it? I hope we shall get it,

and then we can at once put it down for the beginning of the season (end of September). I feel more eager about it than I have about any piece of music for a long time; just as I do about your Italian life and doings altogether. I fancy you now sitting beside the Lake of Como with your mother; it must be a delicious kind of life. And I suppose you also go lounging about with Liszt, and paying court to the Novello, who, I hear, is in Milan, taking lessons; is she still your particular favourite? What do you say to her singing, and to her looks? . . .

The first evening after my arrival we went to the theatre to hear Gluck's "Armida"; I have rarely, if ever, enjoyed anything so much at the opera. The great mass of thoroughly trained musicians and singers, ably conducted by Spontini; the splendid house, full to suffocation, the good mise-en-scène, and above all the beautiful music made such an impression on me that I was obliged to say to myself that nothing can be done with small towns and small means and small circles, and that it is quite another matter here. But how often since have I had to retract that! The very next day they gave a so-called Beethoven Memorial Festival, and played his A major Symphony so atrociously that I soon had to beg many pardons of my small town and my small means; the coarseness and effrontery of the players were such as I have never heard anywhere, and I can only explain it to myself by the whole nature of the Prussian official, which is about as well suited to music as a strait-jacket is to a man. And even so it is an unconscious strait-jacket. Well, since then I have heard a good deal in the way of quartets and symphonies, and playing and singing in private circles, and have altogether begged pardon of my little town. In most places here music is carried on with the same mediocrity and carelessness and arrogance as ever, which quite sufficiently explains my old wrath and the very imperfect methods I adopted to cure it. It all has to do with the sand, the situation, and the official life, so that while one may well enough enjoy a good thing here and there, one cannot become really acquainted with anything. The Gluck operas may be reckoned among such good things. Is it not strange that they always draw a full house, and that the public applauds and is enchanted, and recalls the singers? And that it is about the only place in the world where such a thing is possible? And that the next evening the "Postillon" draws just as full a house? And that in Bavaria it is forbidden to have any music in any church, either Protestant or Catholic, because it desecrates the service? And that chorales are becoming obligato at the theatres? Confound it all! However, the chief things are that there should be as much novelty as possible, and plenty of good and beautiful things in the world . . .

. . . You will have heard that I was at Cologne for the Festival. It all went well; the organ was splendidly effective in Haendel and still more so in Bach—it was some newly-discovered music of his, which you don't yet know, with a pompous double chorus. But even that—to my mind at least—was lacking in the interest one feels in something new and untried; I like it so much when there is that kind of uncertainty which leaves room for me and the public to have an opinion. In Beethoven and Haendel and Bach one knows beforehand what is coming, and always must come, and a great deal more besides. You are quite right in saying that it is better in Italy, where people have new music every year, and must also have a new opinion every year—if only the music and the opinion were a little bit better! At this you snort, and say: What is "better"? Well, if you want to know, something more to my taste. But really, Germany seems to be possessed of the devil . . . Perhaps, after all, my taste is perverted—the possibility of this occasionally dawns upon me—but I must make the best of it, though I certainly have about as much difficulty in swallowing most of these things, as the stork had with the porridge in the shallow dish. The stork reminds me of my boy, who is fat, and merry, and takes after his mother in looks and disposition, which is an inexpressible delight to me, because it is the best thing he can do . . .

But I have not told you anything about what I have been writing, I mean, what music: two rondos for piano, one with and one without orchestra; two sonatas, one with violin, the other with cello; one psalm, and just now I am on a third violin quartet, and have a symphony in my head which will soon be launched. In B-flat. And you? Do you mean to send the overture? Enjoy your life in that heavenly country and think nicely of me.

Your

F.M.B.

Berlin, August 17, 1838.

. . . My time in Berlin is almost over now, and I think of going back to Leipzig in four days; on September 19th they are going to do my "St. Paul" there in the church, and the rehearsals begin next week. Our family life here has been most pleasant; yesterday evening, when I went over to tea and found them all assembled, I read them quite a little out of your letter, which gave them great pleasure and they told me to remember them to you. We were together in that way every evening, talking politics, arguing, and making music, and it was so nice and cheerful. We had only three invitations the whole time, and of music in public I heard little more than I was obliged to; it is too bad, in spite of the best resources; I went to a performance of "Oberon" last week which was beyond conception; I believe the thing never once went together all through. At the Singakademie a piece of my own was sung in such a manner that I should have got seriously angry if Cécile had not sat beside me and kept on saying: "Dear husband, do be calm!" They also played me some quartets and invariably bungled the very same passages that they had bungled ten years ago, and which made me furious ten years ago—another proof of the immortality of the soul.

My third violin quartet in D major[1] *is finished; I like the first movement immensely, I wish I could play it to you—especially a forte passage at the end which you would be sure to like. I am also planning to compose an opera of Planché's next year; I have already got two acts of the libretto, and like them well enough to begin to set to work. The subject is taken from English history in the Middle Ages, rather serious, with a siege and a famine; I am eager to see the end of the libretto which I expect next week. I also still hope to get words for an oratorio this year. You see that I was going to follow your advice of my own accord, but, as I said before, the aid and inventiveness of a poet is wanting, and that is the chief thing I lack. Piano pieces are not the most enjoyable form of composition to me right now; I cannot even write them with real success; but I sometimes need a new piece to play, and if now and then something really suitable for the piano comes into my head, why should I be afraid of writing it down? Moreover, a very important branch of piano music, and one of which I am particularly fond—trios, quartets and other pieces with accompaniment, genuine chamber music—is quite forgotten now and I feel a great urge to do something new of this kind. It was with this idea that I recently wrote the sonata for violin, and the one for cello,*[2] *and I am thinking of writing a couple of trios next. I have also got a Symphony in B-flat in hand, and mean to have it finished soon. I only hope that we shall not have too many foreign virtuosi in Leipzig this winter and that I shall not have too many honours to enjoy—which means concerts to conduct . . .*

1. *Op.* 44, No. 1. *The autograph is dated "Berlin, July 24, 1838".*
2. *Sonata for piano and violin, F major, never published. Sonata for piano and violoncello in B-flat.*

FROM LETTERS TO IGNAZ MOSCHELES

Leipzig, December 10, 1838.

. . . Now to the most important part of your letter—that which refers to Weimar. Upon my word, it is not an easy matter to give you a proper answer to your questions. When I think of your life in London, your independent position at the head of the musical profession, and your never-ceasing activity in public, and then again of Weimar, with its petty court and its still pettier "Hofmarschall" and "Intendanz" that superintend nothing, when I think of the littleness that pervades everything, it would be madness to advise you to go. When I remember, on the other hand, your telling me that you never wished to remain all your life in England, but rather to return to your country and devote yourself to art and to your friends (and I believe that in your place I should feel as you do), and when I take into account that in Germany one town is as good as another—all small, but sociable—that the appointment is one of the best of its kind, that to you it would also be an acquisition to have an orchestra at your disposal, to us to have a man like you in Hummel's place, and to secure a musician of your standing for Germany—then I cannot help being in favour of Weimar. As far as I know, social resources are very limited there. The court circle is the best, not to say the only one; there you still meet with intelligence and culture—a relic of former days—but that, too, is on the decline, and whether your wife would like it seems to me very doubtful. On the other hand, the orchestra is said to be excellent, and the singers at the opera good; the Grand Duchess is a staunch friend of anybody she once likes, and with that, fairly musical herself. There is not very much to do, but enough opportunity to do much good—just what would suit you.

It is very difficult to put it impartially. You see, it would be glorious to have a musician like you amongst us, giving his best work to Germany; only it seems selfish to press you. Yet not to press you is decidedly too unselfish. Would it not be best for you to come over and look into the whole matter yourself? A great deal would be gained if you did not send an absolute refusal, were it only for the present.

I have been rather lazy of late. From the measles I dropped straight into so much conducting that I could scarcely do anything else, save take an occasional rest. Still, I have composed a new sonata for the piano and violoncello [1] and three violin quartets [2] which are shortly to appear. As soon as these four works are out I shall send them to you, and hope you will give me your candid opinion; but mind you criticise, and tell me what should have been done differently, and what I ought to have done better . . .

Leipzig, April 4, 1839.

. . . We recently played a most remarkable and interesting symphony by Franz Schubert. It is without doubt one of the best works we have lately heard. Throughout bright, fascinating and original, it stands quite at the head of his instrumental works.[3] . . . I have written a new dramatic overture [4] that has been quite a pleasure to me; also a psalm, some songs without words and some with words, and now a trio in D, and a symphony in B, of which I will tell you more when they are finished . . .

1. *Sonata in B-flat, op. 45.*
2. *Three Quartets, op. 44.*
3. *Symphony in C major.*
4. *Overture to "Ruy Blas".*

Chorus from the opera "Ruy Blas", composed in 1839.

TO PROFESSOR NAUMANN

Leipzig, September 19, 1839.

Sir,

Pray accept my thanks for the great proof of confidence in me that you show in your esteemed letter of the 12th of this month. Believe me, I appreciate it deeply, and can indeed feel how important the development and future destiny of a child so beloved and so talented must be to you. My sole wish, like your own, is that only such steps should be taken as are best calculated to reward his assiduity and to cultivate his talents. As an artist, I consider this to be my duty; in this case it would also give me pleasure because it would recall an earlier and friendly period of my life.

But I should respond to your confidence unworthily, did I not tell you frankly of the many and great scruples which prevent my unreserved acceptance of your proposal. In the first place, I am convinced, from repeated experience, that I totally lack the talent requisite for a practical teacher, and for giving regular progressive instruction; whether it be that I take too little pleasure in tuition, or have not sufficient patience, the fact remains that I do not succeed in it. Occasionally, young people have stayed with me, but any improvement they have derived was solely from our studying music together, from unreserved intercourse or casual conversation on various subjects, and also from discussions; and none of these things is compatible with actual teaching. Now the question is whether, in such early youth, a consecutive, unremitting, strict course of discipline is not of more value than all the rest? It also seems to me that the estrangement of your son from the paternal roof just at his age forms a second, and not less important objection. Where the rudiments of instruction are not wholly wanting (and the talents of your wife alone are a security against this), then the vicinity of his parents, the prosecution of the usual elements of study, the acquisition of languages and of the various branches of scholarship and science, are of more value to a boy than a one-sided, even though perfect, cultivation of his talent. Such talent is in any case sure to force its way to the light, and in later years will submit to no other permanent vocation, so that the treasures of interest acquired, and the hours enjoyed in early youth under the paternal roof, become doubly dear.

I speak thus from my own experience, for I can well remember that in my fifteenth year there was a question of my studying with Cherubini in Paris, and I know how grateful I was to my father at the time—and often since—that he at last gave up the idea and kept me with him. It would of course be very different if there were no means in Bonn of obtaining good, sound instruction in thorough-bass and the piano; but this I cannot believe, and whether that instruction is a little better or more intellectual (provided it be not positively objectionable) is not important when compared with the advantages of remaining longer in his own home . . .

FROM A LETTER TO IGNAZ MOSCHELES

Leipzig, November 30, 1839.

. . . Your Paris letter gave me much pleasure although what it describes is anything but pleasant. What a curious state of things seems to prevail there! To tell the truth, I never felt very sympathetically disposed towards it; and all I have heard lately, through you and others, does not tend to improve my opinion.

Vanity and outward show nowhere seem to play so prominent a part; and the fact that people assume poses not only to become stars, to acquire decorations and wear stiff neckties, but also to reveal their interest in high art, and a soul replete with enthusiasm, does not mend matters. When I read your description of the soirée at Kalkbrenners, I see and hear it all; that anxiety to shine at the piano, that greed for a poor little round of applause, the shallowness that underlies it all and is as pretentious as if such petty exhibitions were events of world-wide importance! To read about it is more than enough for me. After all, I prefer the German philistine, with his nightcap and tobacco; although I am not the one to stand up in his defense, especially since the events in Hanover, which I followed with great interest and which, I am sorry to say, do not reflect much credit on the German fatherland. So, on the whole, there is not much to be proud of on either side; and one cannot help being doubly grateful for that Art which has a life of its own, far away from everything—a solitude to which we can flee and be happy . . .

I want to write a new concerto, but so far it is swimming about in my head in a shapeless condition. A new oratorio, too, I have begun; but how it is to end, and what is to come in the middle, heaven only knows. I should so like to show you my trio;[1] it has grown quite dear to me, and I am confident there are things in it with which you would be satisfied. The publishers are pressing me to let them have it; I only wish I could just play it once to you before . . .

. . . I declined to give anything to Pott in furtherance of his scheme; nor would you have done so, had you known all their doings and dealings in Germany with regard to monuments. They speculate with the names of the great men in order to give themselves great names; they do a deal of trumpeting in the papers, and treat us to ever so much bad music with real trumpets. If they

1. *Trio in D minor, op. 49.*

wish to honour Haendel in Halle, Mozart in Salzburg, and Beethoven in Bonn by founding good orchestras and performing their works properly and intelligently, I am their man. But I do not care for their stones and blocks as long as their orchestras are only stumbling-blocks, nor for their conservatories in which there is nothing worth conserving. My present hobby is the improvement of our poor orchestra. After no end of letter-writing, soliciting and importuning, I have succeeded in getting the salaries raised by five hundred thalers; and before I leave them I mean to get them double that amount. If that is granted, I will not mind their setting up a monument to Sebastian Bach in front of the St. Thomas school; but first, mind you, the grant! You see, I am a regular small-beer Leipziger. But really you would be touched if you could see and hear for yourself how my good fellows put heart and soul into their work, and strive to do their best.

I am very glad you improved your acquaintance and friendship with Chopin. He is certainly the most gifted of them all, and his playing has real charm. They say Liszt is coming here, and I should be very glad; for notwithstanding his unpalatable contributions to the papers, I am thoroughly impressed both by his playing and his striking personality. Berlioz's programme that you sent me is a very silly production. I wish I could see any pluck or originality in it, but to me it seems simply vapid and insipid. Has not Onslow written anything new? And old Cherubini? There is a man for you! I have got his "Abencerages", and am again and again enjoying his sparkling fire, his clever and unexpected transitions, and the neatness and grace with which he writes. I am truly grateful to this fine old gentleman. It is all so free, so bold and bright.

Now I must end, my dear friend. I have been jumbling everything together, and chatting away as if I were sitting next to you by the piano . . . Write to me and let me know what you are doing and what composing; and above all, tell me that you are my friend, as I am your

F.M.B.

TO I. FUERST

Leipzig, January 4, 1840.

Dear Fuerst,

You scold me extravagantly at the beginning of your welcome letter, but at its close you draw so admirable a moral that I have only to thank you anew for the whole. You do me an injustice in suggesting that my sole reason for wishing to see the scenario is to raise difficulties from the start, in order to bring the child into the world already infected with the germs of disease.

It is precisely on opposite grounds that I desire this; it is in order to obviate subsequent difficulties and developed maladies. If these are, as you declare, born with him, it is best to forget about the whole child while it might still be possible, without giving offense to all the parties involved. Whereas, if the maladies admit of a remedy at all, they might be cured before they attack the whole organism.

To cease speaking figuratively, what can deter, and has hitherto deterred me from composing a libretto, is not the verse, nor the individual words, nor the method of treatment (or whatever you call it), but the course of the action, the dramatic essence, the march of events—in short, the scenario. If I do not consider this good and solid in itself, then it is my firm conviction that the music will not be so either, and the whole cannot satisfy the demands I must make of such a work, though they may indeed differ entirely from those which are usually made, and from those of the public. But I have long since given up all idea of conforming to those tastes, for the simple reason that it is impossible; so I must follow the dictates of my own conscience, now as always.

Planché's text can never, even with the best will on both sides, become the kind of work I want; I am disposed to give up this attempt, too, as being utterly hopeless. I would rather never compose an opera at all, than one which I considered mediocre from the very start. Moreover, I could not possibly write such a work were you to give me the whole kingdom of Prussia. All this, and the many annoyances certain to occur at the completion of a text, if I should not feel attracted to it, render it my duty to move step by step, rather too slowly than too hastily; on this account, I have resolved, unless we first agree about the scenario, never to beguile any poet into undertaking so laborious a work, which may, after all, prove vain. This scenario may be prolix or brief, detailed or merely sketched, on these points I do not presume to dictate, nor to decide whether the opera should be in three, four or five acts. If it is really good—just as it is written—then eight acts would not be too much for me, nor a single act too little. The same holds true as to whether or not there should be a ballet, the only criterion being whether or not it harmonises with the musical and general feeling of the work. I believe that I am able to tell this quite as well from the scenario as from the finished text, and that is a point which no one but myself can decide.

I have thus placed the whole truth before you, and heaven grant that all these things may not deter you from writing an opera, that you may also intrust it to me for composition, and that I may at last, through you, see a long-cherished wish fulfilled. I need not tell you how eagerly I await your decision.

Your

F.M.B.

FROM A LETTER TO HIS MOTHER

Leipzig, March 30, 1840.

. . . There has been too great a hither and thither in the last few weeks. Liszt was here for a fortnight and was the cause of a tremendous uproar in both a good and a bad sense. I consider him to be fundamentally a good, warm-hearted man and an admirable artist. There is no doubt that he plays most of all of them, yet Thalberg, with his composure, and within his more restricted sphere, is more nearly perfect as a real virtuoso; and after all this is the standard by which Liszt must also be judged, for his compositions are inferior to his playing, and, in fact, are calculated solely for virtuosi. A fantasia by Thalberg (especially that on the "Lady of the Lake") is an accumulation of the finest and most exquisite effects, and a crescendo of difficulties and embellishments that is astonishing. Everything is so calculated and so polished and shows such assurance, skill and superlative taste. At the same time the man has incredibly powerful hands and such practiced, light fingers that he is unique.

Liszt, on the other hand, possesses a certain suppleness and differentiation in his fingering, as well as a thoroughly musical feeling that cannot be equalled. In a word, I have heard no performer whose musical perceptions extend to the very tips of his fingers and emanate directly from them as Liszt's do. With his directness, his stupendous technique and experience, he would have far surpassed all the rest, were not a man's own thoughts in connection with all this the main thing. And these, so far, at least, seem to have been denied him by nature, so that in this respect most of the great virtuosi equal, or even excel him. But that he, together with Thalberg, alone represent the highest class of pianists of the present day, seems to me indisputable. Unhappily, Liszt's behaviour here towards the public, has not made a favourable impression. The whole wrangle gives one the feeling of listening to the perorations of two people, both of whom are wrong, and whom one would fain interrupt at every word. The philistines who are mostly concerned with the high prices and who never wish to see a clever fellow get on too well, and who grumble accordingly—they can go to the dickens. But the newspaper articles, on the other hand, there you had explanations, and counter-explanations, criticisms and complaints, and all kinds of stuff dragged in, that was totally unconnected with music; so that his stay here caused us almost as much annoyance as pleasure; though the latter was often great beyond words.

Then it occurred to me that this unpleasantness might be most effectually allayed if people could see and hear Liszt at close quarters. So I suddenly determined to give a soirée for him in the Gewandhaus (for three hundred and fifty people) with orchestra, chorus, bishop, cakes, "Meeresstille", "Psalm", triple concerto by Bach (Liszt, Hiller and I), choruses from "St. Paul", a fantasia on "Lucia di Lammermoor", "Erl King", devil and his grandmother, and all the people were so delighted, and played and sang with such enthusiasm, that they swore they had never had a jollier evening. So my object was happily effected in a most agreeable manner.

Today I made a resolution over which I am as happy as a bird, and that is, never again to participate in any way in the awarding of prizes at a musical competition. Several proposals of this kind were made to me and I did not know why I was so annoyed, until it became clear to me that fundamentally it would be sheer arrogance on my part, which I would not tolerate in others. I should therefore be the last person to set myself up as a criterion and my taste as incontrovertible, and, in an idle hour passing in review all the assembled competitors, criticising them, and—God knows—

possibly being guilty of the most glaring injustice towards them. So I have renounced such activity once and for all and since then have been very happy.

TO THE KREISDIREKTOR VON FALKENSTEIN

Leipzig, April 8, 1840.

Sir,

Emboldened by the assurance of your kind feelings, in our recent conversation, and by the conviction that you have sincerely at heart the condition of art here and its further cultivation (of which you have already given so many proofs), I permit myself to put before you a question which seems to me of the highest importance in the tonal art.

Would it not be possible to entreat His Majesty to devote the sum bequeathed by the late Herr Bluemner for an institution of art or science—the disposal of which was left to the discretion of His Majesty—to the erection and maintenance of a basic Music Academy in Leipzig? Permit me to make a few observations on the importance of such an institution, and to state why I consider that Leipzig is peculiarly entitled to aspire to one of her own, and also what I consider to be the fitting principles for its organisation.

For a long time, music has been indigenous to this country, and just that trend which must lie nearest the heart of every ardent and thoughtful friend of art, namely the feeling for what is true and genuine, has always been able to strike roots in this soil. Such universal sympathy is certainly neither accidental nor has it been without important results for general education. Music has thus become an important factor—not a mere fleeting pleasure, but a spiritual and intellectual necessity. Whoever has a sincere interest in this art must eagerly desire to see its future in this land established on the most solid foundations possible. But the positive, and technically materialistic tendencies of the present day render the preservation of a genuine sense of art, and its further development, a doubly important, but also a doubly difficult task. It seems that this can be achieved only by working from the ground up; and as the expansion of sound instruction is the best mode of preserving every species of intellectual development, so it certainly is with music, too. If we had a good Music Academy which embraced all the various branches of this art, and taught them from one sole point of view, merely as the means to a higher end, and guided all its students as far as possible toward this goal, then this practical, materialistic tendency which, alas! can number, even among our artists, many influential followers, might yet be effectually checked.

Mere private instruction, which once bore much good fruit, also for life in general, now, for many reasons, no longer suffices. Formerly, music students who learned to play various instruments were to be found in every class of society, whereas now the number of amateurs has become more and more reduced and those that are left confine themselves preferably to one instrument, the piano.

The students who desire further instruction are almost invariably those who intend to devote themselves to this profession but who lack the means to pay for good private lessons. It is true that the best talents are often to be found amongst them, but, on the other hand, teachers are seldom placed in such fortunate circumstances as to be able to devote their time, without remuneration, to the training of even the greatest talents; thus both sides suffer; the former are deprived of the longed-for instruction, and the latter of the chance to impart their knowledge and keep its influence alive. A public institution would, therefore, just now be important to teachers as well as to pupils. These latter would be given the means of cultivating abilities which otherwise would often be wasted. But for the teachers of music it would be equally important; for to work in a group which has a common point of view and a common goal is the best means of preventing indifference and isolation, whose unfruitfulness these days can become genuinely harmful all too quickly.

Here in Leipzig there is a deeply-felt need for such a school, in which music may be pursued with conscientious study and an earnest mind; and on several grounds Leipzig seems to be a peculiarly suitable place for it. The university already provides a centre for intelligent, aspiring young people, and such a school of science would have many points of contact with one of tonal art. In most of the other large towns of Germany, public amusements dissipate the mind and exercise an injurious influence over the young; here, however, where most of these amusements are more or less connected with music or consist of it wholly, and where few other public recreations are offered, this institution would benefit both the cause and the individual. Moreover, in that particular branch of art which must always provide the chief basis for musical study —namely instrumental and sacred compositions of higher quality— Leipzig, with her great wealth of concerts and church music, provides educational material for potential musicians that few other cities can boast to that degree. Because of the lively sympathy with which, for the last fifty years, the principal works of the great masters have been received and acknowledged here (often for the first time in Germany) and because of the care with which these works invariably have been performed, Leipzig has assumed an important place among the musical cities of our fatherland.

Lastly, in support of this petition I may add that His Excellency, Kriegsrat Bluemner, who cherished so great a love for poetry and whatever was poetical in all the arts, always devoted special attention to musical conditions here, and even took an active part in the management of the concerts in which he was warmly in-

terested; so that such an apportionment of his bequest would undoubtedly be in accordance with the artistic feelings of the testator.

Whilst other establishments of public utility are constantly encouraged, and some even richly endowed, musical activity here has never received the smallest aid from any quarter. Since musical institutions in the capital are supported by the state, would it not be particularly desirable that the sum bequeathed by one of its inhabitants should be turned over to the city: would not such a boon be received with particular gratitude on all sides? For these reasons, may His Majesty be graciously disposed not to refuse the fulfilment of a wish so warmly cherished, and thus grant a new stimulus and a fresh impulse to art. It would give an impetus to musical life here, the effects of which would be speedily and enduringly disseminated with greatest benefit.

Allow me to enclose in this envelope a general outline for the organisation of such a musical Academy, and receive the assurance of the distinguished esteem with which I have the honour to remain

Always your devoted

F.M.B.

FROM LETTERS TO HIS MOTHER

Leipzig, August 10, 1840.

. . . On Thursday I gave an organ concert here in St. Thomas's Church, from the proceeds of which old Sebastian Bach is to have a monument erected to his memory in front of the St. Thomas School. I gave it solissimo, and played nine pieces, finishing up with an extempore fantasia. This was the whole programme. Although

my expenses were considerable, I had a clear gain of three hundred thalers. I shall repeat this pleasure in the autumn or spring, and then a fine stone can be erected.[1] I practised for eight days before, so that I could scarcely stand up straight on my feet any longer and walked along the street only in organ passages . . .

Leipzig, October 27, 1840.

Dear Mother,

You will already know from the newspapers that we recently had a second performance of the "Hymn of Praise" for the King of Saxony at an extra subscription concert, and it went off famously. All the music was given with such precision that it was a joy to listen to it. The King even sent for me in the intermission which obliged me to pass through a double row of ladies (you know the arrangement of our hall) in order to reach the place where the King and his court were seated. He conversed with me for some time in the most good-natured and friendly manner, and spoke very well about music. The "Hymn of Praise" was given in the second part, and at the end, when I had already left my desk, I suddenly heard people round me saying, "Now the King is coming to him"; and he had in fact passed through the row of ladies. He came up to my desk (you can imagine the general jubilation) and spoke to me in so animated a manner and with such cordiality and warmth that I really did feel pleased and honoured. He mentioned the particular passages he had liked best, thanked all the singers and then departed whilst the whole orchestra and the whole audience made the very best bows and curtsies they could possibly muster up. Then there arose a hubbub and confusion like in

1. *This has been done. The monument is on the promenade, under the windows of Sebastian Bach's rooms in the St. Thomas School.*

Noah's ark. Perhaps the King will now donate the twenty thousand thalers which I long ago petitioned might be given for music here. In that case I could honestly say that I have rendered a good service to the music of Leipzig.

Farewell, dearest mother—ever your

Felix.

FROM A LETTER TO HIS SISTER FANNY

Leipzig, November 14, 1840.

Dear Fanny,

. . . My best thanks also for your last letter. Do you know that your suggestion as to the "Nibelungen" seems most interesting to me? It has been constantly in my head ever since, and I mean to spend my first day of leisure reading the poem, for I have forgotten the details and can only recall the outlines and the general colouring which seem to me gloriously dramatic. Will you kindly give me your more specific ideas to the subject? Evidently the poem is more present in your memory than in mine. I scarcely remember what your allusion to the "sinking into the Rhine" stands for. Could you point out to me the various passages which struck you as particularly dramatic when the idea first occurred to you? And above all, say something more definite on the subject—the whole tone, and the pictorial qualities and the characteristic features impress my imagination strongly; and I beg you to do it, and to do it soon; you will render me an essential service. You can refer directly to the poem, because I shall certainly have read it before your next letter arrives, but anyhow I will not await your opinion the less eagerly. Thanks so much for this thought, as for everything else . . .

When you meet Herr von Zuccalmaglio, thank him for his package and the letter I received from him. Quite between ourselves—I will not be able to compose the songs he sent me. They are patriotic, and at this moment I do not feel in the least disposed toward this kind of "patriotism". Such songs might cause a great many misunderstandings just now, at a time when people are beginning to sing against the French, although they have just discovered that the French do not want to fight against them. I do not wish to make music for such a purpose. But adieu for tonight—I do wish that instead of having to dress and to go through such a terrible lot of music, I could just cross the street to your house—and we could play "Black Peter", and eat cakes, and have some fun.

Your

Felix.

TO KARL KLINGEMANN

Leipzig, November 18, 1840.

My dearest Friend,

I am living here in as complete quiet and solitude as I could possibly desire; thanks be to God, my wife and children are well, I have plenty of work, and what more can man desire? I do not ask Heaven to grant me anything else, and I start every day by enjoying anew my peaceful and monotonous life. I admit that at the beginning of the winter I generally have difficulty avoiding the somewhat philistine social gatherings which bloom and thrive here and in which one might be enticed to participate and thus lose much time and pleasure. By now I have pretty well succeeded in getting rid of them. Moreover there is a fast this week, so we have no subscription concert, but a pleasant period of domestic rest instead.

My "Hymn of Praise" is to be performed the end of this month for the benefit of old invalided musicians. I have decided that I do not want to produce it again in the imperfect form in which, owing to my illness, it had to be given in Birmingham, and so I have to work rather hard. Four new pieces are to be added, and I have also much improved the three symphonic parts which are now being copied. As an introduction to the chorus, "Die Nacht ist vergangen", I have found words in the Bible which could not be more beautiful, nor better adapted to this music. By-the-way, you have assumed a great responsibility by finding such an admirable title; for not only shall I send the piece into the world as a "Symphony-Cantata", but I am thinking seriously about resuming the "First Walpurgisnacht" (which has been stored away for so long,) under this name too, finishing the work and finally getting rid of it. It is strange enough that after my first conception of it, I should have written to Berlin that I wanted to compose a symphony with chorus and then subsequently have lacked the courage to begin, because the three movements seemed too long for a mere introduction and yet nonetheless could never overcome feeling that something was lacking in that same introduction. Now the movements are to be inserted according to the old plan, and then the piece can be brought out. Do you know it? I do not believe that it is worth much for a performance, and yet I am so fond of it!

The whole town is ringing with a song, supposed to have a political tendency against the French, and the papers try very hard to make it popular. In the actual dearth of public topics they succeed without much difficulty, and everybody is talking about the "Rheinlied" or the "Colognaise", as the song is significantly *called. The thing is characteristic, for the first lines begin with "Sie sollen ihn nicht haben, den freien, deutschen Rhein", ("They shall never have it, the free, German Rhein") and each verse repeats "They shall never have it!" as if there were the least sense in such words! If they were at least changed to "We mean to keep it" —but just "They shall never have it", seems to me all too sterile and futile. One might well call it just a puerile affair, because if I actually and definitely possess an object, it is useless to go on saying and singing that it belongs to nobody else. This song is now sung at the court in Berlin, and in the clubs and casinos here, and of course, the musicians pounce on it like mad and are immortalising themselves by setting it in their own way. The Leipzig composers have already fitted to it not less than three melodies, and the song is alluded to daily in one paper or the other. Yesterday it was even announced that I had also composed the poem, whereas I never dreamt of meddling with such a defensive enthusiasm—and people here lie like a book, right and left.*

TO CHARLOTTE MOSCHELES

Leipzig, March 14, 1841.

Dear Mrs. Moscheles,

What a delightful letter of yours I received the day before yesterday, written beside the singing tea-urn and taking me straight to Chester Place! By rights, my thanks ought to come in shape of a song on one of these pages; but I cannot manage it today, and you must take these unmusical, prosaic, dry thanks for your musical, bright, poetical letter.

For now, when our season is drawing to a close, you know from experience how hard-driven a man is—and, to keep up the usual distinction, a musician into the bargain. Since January we have been having an uninterrupted succession of musical events, besides which the Leipzigers are so very sociable that at this time one is hardly allowed a quiet evening at home. Our own house has become a lively centre too . . . We invite our friends and they return the compliment. We speak German, French and English all in one breath; and all the while the orchestra is fiddling, trumpeting, and drumming every day, whilst one is expected to sit an hour and a half at supper, and sing four-part songs to a roast-beef accompaniment.

The only thing I regret in your charming letter is that you should have countenanced the strange attempts at making comparisons between Spohr and myself, or the petty cockfights in which, for some inconceivable reason and much to my regret, we have been pitted against each other in England. I never had the slightest idea of such competition or rivalry. You may laugh at me, or possibly be vexed, at my taking up such a silly matter so seriously. But there is something serious at the bottom of it; this pretended antagonism, imagined and started by heaven knows whom, can in no way serve either of us, but must rather be detrimental to both. Besides, I could never appear as the opponent of a master of Spohr's standing, whose greatness is so firmly established; for even as a boy, I had the greatest esteem for him in every respect, and with my riper years this feeling has in no way been weakened.

My wife has been in such good health all this time that I cannot be sufficiently thankful. There is however much to manage and arrange with three little soprano singers in the house, and that is why she returns your kind messages through me. Should you ever feel inclined to write another such truly charming letter by the side of the tea-urn, so enjoyable to your distant friends and drawing them into your family circle, then think of yours

F.M.B.

FROM A LETTER TO KARL KLINGEMANN

Berlin, September 6, 1841.

. . . You would like to have more detailed news about my position here in Berlin, but I cannot tell you more than I have already written from Leipzig. As to what people expect of me, now or later, I have not the faintest idea, nor, do I actually believe, have they. You know that I had promised to stay for one year; in order to do that I arrived at the end of July, and was received in the most cordial manner by everybody; the Minister discussed everything with me thoroughly, the Privy Councillors did the same, Herr von Massow, who had carried on the negotiations with me, proved himself to be a genuinely sympathetic and benevolent friend, the King invited me for dinner, the Queen asked for a piano-arrangement of my Hymn-of-Praise Symphony which, of course, I made for her—and in this way nearly two months have passed since I arrived and I know no more about what I am supposed to do than I did before—if anything, less. And about the salary, the position and the title that they desire to give me here, and about which the people and the papers are talking, and which were offered me half a year ago, not another word has been said since I arrived. I do not doubt that those promises are going to be kept; nevertheless, anybody else could have been devilishly embarrassed by it. At the same time I am lucky enough to be able to live here in the Leipziger Strasse quite retired and with nothing to bother about. Meantime I have begun a big symphony, and am already in the third movement, and work at it every day with delight; I also continue my sketching, drink mineral water which agrees with me splendidly, and spend the evenings happily with my family. Thus I can wait quietly and see what they are brewing. It is the urgent desire of the King to have the "Antigone" of Sophocles produced in the palace; he wants me to write the choruses and Tieck to stage it. If only something would come of it. But neither is this plan definite, although they talked about it four months ago, the same as now. I am going honestly to work and am acting as though it meant a great deal to me to bring the matter to fulfilment. I am hustling and pushing and rushing people as much as I can, so at least, if nothing comes of it, (which I believe, and almost know) I will at least have done my part. And then next year I shall return to my jolly home in Leipzig, which will not make me unhappy, as you know, and I will be justified in the eyes of my mother, and my brother and sisters, if I cannot stay in a place that is not for me.

TO HIS MOTHER

London, June 21, 1842.

Dear Mother,

Your letter of yesterday was again so lovely and gave us so much pleasure that I must thank you for it in detail today; I was scarcely able to do so for the previous one, which contained a real kaleidoscope of Berlin conditions, and which, through the glasses of your description, assumed perpetually novel and delightful forms. If I could write half as well, you would today receive the nicest letter, for we daily see the most beautiful and splendid things. But I am somewhat fatigued by the all-too-mad activities of the last week, and for two days past I have been chiefly lying on the sofa reading "Wilhelm Meister", and strolling through the fields with Klingemann in the evening, to try to restore myself.

So, if the tone of this letter is rather languid and weary, it accurately paints my feelings. They have really asked a little too much of me. Recently when I played the organ in Christ Church, Newgate Street, I thought for a few moments that I would suffocate, so great was the crowd and pressure around my bench at the organ. Then, too, several days later I had to play in Exeter Hall before three thousand people, who shouted hurrahs and waved their handkerchiefs, and stamped their feet till the hall quaked. At that moment I felt no bad effects, but next morning my head was dizzy and as if I had had a sleepless night. Add to this the pretty and most charming Queen Victoria, who looks so youthful and is so shyly friendly and courteous, and who speaks such good German and who knows all my music so well: the four books of songs without words, and those with words, and the symphony, and the "Hymn of Praise". Yesterday evening I was with the Queen, who was practically alone with Prince Albert and who seated herself near the piano and made me play to her; first seven "Songs Without Words", then the Serenade, two impromptus on "Rule Britannia", Lutzow's "Wilde Jagd", and "Gaudeamus igitur". The latter was somewhat difficult, but remonstrances were out of question, and as they gave me the themes, of course I was able to play them. And besides, the splendid grand gallery in Buckingham Palace where they drank their tea, and where two boars by Paul Potter are hanging, and a good many other pictures which did not displease me. And besides, my A minor Symphony has had great success with the people here, who one and all receive us with a degree of amiability and kindness which exceeds everything I have ever known in the way of hospitality. All this sometimes makes my head feel quite bewildered and wild, and I have to pull myself together in order not to lose all self-control.

June 22nd.—Today, however, I can continue my letter in a more cheerful spirit; I have slept away my weary mood and feel again well and fresh. Yesterday evening I played my concerto in D minor and directed my "Hebrides" in the Philharmonic where

I was received like an old friend and where they played with a degree of enthusiasm which gave me more pleasure than I can say. The people make such a fuss over me this time that I am quite dumbfounded; I believe they clapped their hands and stamped for at least ten minutes after the concerto, and insisted on the "Hebrides" being repeated. The directors are to give a dinner for me at Greenwich next week, and we are to sail down the Thames in corpore and to make speeches. They talk of bringing out "Antigone" at Covent Garden as soon as they can procure a tolerable translation. Lately I went to a concert in Exeter Hall where I had nothing whatever to do, and was sauntering in quite coolly with Klingemann—it was already the middle of the first part and there was an audience of about three thousand present—and no sooner had I come in the door, than such a clamour, and clapping and shouting, and standing-up ensued, that at first I had no idea that it concerned me; but I discovered it did when on reaching my place, I found Sir Robert Peel and Lord Wharncliffe close to me, and they continued to applaud with the rest till I made my bow and thanked them. I was devilishly proud of my popularity in Peel's presence. When I left the concert they gave me another hurrah.

Oh! and how splendidly Mrs. Butler, at Chorley's, recently read aloud Shakespeare's "Anthony and Cleopatra"! We have always been on friendly terms since our acquaintance twelve years ago, (it is Miss Fanny Kemble) and she gave this reading in honour of me, but it was much too beautiful. Lady Morgan was there, and Winterhalter, and Mrs. Jameson, and Duprez, who afterwards sang a French romance of an old beggar who was so hungry, and another of a young man losing his reason, with the refrain, "Le vent qui vient à travers la montagne me rendra fou!"—("The wind which comes over the mountain will drive me mad")—"Sweet!" said the ladies; and Benedicts and Moscheles, and the Grotes—who can count them all! This evening at seven o'clock we dine with Bunsen, and as we do not know what to do with our evening afterwards, we shall probably drive to Charles Kemble's about eleven o'clock and be among his early guests; the late ones will not arrive till after midnight. And the persistently bright and beautiful weather besides all this! The other morning we first went to see the Tower, then the Katherine Docks, then the Tunnel, then ate fish at Blackwall, had tea at Greenwich, and came home by way of Peckham; we travelled on foot, in a carriage, on a railway, in a boat, and in a steamboat. The day after tomorrow we intend to go to Manchester for a couple of days, and next week be on our way back to Frankfort. I have given up the music festival at the Hague, though they pestered me to go there for my "Hymn of Praise". I wish to have nothing to do with music for the next four weeks.

But I must conclude. May we soon have a happy meeting, dearest Mother, and dearest Brother and Sisters!

Your

Felix.

FROM A LETTER TO HIS MOTHER

Frankfort, July 19, 1842.

My dear little Mother,

Here we are back again,[1] jolly and happy after a jolly, happy trip, and we found the dear children well and blooming, and your sweet letter tells us the same of all of you. A blue sky and warm, clear air are brought by one unforgettably beautiful day after the other—

1. *Mendelssohn and his wife had just returned from one of his most successful trips to England.*

if one only knew how to prove himself sufficiently thankful for such great happiness.

Moreover, I especially enjoy being in Frankfort, among so many good friends and relations in this beautiful part of the world . . .

I owe you further particulars of our time in London, after our trip to Manchester . . . All this I can describe better when I see you, but the details of my last visit to Buckingham Palace I must write you at once because they will amuse you so much, and me, too. As Grahl says—and it is true—the only friendly English house, one that is really comfortable and where one feels at ease, is Buckingham Palace—as a matter of fact, I know several others, but on the whole, I agree with him. Joking apart, Prince Albert had asked me to go to him on Saturday at two o'clock, so that I might try his organ before I left England. I found him all alone; and as we were talking away, the Queen came in, also quite alone, in a house dress. She said she was obliged to leave for Claremont in an hour; "But, goodness! how it looks here", she added, when she saw that the wind had littered the whole room, and even the pedals of the organ (which, by the way, made a very pretty feature in the room), with leaves of music from a large portfolio that lay open. As she spoke, she knelt down and began picking up the music; Prince Albert helped, and I too was not idle. Then Prince Albert proceeded to explain the stops to me, and while he was doing it, she said that she would put things straight alone.

But I begged that the Prince would first play me something, so that, as I said, I might boast about it in Germany; and thereupon he played me a chorale by heart, with pedals, so charmingly and clearly and correctly that many an organist could have learned something; and the Queen, having finished her work, sat beside him and listened, very pleased. Then I had to play, and I began my chorus from "St. Paul": "How lovely are the Messengers!" Before I got to the end of the first verse, they both began to sing the chorus very well, and all the time Prince Albert managed the stops for me so expertly—first a flute, then full at the forte, the whole register at the D major part, then he made such an excellent diminuendo with the stops, and so on to the end of the piece, and all by heart—that I was heartily pleased. Then the Crown Prince of Gotha came in, and there was more conversation, and among other things the Queen asked if I had composed any new songs, and said that she was very fond of singing the published ones. "You should sing one to him", said Prince Albert; and after a little begging she said she would try the "Fruehlingslied" in B-flat. "Yes, if it were still here, for all my music is packed up for Claremont." Prince Albert went to look for it, but came back saying it was already packed. "Oh, perhaps it could be unpacked", said I. "We must send for Lady N. N.", she said. (I did not catch the name.) So the bell was rung, and the servants were sent after it, but came back embarrassed; and then the Queen went herself, and whilst she was gone Prince Albert said to me: "She begs you will accept this present as a remembrance"—and gave me a case with a beautiful ring, on which is engraved "V. R., 1842".

Then the Queen came back and said: "Lady N. N. has left and has taken all my things with her. It really is most unseemly." (You can't think how that amused me.) I then begged that I might not be made to suffer for the accident, and hoped she would sing another song. After some consultation with her husband he said: "She will sing you something of Gluck's". Meantime the Prince of Gotha had come in, and we five proceeded through the corridors and rooms to the Queen's sitting-room, where, next to the piano, stood an enormous, thick rocking-horse, and two great bird-cages and pictures on the walls and beautifully bound books lay on the tables, and music on the piano. The Duchess of Kent came in, too, and while they were all talking I rummaged about a little amongst the music and found my first set of songs. So, naturally I begged her to choose one of those rather than the Gluck, to which she very kindly consented; and which did she choose? "Schöner und schöner"; sang it beautifully in tune, in strict time, and with very nice expression. Only where, following "Der Prosa Last und

Mueh' ", where it goes down to D and then comes up again by semitones, she sang D-sharp each time; and because the first two times I gave her the note, the last time, sure enough, she sang D— where it ought to have been D-sharp. But except for this little mistake it was really charming, and the last long G I have never heard better or purer or more natural from any amateur. Then I was obliged to confess that Fanny had written the song (which I found very hard, but pride must have a fall), and to beg her to sing one of my own, too. "If I would give her plenty of help she would gladly try", she said, and sang "Lass dich nur nichts dauern" really without a mistake, and with charming feeling and expression. I thought to myself that one must not pay too many compliments on such an occasion, so I merely thanked her very much; but she said, "Oh, if only I had not been so nervous; otherwise I really have a long breath". Then I praised her heartily, and with the best conscience in the world; for just that part with the long C at the close she had done so well, taking it and the three notes next to it all in the same breath, as one seldom hears it done, and therefore it amused me doubly that she herself should have begun about it.

After this Prince Albert sang the Erntelied, "Es ist ein Schnitter", and then he said I must play him something before I went, and gave me as themes the chorale which he had played on the organ and the song he had just sung. If everything had gone as usual, I ought to have improvised dreadfully badly; for that is what nearly always happens to me when I want it to go well, and then I should have gone away vexed with the whole morning. But just as if I were to keep the nicest, most charming recollection of it, without any unpleasantness at all, I have rarely improvised as well. I was in the mood for it, and played a long time, and enjoyed it myself; of course, besides the two themes, I also brought in the songs the Queen had sung; but it all worked in so naturally that I would have been glad not to stop. And they followed me with so much intelligence and attention that I felt more at my ease than I ever have in improvising before an audience. Well, and then she said, "I hope you will come and visit us soon again in England", and then I took my leave; and down below I saw the beautiful carriages waiting, with their scarlet outriders, and in a quarter of an hour the flag was lowered, and the papers said: "Her Majesty left the Palace at 30 minutes past 3". I walked back through the rain to Klingemann's, and enjoyed more than everything giving a piping-hot account of it all to him and Cécile. It was a delightful morning! I must add that I asked permission to dedicate my A minor symphony to the Queen, that having really been the reason for my visit to England, and because the English name would be doubly suited to the Scottish piece; and that, just as the Queen was going to sing, she said: "But the parrot must be removed first, or he will scream louder than I sing"; upon which Prince Albert rang the bell and the Prince of Gotha said, "I will carry him out", upon which I replied, "Allow me to do that", (like cousin Wolf with his "allow me, me, me!") and lifted up the big cage and carried it out to the astonished servants, etc. There is much more to tell when we meet, but if this long description makes Dirichlet set me down as an aristocrat, tell him that I swear that I am a greater radical than ever . . .

TO HIS MOTHER

Interlaken, August 18, 1842.

Dear little Mother,

Do you still remember our staying here twenty years ago in this pretty inn under the big walnut trees (I sketched one of them), and our charming young landlady? When I was here ten years ago, she refused to give me lodgings, I looked so shabby after the pedestrian tour, and I believe that was the only time that I felt vexed on that whole trip. Now we are here again as decent people. The Jungfrau with her silver horn stands out against the sky with just the same delicate, elegant, and pointed outlines, and looks fresh as ever. The landlady, however, has grown old, and it was only because of her posture that I recognised her. I have again sketched the walnut trees, much better than at that time, but worse than I know it ought to be done. The post in Untersee brings our letters from the same office as it did then, and many new houses have been built, and the Aar gurgles and glides along, as rapid and smooth and green as ever—time is, time was, time is past. I have, in fact, nothing else to write to you, except that we are all well and are remembering you daily and hourly.

Descriptions of Switzerland are impossible, and instead of keeping a diary as before, I am sketching furiously this time, and sit in front of a mountain and try to draw its likeness, and do not give it up until I have spoiled the sketch. But I must have at least one new sketch in my book every day. He who has not seen the Gemmi knows nothing of Switzerland; but this is what people say of every new object in this unbelievably beautiful country. With regard to this land, I feel just as I do about the best books. They keep on changing with one's inner aspect, present a new phase with every change but always remain towering with the same loftiness and grandeur. So now, when I see this country with my wife, I have quite different impressions from those in previous times. Then I wished to climb every crested mountain and to dash across every green pasture. This time, on the contrary, I would like to stay on and on everywhere, for months. I am not at all sure that some fine spring day I may not set off for this place bag and baggage, and not return to the North until the last leaf is gone. Such, at least, are now my daily thoughts and air-castles. In a few days we shall leave for the Oberland; I am looking forward to seeing the full moon in Lauterbrunnen. Then we return here, across Furka and

Grimsel, to the Lake of Lucerne, and the Rigi, and then away from the land of all lands, and back to Germany—where it is not so bad either, after all. I confess there are many days when the world pleases me very, very much!

I am writing funny news, dear Mother! When we meet, I shall have a tale to tell that will know no end. Ever your

Felix.

TO N. SIMROCK

Frankfort, September 21, 1842.

Dear Mr. Simrock,

I write to you today about a matter in which I must count on your entire discretion and profound secrecy; your kindness to me I know too well from experience to doubt the fulfilment of my wish, and I put the matter before you, fully relying on your silence. I heard quite by chance, during my stay here, that my friend and fellow-artist, Mr. F. Hiller, has written to you about the publication of some new works, but has as yet received no answer. I wish very much, in the interest of art as well as in that of my friend, that your answer may be favourable; and as I fancy that my opinion may have some weight with you, it occurred to me to write to you about it, and beg you, if you possibly could, to acquaint the German public with some of my friend's works. My reason for begging you to keep the matter secret from everybody and in all circumstances, is that I am certain that Mr. Hiller would be frantic if he had the remotest idea of my having taken such a step. I know that nothing would be more unbearable to him than not to stand altogether on his own feet, and therefore he must never know anything about this letter. But on the other hand, it is a duty and an obligation, which one artist owes another, to help him as much as possible over difficulties and unpleasantnesses and to give him every assistance toward the fulfilment of his efforts, provided that they are honourable and the cause a good one. And certainly this is true in the very highest degree, both of his efforts and his cause. That is why I wanted to beg you to publish some of his compositions, and above all, if possible, to enter into some sort of an agreement with him. I know perfectly well that the German publishers have not done very brilliant business (as it is called) with most of his works as yet, and I cannot insure its being different now; but that this deserves to be otherwise I feel no doubt whatever, and this is my reason and my only reason, for making the request. Were it not so, however great a friend of mine he might be, I would not ask it.

But just because the only consideration which ought reasonably to be entertained is that of intrinsic worth, and because it is the only one which ought to insure success if everything were carried on fairly in this world, and because it is too annoying to hear, forever repeated, the old story of the deserving and clever artists who at first experience the greatest difficulty in having their works brought out and become known, and who, afterward, are fussed over by everybody when one of their works happens to make a hit and gains the ear of the public (though, after all, neither the pleasure nor the fuss can make up for their former troubles), just because of all this I want you to act differently, and to put more belief in real work than chance success. Someone must put a stop to it some day, and the only question in such cases is how soon, and after how much unpleasantness. That is just the point at which a publisher may be of so much value and importance to an artist. Universal applause brings them all to the front, of course; but I feel that you would be just the man to reform this state of affairs and bring about one which should at once be ideal, practical and just. Pray forgive my boldness, and if possible fulfil my request. As far as I understand, the amount of remuneration is of no consequence; the most desirable thing is that you should write in a friendly and artistic tone, and that the works should be published and well disseminated. And finally, if you are willing and able to carry this out, please keep my share in it, my name, and my request completely secret. How happy it would make me if I were to hear from him before long that you had written to him, and made him a kind offer to publish some of his new songs and piano pieces! But after all, perhaps you will only say: "What does this idle composer and still more idle correspondent mean"? In my correspondence I certainly have improved—as may be seen from this—and in the former, I mean to improve very soon, and shall bombard you with music-paper (as soon as it is well filled), and beg you, in my own name, what I have begged so earnestly and fervently for my friend.

Always yours faithfully

F. M. B.

TO MARC-ANDRÉ SOUCHAY[1]

Berlin, October 15, 1842.

. . . There is so much talk about music, and yet so little is said. For my part, I believe that words do not suffice for such a purpose, and if I found they did suffice I would finally have nothing more to do with music. People often complain that music is too ambiguous; that what they should think when they hear it is so unclear, whereas everyone understands words. With me it is exactly the

1. *Souchay had asked Mendelssohn the meanings of some of his "Songs without words".*

reverse, and not only with regard to an entire speech, but also with individual words. These, too, seem to me so ambiguous, so vague, so easily misunderstood in comparison to genuine music, which fills the soul with a thousand things better than words. The thoughts which are expressed to me by music that I love are not too indefinite to be put into words, but on the contrary, too definite. And so I find in every effort to express such thoughts, that something is right but at the same time, that something is lacking in all of them; and so I feel, too, with yours. This, however, is not your fault, but the fault of the words which are incapable of anything better. If you ask me what I was thinking of when I wrote it, I would say: just the song as it stands. And if I happen to have had certain words in mind for one or another of these songs, I would never want to tell them to anyone because the same words never mean the same things to different people. Only the song can say the same thing, can arouse the same feelings in one person as in another, a feeling which is not expressed, however, by the same words.

Resignation, melancholy, the praise of God, a hunting-song, do not conjure up the same thoughts in everybody. Resignation is to the one what melancholy is to the other; the third can form no lively conception of either.. Why, to anyone who is by nature a keen sportsman, a hunting-song and the praise of God would come to pretty much the same thing, and to him the sound of the hunting-horn would actually be the praise of God, while to us it would be nothing but a hunting-song. And however long we might discuss it with him, we should never get any farther. Words have many meanings, but music we could both understand correctly. Will you allow this to serve as an answer to your question? At all events, it is the only one I can give, although these, too, are nothing, after all, but ambiguous words!

TO THE KING OF PRUSSIA

Berlin, October 28, 1842.

Your Majesty,

In the memorable words Your Majesty was pleased to address to me, you mentioned that the intention is to add a certain number of able singers to the existing royal church choirs, in order to form a nucleus for these choirs, as well as for any amateurs of singing who might subsequently wish to join them, serving as a rallying-point and example, and in this manner gradually to elevate and to ennoble church-music and to insure its greater development.

And further, in order to support the singing of the congregation with instruments which produce the most solemn and noble effects—as Your Majesty may remember, during the celebration of the Jubilee in the Nicolai Church—it is proposed that a small number of instrumentalists (probably selected from the members of the Royal Orchestra) should be engaged, who are also intended to form the basis for subsequent grand performances of oratorios, etc.

The direction of a musical body, which would be built up in this manner—a genuine Royal Orchestra—Your Majesty expressed the intention of intrusting to me, but, until its formation, to grant me entire freedom of choice with regard to my place of residence.

The execution of this plan will fulfil to the utmost all my wishes as to public musical activity; I can never cease to be grateful to Your Majesty for it, and I do not doubt that the organisation of such an institution could be effected here without any serious difficulties.

But I would request Your Majesty not to assign the organising to me personally, but permit me to co-operate merely with my opinion and advice, which I shall always most gladly be prepared to give. Until, however, to use Your Majesty's own expression, the instrument is ready, on which I am hereafter to play, I wish to make use of my freedom of action, so graciously accorded to me by Your Majesty, and for the present return to Leipzig, for the direction of the Gewandhaus-Concerts. The orders which Your Majesty was pleased to give me, I shall carry into execution there with the utmost zeal and to the best of my abilities. At the same time, I entreat Your Majesty—as I am not to be engaged in any public sphere of action here till the organisation of the Institute and am, till then, to enjoy entire liberty—to be allowed to give up one-half of the salary previously granted to me; for as long as I take advantage of this freedom from work.

In repeating my heartfelt thanks for all the favours which Your Majesty has so liberally bestowed on me, I am, till death,

Your Majesty's devoted servant.

FROM A LETTER TO KARL KLINGEMANN

Leipzig, November 23, 1842.

. . . We have once again returned to Leipzig and are firmly established here, at least for this winter and until late in the spring. The old rooms where we thankfully passed many happy days have once more been arranged as attractively as possible and are very comfortable. I could no longer endure the state of suspense in Berlin; nothing was certain there except that I received so and so much money, and that alone should not suffice for one whose avocation is music. I, at least, felt more oppressed from day to day, and I

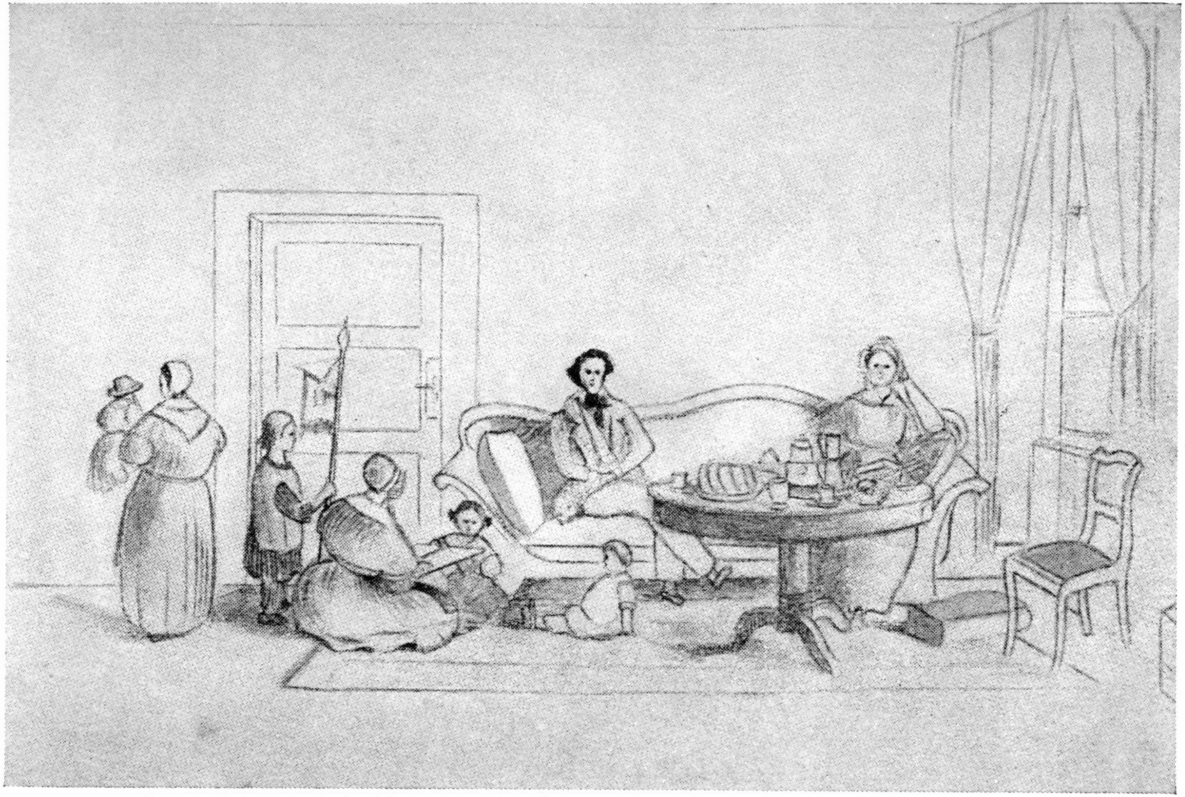

Family Group.
Sketch by Mendelssohn, Soden, 1844.

Mendelssohn.
Painting attributed to Edouard Magnus, 1844.

requested either to be told plainly that I should do nothing (that would have been satisfactory for then I could have worked with an easy mind at whatever I chose), or be told exactly what to do. As I was again assured that the results would certainly insure my having employment, I wrote to Herr von Massow, begging him to procure me an audience with the King that I might thank him verbally and endeavour to obtain my dismissal on such and such grounds, requesting him to communicate the contents of this letter to his Majesty. This he did and appointed a day for the audience, at the same time saying that unfortunately, the affair was now at an end, the King very much displeased with me, and that it was his intention to take leave of me in very few words. He made some proposals in the name of the King, none of which I could accept, and with which I will not detain you now as they led to nothing and could only lead to nothing. So I was prepared to take my leave of Berlin in ill-will, however painful it would be to me. Then, finally I was obliged to speak to my mother about it and break the news to her that I had to return to Leipzig in eight days. I had not believed that this would affect her as terribly as it actually did. You know how calm Mother generally is, and how seldom she allows anyone to get a real glimpse into her heart; and therefore it was doubly and trebly painful for me to cause her such unhappiness. And yet, I could not do otherwise. So next day I went to the King with Massow, who is my kindliest friend in Berlin, and who took formal leave of me in his own house. The King must have been in an especially good humour, for, instead of finding him angry with me, I never saw him so amiable and so genuinely confidential. To my farewell speech he replied: he could not compel me to remain, but he did not hesitate to say that it would cause him heartfelt regret if I left him; that, by doing so, all the plans which he had built around my presence in Berlin would be frustrated, and that I should leave a void which he could never fill. As I would not concur in this, he said that if I would name anyone capable of carrying such and such plans into execution as well as he believed I could, then he would intrust them to the person I selected, but he felt sure I should be unable to name one of whom he could approve. The following are the plans which he disclosed at length and in detail. First of all to form a kind of real theatre organisation, that is, a small chorus of about thirty first-rate singers, and a small orchestra (to consist of the élite of the theatre orchestras); their duties would be to perform church music on Sundays and at festivals, and also to give oratorios and so forth; that I was to direct these and compose music for them. "Yes", said I, "if there had been any talk of this earlier, and if there were any chance of such a plan being realised; but that that was the very point at issue; it was what I lacked". To which he again replied that he realised perfectly that I must have an instrument to make music on, and that it would be his care to procure such an instrument of singers and players. But he had to be sure that when he had procured it that I would be prepared to play on it. Till then I might do as I liked, return to Leipzig or go to Italy—in short, be entirely unfettered. Only he wanted the certainty that he could depend on me whenever he needed me, and this could be assured only if I remained in his service. Such was the essential substance of the long conversation; we then separated. He said I need not give him my decision immediately, because all the difficulties could not be foreseen in a moment; I was to take time to consider and to send my answer to Massow, who was present during the whole time of the hour-and-a-quarter conversation. He was quite flushed with happiness when we left the room, and could not contain himself but kept repeating over and over again: "Surely, you cannot still think of leaving!" And, to tell the truth, I thought more of my little mother than of all the rest. In short, two days afterwards I wrote to the King and said that after his words to me I could no longer think of leaving his service but that, on the contrary, my best abilities should be at his command as long as I lived. He had mentioned so and so (and I repeated the substance of our conversation), that I would take advantage of the liberty he had granted me and remain in Leipzig until I was appointed to some definite sphere of work; on which account I begged to relinquish one-half of my salary so long as I was not really engaged in that work. This proposal he accepted, and so here I am again with wife and child.

I have now been obliged definitely to decline the offers of the King of Saxony; but, in order to do so in the most respectful manner, I went to Dresden for a few days after my return here, thanked the King once more personally and entreated him nonetheless to bestow the twenty thousand thalers (which an old Leipziger bequeathed in his will to the King for the establishment of an Academy of Art) to found a school for music in Leipzig, to which he graciously acceded. The official announcement came the day before yesterday. This music school is to be organised next winter, at least in its chief features; when it is established, I may well say that I have been the means of procuring a permanent advantage for music here. If they begin anything worth while in Berlin, I can settle there with a clear conscience . . .

FROM A LETTER TO HIS MOTHER

Leipzig, November 28, 1842.

Dearest Mother,

As pen and paper must serve again instead of our usual evening hour for tea, I begin by making a suggestion, which is to ask whether you would like me to write to you regularly every Saturday (perhaps only a few words, but of this hereafter), and to have one of the family undertake to send me a punctual reply (whenever you cannot or prefer not to write). Besides the pleasure of knowing beforehand what day I am to hear from you, it is indispensable for my writing. For time must be found for a weekly letter; and I would otherwise be ashamed to send you only a few lines, should it happen that I were unable to write more. You have no idea of the mass of affairs—musical, practical, and social—that have passed over my writing table since my return here. The weekly concerts; the extra ones; the money which the King has at last bestowed, at my request, on the Leipzigers, and for the judicious expenditure of which I only yesterday had to furnish the draft; the proof-reading of "Antigone" and of the A minor symphony—score and parts—and a huge pile of letters. These are the principal things, which, however, branch off into a mass of secondary ones. Besides, Raupach has already sent me the first chorus of "Athalie". The "Midsummer Night's Dream" and "Oedipus" are revolving more busily in my head every day; I am really anxious at last to make the "Walpurgisnacht" into a symphony-cantata—for which it was originally intended, but did not become one from want of courage on my part—and also to complete my cello sonata . . .

Has somebody read to you aloud one day at the tea-table the passage from the last of Lessing's "Antiquarian Letters": "Wenn ich Kunstrichter wäre", etc., ("If I were to judge art"), and tell me whether any of you dispute the point, or whether you all agree with me that it is the most exhaustive address which can be made to a critic, indeed to every critic. At this moment, when so many artists, young and old, good and bad, appear here, this passage daily recurs to me . . .

Your

Felix.

TO JULIUS SCHUBRING

Leipzig, December 16, 1842.

My dear Schubring,

I send you herewith, having had your permission, the text of "Elijah" as far as I have done it . . . In the first of these letters you very rightly allude to the chief difficulty of the text, and the point in which it is still most deficient, that is, the lack of universally valid and impressive thoughts and words. For of course, as you point out, it is not my intention to compose what you call "a Biblical Walpurgis Night". I have endeavoured to obviate this deficiency by the passages written in Roman letters but there is still something wanting to develop these, and also to find really pregnant words for the motives. This is the first point which I ask you to think about and where your assistance is urgently needed. Secondly, in the "dramatic" arrangement. *I cannot endure the half operatic style of most oratorio texts (where recourse is sought by introducing general figures, as, for example, an Israelite, a maiden, Hannah, Micaiah, and similar characters, and where, instead of saying "this and that occurred", they are made to say, "Woe is me! I see this and that occurring"). To my mind that is very weak and I will not follow such a course. But surely the everlasting "he spake" etc., is not correct either. Both these mistakes have been avoided in the text; but that, too, is still—and always will be—one of its weak sides.*

Think over, too, whether it is justifiable that, except for Elijah, no other really dramatic figure appears. I believe it is. But in that case he should have something to say (sing) at the close, on his ascension to heaven. Can you find appropriate words for this? Altogether, the second part, especially towards the end, is as yet very uncertain. I still have no final chorus at all; what do you think about it? Pray, study the whole thing carefully, and write on the margin a great many beautiful arias, reflections, pithy utterances, choruses, and all sorts of things, and let me have it back as soon as possible.

Talking is after all a very different thing from writing. The few minutes the other day with you and yours were more enlivening and stimulating than any number of letters. Ever your

Felix M. B.

FROM A LETTER TO KARL KLINGEMANN

Leipzig, January 17, 1843.

My dearest friend,

Thank you for your dear, kind letter. You are right: this has been a very, very difficult year . . . There is not much to say or to write. May heaven protect our nearest and dearest ones and give us strength to get better ourselves . . .

Mother was in the midst of her usual Sunday gathering which on that day (it was December 11th—father's birthday)—was livelier and merrier than it had been for years, and she felt so well that she said to my sister-in-law, Albertine, that, for once, we should dance again. During the night she woke up, said it was nothing but an upset stomach, she was feeling much better, and everybody should go to bed. So the physicians left and assured us that there *was not the slightest danger. After awhile Mother again awakened from a quiet sleep, but this time she was unconscious, so that the physicians said there was no hope. She went quietly to sleep again and passed away after a few hours, at half-past nine in the morning, to all appearance without having had the slightest feeling of illness. That had been always her wish, and it was like a soothing comfort for me when my brother and sisters told me about it the following evening in Berlin. I had Paul's letter, written when Mother was still alive, early in the morning on the 13th, left with the eleven o'clock train and thought, as one always does, to find better news on my arrival. I arrived too late—but still I saw her once more . . . And the very bitterness of seeing her again thus is better than the dull indifference of daily life elsewhere . . . I am, as yet, totally unable to accustom myself to daily intercourse with people to whom I really do not matter very much and who regard as a piece of news something that I can never forget nor recover from, and equally unable to take part in what they call diversion . . . But I feel more vividly than ever what a heavenly calling art is. For this too I have to thank my parents! At a time when everything else which ought to interest the mind appears repugnant, empty and vapid, the smallest real service to art takes hold of one's innermost being, leading one away from town and country, and the earth itself, and seems a blessing sent by God. A few days previous to the 11th, I had undertaken to transcribe my "Walpurgisnacht", a work I had intended to do for a long time, and I had the vocal parts of the voluminous score written out and copied afresh. Then I was summoned to Berlin, and after an interval of several weeks began to write the instrumental parts in my little study which has a pretty view on fields and meadows and a village. The pleasant intercourse with the old familiar oboes and violas and the like which live so much longer than we do and are such faithful friends, so fascinated me that I often could not leave my desk for hours. I was much too upset and sore to think of composing, but even this merely mechanical pursuit of and preoccupation with art was* my consolation the entire time I was alone, when the beloved faces of my wife and children did not make me forget even music and remember only my blessings, for which I thank God daily, on my knees.

FROM A LETTER TO FERDINAND HILLER

Leipzig, March 3, 1843.

. . . How can you wonder at N.'s success? They put all that into the newspapers themselves; and you who read them don't know what to think of it all, whilst I, meantime, am much better off, for I have become such a Septembrist[1] as regards all newspapers that I believe nothing, absolutely nothing, except what I see with my own eyes on the music paper, or hear with my own ears. Unfortunately the case is almost the same with Wagner; I am afraid that a great deal becomes exaggerated in that quarter; and just those musicians whom I know to be conscientious people, increase my fear not a little. Still I have not yet heard any connected passages of his operas, and I always think that they must be better than people say. Talent he most certainly has, and I was delighted that he got that position[2] even though it won him enemies enough in the course of those few weeks, as I will tell you when we meet . . .

You remind me to choose a good singing teacher for our Music School. Please, tell me whether there is one to be found in all Germany. Meantime I have had hard work to prevent them from doing away altogether with the teaching of singing, which is almost more necessary than anything else. Thirty-four pupils have sent in

1. *This evidently refers to the French revolutionists of September, 1789.*
2. *The post of a Hofkapellmeister at the Dresden opera.*

their names, and the school is to be opened the middle of April. Schumann will teach piano, and so shall I . . .

I have written the "Walpurgisnacht" all over again from A to Z; in fact it is a different work now, and a hundred times better. But I am still in doubt about having it engraved . . .

FROM A LETTER TO KARL KLINGEMANN

Leipzig, June 12, 1843.

. . . You want me to write you about new music? I am shortly going to send four manuscripts at once to publishers in various parts of the world: The "Walpurgisnacht", a sonata for piano and violoncello, four songs for a single voice, and six songs to be sung in the open air, for four mixed voices. As long as the compositions remain here with me they never cease to torment me, because I so much dislike to see such nice, clean manuscript pass into the dirty hands of engravers, customers and the public, and I bolster up a little here, smooth out a little there and go on improving them just in order to keep them here. But when the proofs are once here, they are as foreign and indifferent to me as if they had been written by a stranger. But what good does that do? Recently, I again did a big work on the private order and for the private use of the King of Prussia, namely the choruses for Racine's "Athalie". I composed them in French, for female voices only, but for a large orchestra, and now they have to be translated into German, in order to be performed privatissime for His Majesty. If from time to time, I carry out some of his musical ideas, on which nobody else wants to break his teeth, it is because I think he will be satisfied and let me live where and how I like, and thus we would both benefit. If that does not satisfy him, then I must wait and see whether he gives me something real to do there, in which case I shall have to go to Berlin, however much I may grumble. Or, if he wants to have me there without something really definite to do, I shall not go, however much he may grumble. But I hope, and wish with all my heart, that the latter will not be the case because I am sincerely devoted to him and certainly owe him gratitude and acknowledgement for all he has done, and still wants to do for me.

The score of "Athalie" is going to be published in the course of this year, too, I believe; there are still many things in it to be combed out and brushed up. I am going to dedicate the "Songs to be sung in the Open Air" to Jette Henecke. I thought of her so often while I wrote them; first because of the open air and the whole breath of spring and the garden which I wished to put into the music, and because, whenever I think of it—the breath of spring—more than of anything else I have a vision of her and her children on the lawn; and secondly because I never wrote a second voice without also thinking how she complained that with me everything had to sound so "superfine" that even the second parts were difficult to sing. That rankles! . . .

TO HIS BROTHER

Leipzig, July 26, 1843.

Dearest Brother,

I have just received your kind letter, and indeed, at this very moment I was about to write to you and beg you to give me quarters. Next Tuesday, the 1st of August, I am obliged to return to Berlin to rehearse and perform the "Tausendjährige Reich" and to have the King give me his views on the composition of the psalms. Yesterday he summoned me for this purpose, and of course I must go, and of course I must stay with you; but is it also "of course" that my visit is convenient to you? This time I shall remain at least eight days; on the sixth is the celebration of the abovementioned "Reich". Give me a line in reply.

I have an answer to my letter from von Massow, who sends me the King's invitation; he says we are sure to agree, and that the only things in question are some matters of form; that I shall spare myself the annoyance and vexation which such a tiresome correspondence must entail, and that as I am coming in any case for the "Tausendjährige Reich", I can also reply personally to the zehntausendjährige affair. Herr von Massow, in fact, says pretty plainly: "Asking and bidding make the bargain"; that he wished to see whether I would sign; and this not being the case, the others would no doubt give way, etc. etc. All this is very confusing and I do not like it at all. To be sure, it is true that his head must also be in a daze and he seems to take all imaginable trouble about the affair. I mean to bring the whole of the everlasting papers for your inspection; we can read them together when we meet. I hope on this occasion not merely to have a court dinner with the King but a satisfactory discussion on business—probably the easiest way of producing a result. I wish, if possible, to defer this till after the celebration of the tausendjährige festival; the chorale I wrote for it is, I believe, just what the King wishes; at all events, it furnishes an opportunity for a complete understanding.

My anger (which was indeed greater on this occasion than for a long time past) I shook off in a defile on the way to Naumburg, close to Rippach, where you drive down to Weissenfels. And now I am writing music once more instead of painting fir-trees . . . It is a year tomorrow since we set off for Switzerland!

Your

Felix.

FROM A LETTER TO HIS SISTER REBECCA

Leipzig, October 29, 1843.

. . . From early morning till late at night I have sat at my desk writing out scores till my head felt as if it were burning; and so I have had to let several Saturdays pass without keeping punctually to my post day. My previous stay in Berlin, too, was very strenuous for me. I had eleven dress rehearsals and four performances in a fortnight,[1] and got a little homesick towards the last; and since my return, eight days ago, I have done nothing but recuperate; and now a fellow can take up his correspondence again. With that I do not mean this letter; for it does not come under that, to me hateful, term "correspondence" at all, but the ones I wrote before this, and those that I am about to write. I am really incapable of talking to you about anything but oboes and trumpets, and they are the least worthy of attention. There are twelve numbers in the "Midsummer Night's Dream", and the funeral music for Thisbe is quite in the style of my mock preludes which used to make you laugh so; it is written for a clarinet, a bassoon, and a kettledrum, but it is no good trying to describe it . . . I assure you that a couple of times during each rehearsal and each performance I felt a special, extra pang of regret at your absence. It was so exactly your dish, and you would so heartily have enjoyed what succeeded, and been so vexed with what failed. It is amusing though that the public of Berlin should be so surprised and delighted with our favourite amongst old Will's beloved plays. Yesterday it was performed for the seventh time in ten days, and in the morning not a ticket was to be had . . .

1. *The music to the "Midsummer Night's Dream" had been performed in Berlin for the first time.*

FROM A LETTER TO FERDINAND DAVID

Berlin, December, 1843.

. . . We have a concert again on the tenth of January for which I must be here, and I would prefer to wait for a couple of free weeks instead of coming now for just a few days. There is much to be praised in these concerts but there are also a few things to be criticised; moreover, there is one small item which they lack and which is generally overlooked here, but which I prefer not to do without, namely an innate vigour and hearty enthusiasm. These people are living, playing and listening in a style of utmost refinement and detachment; no fault can be found with them, but real joy is lacking. I cannot find pleasure in that. There is no dearth of good will, but there is no solid groundwork, no genuine feeling, no sincere conviction. With all this their technical achievement is not to be compared with the perfection heard in Paris; and if our people dream of an Orchestre du Conservatoire, they will have to dream on for all eternity. I would not mind that so much, if only the deficiencies were made good by the qualities in which German musicians are infinitely superior—you may call it thoroughness, or honesty, or musical instinct, or decency, or philistinism, or whatever you like—but as both extremes are wanting, they fall between two stools in this, as in many another respect. They want to pose as French and they fail to be German. I am most nearly satisfied with the basses, because I have not been spoiled in that respect; sometimes I really enjoy the abundant sonority of the eight violoncelli and the four double basses.

Next Sunday for the first time we shall have grand church music, consisting, however, only of smaller pieces, namely a Psalm in eight parts without orchestra—composed by myself expressly for this occasion—one chorus from the "Messiah" and three chorales with "trombones, etc." Such is the King's will and it caused us considerable distress; but now we may have wind instruments of every kind, so I have made the instrumentation after my own taste, and we will keep to the oboes, etc. We have managed to get thus far with great difficulties—which elsewhere they do without—and at last that much-heralded "grand" church music will have shrunk to a single piece before the beginning of the service—and you achieved this long ago. "Alas!" you will say—if at least it is not just advent time. How the musicians keep an eye on the instrumental solos, and singers on their solos in choral works, and Schlesinger [1] on the publishing of new compositions which may, perchance, crop up, and the clergy on greater crowds in the churches, and what an extensive pottering goes on all the while over all this business—about all this I will tell you a good tale one day when we play billiards, or take a stroll, or sit on the sofa with Schleinitz,[2] or at your desk before a new composition of the successor of M. Baillot,[3] or wherever else we find a cheerful place for a chat . . .

1. *Noted music publisher in Berlin.*
2. *Konrad Schleinitz, Leipzig lawyer and great music lover, one of Mendelssohn's closest friends.*
3. *Flattering comparison for David. Pierre Baillot, most renowned Paris violinist and professor at the Paris Conservatoire.*

TO EDWARD BUXTON

Berlin, January 27, 1844.

My dear Sir,

My friend, Dr. Schumann, wishes for an opportunity to publish his new work "Paradise and the Peri" in your country, and has desired me to write to you my impression of the work while I think he intends communicating himself with you his ideas about the publication.

I must accordingly tell you that I have read and heard this new work of Dr. Schumann with the greatest pleasure, that it has afforded me a treat which made me easily foretell the unanimous applause it has gained at the two performances at Leipzig and the performance at Dresden (which took place last month), and that I think it a very impressive and noble work, full of many eminent beauties. As for expression and poetic feeling it ranks very high, the choruses are as effectively and as well written as the solo parts are melodious and winning. In short, it is a worthy musical translation of that beautiful inspiration of your great poet Moore, and I think the feeling of being indebted to that poet for the charm that pervades the whole music has induced the composer to wish your countrymen to become acquainted with his work. He intends visiting England next year, when, I am sure, he and his music will be received as they so highly deserve.

I am, dear Sir, yours very truly

F. M. B.

TO WILLIAM STERNDALE BENNETT

Berlin, March 4, 1844.

My dear Bennett,

Since yesterday I have the certainty of being able to come over to you; and this morning I received Mr. Watts' letter.[1] There is a superstition for you and me. I have written to him with how great a pleasure and how thankfully I accept the honour the Philharmonic Society will do me, and that I shall come—if possible, in time for the 29th April—if not, certainly for the five last concerts. And that I anticipate such a happy time, such a treat from England. The same I must write to you and for you. And do that from my heart! . . . So then, my first questions:

When do you fix the programmes for each concert? Are there some pieces fixed already, and which? Will the directors allow me a vote or opinion in the composition of the programmes?

Who are the vocal artists on which you can depend? Is the choice of their pieces left to them or not? Have you a chorus at your disposal for every concert? or for several, or for none?

Have you something new for these concerts? And do you know of something, besides yours? Have the two overtures to Leonore, of Beethoven, that he composed before the one in C, (and the one in E to Fidelio) been performed in England? And has the second Finale to Leonore (manuscript) been ever performed at the Philharmonic? I possess the last, and could perhaps send it over and have an English translation made for it. Should I perhaps bring some new unpublished music, and could we have a trial-night of it after my arrival? But even if this were not possible (for which I would be very sorry, should I not bring a copy of the Symphony

1. *Secretary of the Philharmonic Society. The directors had decided to invite Mendelssohn to conduct six concerts of the season.*

Mendelssohn's living-room in Leipzig.
Watercolour by Mendelssohn, 1846.

Thun, Switzerland.
Watercolour by Mendelssohn, 1847.

of Schubert, of that of Gade, and some other good new things that I might get here or at Leipzig, to make our choice of them? I intend also to bring several things of mine, but am not yet quite sure whether I shall finish all I have in my mind, however, I hope so!

Ever your

F. M. B.

Berlin, March 10, 1844.

My dear friend,

The bearer of these lines, although a boy of thirteen, is one of my best and dearest friends and one of the most interesting people I have met for a long time. His name is Joseph Joachim. He was born in Hungary at Pesth, and he is going to London. Of all the young talents that are now going about the world, I know none that is to be compared with this violinist. It is not only the excellence of his performances, but the absolute certainty of his becoming a leading artist—if God grants him health and leaves him as he is—which makes me feel such an interest in him . . . He is not yet very far advanced in composition, but his performances of the Vieuxtemps, Bruch and Spohr concertos, his playing at sight (even the second violin parts of difficult quartets I have heard him play in the most masterly manner), his accompanying of sonatas, etc., is in my opinion as perfect and remarkable as may well be.

I think he will become a yeoman in time, as both of us are. So pray, be kind to him, tell him where he can hear good music, play to him, give him good advice, and for everything you may do for him, be sure that I shall be as much indebted to you as possible. Farewell.

Very truly yours,

F. M. B.

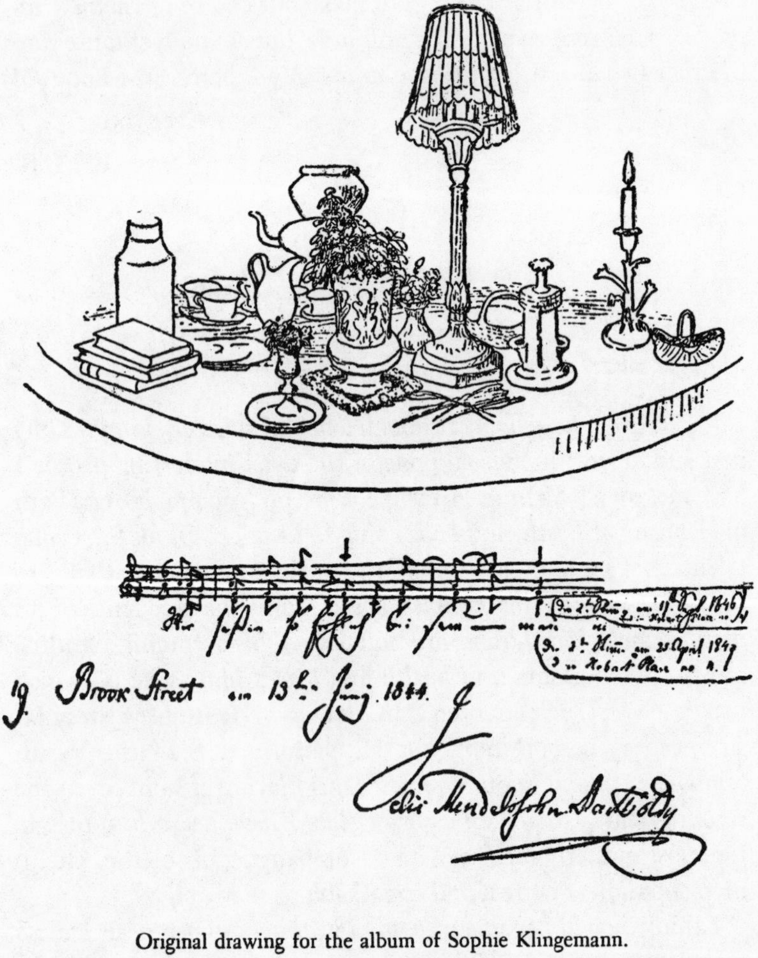

Original drawing for the album of Sophie Klingemann.

TO HIS SISTER FANNY

Soden, July 25, 1844

Dear Fanny,

If you refuse to come to Soden for a fortnight, to enjoy with me the incredible cosiness of this country and locality, all my descriptions are of no avail. And alas! I know too well that you will not come. So I will describe but little. My family improves every day in health, and I lie under apple-trees and huge oaks. In the latter case I request the swine-herd to drive his animals under some other tree, not to disturb me (this happened yesterday); further, I eat strawberries morning, noon and night; I drink the waters of the Asmannshaeuser spring, rise at six o'clock, and yet sleep nine and a half hours. (When do I go to bed, Fanny?) I visit all the glorious environs, I meet Herr B. in the most romantic spot (happened yesterday), who gives me recent and good news of all of you and addresses me as Herr General Musikdirektor, which sounds as strange here as Oberursel, and Lorschbach, and Schneidheim would to you. Towards evening I have visits from Lenau, and Hoffmann von Fallersleben, and Freiligrath, and I accompany them for ¼ hour through the fields on their way home, and find fault with the system of the world, utter prophecies about the weather, and am unable to say what England can do in the future. Further, I sketch busily, and compose still more busily. (A propos, look out the organ piece in A major, that I composed for your wedding, and wrote in Wales, and send it to me by return of post; you shall positively have it back, but I need it. I have promised an English publisher a whole book of organ pieces, and as I was writing out one after another, that old one suddenly recurred to me. I love the beginning, but detest the middle, and am completely rewriting it with another choral fugue; but I should like to compare it with the original, so pray, send it here!) Further, I unfortunately have to go to Zweibruecken tomorrow, to direct the Music Festival there, and I am not at all in the mood for it. Still there is very good wine at Duerckheim (as credible witnesses inform me), and I hear the country is very beautiful, and tomorrow week, (God willing), I shall be back again. Then I shall once more lie down under the apple-trees, etc., dal segno. Ah! if it could always be like this.

Jesting apart, the contrast of these days with my stay in England is so remarkable, that I can never forget it. There, not one hour was free three weeks ahead, and here, all the bright, livelong days are free, without a single occupation of any kind, except what I choose for myself (and those alone are fruitful and worth while) and what is not done today is done tomorrow, and there is leisure for everything. In England, by the way, it was really wonderful this time; but I will describe to you personally each concert there, and every bramble-bush here . . .

Farewell, dear sister, may we soon meet again. Do not forget the piece for the organ, and still less its author; forget, however, the stupidity of this letter, and that I am such a lazy correspondent.

Your

Felix.

FROM LETTERS TO MR. COVENTRY

Frankfort, August 29, 1844.

. . . According to your wishes I send you a copy of my collection of organ pieces by Sebastian Bach, which I have carefully looked over and corrected:

1) 15 grand Choral Préludes, 2) 44 little Choral Préludes, 3) Six Variations, 4) Eleven Variations, 5) Four Préludes and Fugues. Of the last I think several (if not all) have been already published in Germany or England. Both the Variations, I believe, have never been published, as also the greater part of the 44 or of the 15 Préludes. Perhaps 9 out of these 59 are known; all the rest is not . . . I have also been very busy about the organ pieces and they are nearly finished. I should like to call them "Three Sonatas for the Organ", instead of Voluntaries. Tell me if you like this title as well, if not, the name of Voluntaries will suit the pieces also, the more so, as I do not know what it means precisely.[1]

December 17, 1844.

. . . Pray, alter the inscription which is to be found at the bottom of every page, "Fugue", etc. Why is Bach's name always connected with fugues? He has had more to do with psalm-tunes than with fugues, and you call the beginning of your collection "Bach's Studies", which I like much better. Pray, alter this, and call it either Studies, Organ Préludes, or Chorales, as you like, but not Fugues. Let me know before it is issued, the title which the work is to have in English; perhaps you will send me a copy of it with the next proofs.

I hope to send you soon the promised organ pieces. 9 are ready, but I want to have 12 before I make a parcel of them.

February 17, 1845.

. . . As a title I should propose: "Johann Sebastian Bach's Organ compositions, or Chorales, (Psalm Tunes)", edited by F.M.B. Vols. I and II., 44 short Préludes, vols. III. and IV., 16 Grand

1. *According to Grove's Dictionary of Music, "Voluntary" is the name given to organ music played before, during and after divine service.*

Préludes, vol. V., 2 Chorales with variations. But as for this title, as well as for the preface, I make it a condition, that you submit them first to my friend Klingemann and get his "imprimatur", as I dare not appear before the English public without this sanction.

May 26, 1845.

. . . I have no objection to your dividing my sonatas into two books, I was only glad to see that they are to appear altogether at your house. I even think it would be well to sell each one separately, if somebody wants to buy them so; but it must always be with the title: "Six Sonatas, etc., Nos. 1.2., etc." Pray, if you place them into the engraver's hands, let him be most careful, in order to get a correct edition. I attach much importance to these Sonatas, (if I may say so of any work of mine), and accordingly wish them to be brought out as correctly as possible. Perhaps some one of my English friends and brother organists would look them over for me . . .

August 8, 1845.

. . . You will see that in the prélude and fugue in G major, (particularly in the prélude) I have made a great many corrections; this is owing to my having seen a new edition of the piece, which appeared some months ago (at Peters, Leipzig and Ewer's, London), and in which the editor says, he has had Bach's autograph as an authority. Accordingly I adopted many readings which I thought eventually better than those of my copy, although this may have been taken from another autograph of Bach's, (as he used to copy out his things and introduce alterations in every new copy).

TO FERDINAND DAVID

Frankfort, December 17, 1844.

Dear David,

Today I must ask you a favour. I have sent the score of the violin concerto to Breitkopf and Haertel and I have lately made several alterations in it with pencil, which can be copied into the parts. I have changed a number of things in the solo part, too, and I hope they are improvements. But I would particularly like to have your opinion about all this before I give up the music irrevocably to the printer.

First of all, do you agree with the alteration in the cadenza and its being lengthened in this way? I like it far better, but is the part now written correctly and smoothly? The arpeggios have to begin immediately in tempo and continue four-four till the entrance of the tutti; is this too exhausting for the player? Also the diminuendo to the pp should be quite feasible now.

How about the two measures on sheet 15?

Further, is the alteration at the end of the first movement easily playable? I should think so.

One important thing that is not clear to me (I really ought to be ashamed that it isn't!) is the pizzicato accents in the theme of the adagio. I originally intended to write it this way but later was dissuaded from doing it; I do not know why. Actually the problem is NOT how the pizzicato sounds because that I know, but how it sounds together with the coll'arco of the basses and the solo violin. Will these accents not bring about a confused effect through the alternating of coll'arco and pizzicato in such a combination?

Pray, let Gade [1] have a look at this phrase in the score, and let me know his opinion of it. Do not laugh at me too much, I feel ashamed in any case, but I cannot help it; I am just groping around.

The alterations in the solo part on sheet 18 (pages 2-3) ought certainly to be an improvement. Is the return into C major (sheet 20, page 4) without the flute now all right? Quite all right? because I want it to be played very delicately. The close, too, ought to be less awkward now.

You will certainly not mind that I am covering the solo violin less in the last movement, nor that I have added two measures (sheet 30), more, perhaps, the one measure I have eliminated (sheet 32), but that had to be done, too. Again I had the right feeling the first time, and the wrong one, later. How playable are the four last measures on sheet 32, and the first one on sheet 33? You see that here, too, I have tried to subdue the accents—everything to please you!

Finally: how about sheet 33, last page? It seemed to me a trifle too risky; will it be possible to bring the passage into prominence thus, or ought I to add the lower octave?

Thank God that the fellow is through with his concerto! you will say. Excuse my bothering you, but what can I do? . . .

1. Niels Gade conducted the first performance of the violin concerto played by David at the Gewandhaus in Leipzig on March 13, 1845.

TO MINISTER EICHHORN

Frankfort, March 6, 1845.

Your Excellency,

I must first of all thank Your Excellency for the flattering proof of confidence contained in the letter I have received from Your Excellency, and also for your wish to hear my opinion in so important a matter.[1] *That the reform of the Academy of Art and its music department, of which Your Excellency writes, can be of great importance to the whole musical condition of Berlin, does not admit of doubt. Your Excellency informs me that it is your intention to effect this by placing at the head of the music section a composer who, through his own creativeness, should be an example to the students, like the master in a studio of plastic art; and you do me honour to mention my name on this occasion, or, in the event of my being prevented from accepting this offer, you commission me to point out one of my colleagues in art whom I consider best suited for such a situation. But in order to form a definite opinion on the matter, I must beg for a fuller explanation of various points which, in this and every similar affair, appear to me most important, and which must, for the present, take precedence over all personal considerations.*

Is the reform which Your Excellency has in mind in the musical section, to consist solely in the appointment of such a composer,

1. *In a preceding letter, the Prussian Minister for Education, Eichhorn, had told Mendelssohn of a project to establish—at the Berlin Academy of Art—a newly organised section for music, headed by a composer of world fame, and had suggested that Mendelssohn himself might accept the offer of such a post. The correspondence led to no results.*

and is the musical section to continue on the same lines as formerly? And if this be the case, what will be the relationship of such a director to the former members of the senate or section? And to the director of the entire academy? Will the distribution of the different branches of instruction remain the same, or is a reform also proposed in this respect? And in what will the practical efficacy of such a teacher consist? It is hardly possible to demonstrate the process of composition, as the master in a studio demonstrates the planning of a picture or the forming of a model; and, according to Your Excellency's words, it is to be chiefly a question of intellectual stimulus. I am convinced that such stimulus can only be effective in an art school when the whole course of instruction has already laid a faultless foundation, when all the teachers in their particular subjects strive towards the same goal, when there has been no serious deficiency anywhere in the students' education, and when finally, like the setting of a key-stone, all the harmonious impulses of this education are once more combined in their practical application and demonstrated to the students and are thus more deeply impressed on their minds. In this sense, I could well imagine such a newly created organisation rich in its influence and blessing; but it seems to me that for this purpose it is not merely the situation itself which is essential, but rather a drastic reform of the whole inner constitution of the academy; and I do not know whether this is what Your Excellency had planned, or indeed whether it is within the realm of possibility. Without this, the position would still be highly honourable, but would be devoid of all really practical use. Just a general stimulation, no matter how great, can at best only call forth an unfruitful enthusiasm in the minds of the students, if indeed it ever calls forth anything at all. The teachers of concrete subjects alone would, in such a case, acquire a decisive influence on the development of the young artists; the man at the head, who would exert his influence only through his example, would, by contrast, be left hanging in the air, and there would be no connection between the head and the rest of the body; and without that contact neither the head nor the limbs can live and thrive.

If Your Excellency will be so kind as to give me somewhat more precise information on this matter, I would be put in a position to form a clearer view of the affair itself, as well as of the personal questions connected with it; a view which I should consider my duty (on this as on every other subject) to put at the service of Your Excellency.

Your devoted

F. M. B.

TO CABINETSRATH MÜLLER

Frankfort, March 12, 1845.

. . . His Majesty the King never spoke to me on the subject of the choruses in the combined and curtailed trilogy of "Agamemnon", the "Choephorae", and the "Eumenides".[1] His Majesty certainly was pleased to appoint me last winter to the task of composing music for the choruses in Aeschylus's "Eumenides". I could not promise to supply this music because it seemed to me immediately to be beyond my capabilities; still I promised His Majesty to make an attempt, but without concealing the almost insuperable difficulties which caused me to doubt the success of the attempt.

Since then I have occupied myself most earnestly with the tragedy for a considerable time. I have endeavoured by every means in my power to find a musical aspect in these choruses, in order to render them suitable for composition; but I have not succeeded,

1. *The King of Prussia had requested Mendelssohn to set to music the choruses of the Aeschylus Trilogy, to be combined and curtailed for one single performance.*

even in a single case, to fulfil the task in such a manner as the loftiness of the subject and the refined artistic perceptions of His Majesty demand. For naturally, the problem was not that of writing tolerably suitable music for the choruses, such as any composer conversant with the forms of art could write for almost any words, but the task was to set the Aeschylus choruses to music in the modern (good) sense, which would enliven them and express their importance with the means at our command today. I wanted to attempt this in my music to "Antigone", with the Sophocles choruses; with regard, however, to the choruses of Aeschylus, in spite of all my efforts, I have not succeeded so far in a single attempt.

The contraction of these pieces into one, augments the difficulties to an extraordinary degree, and I venture to assert that no living musician would be able to solve this gigantic task conscientiously; how much less, then, could I do it.

In requesting Your Excellency to communicate this to His Majesty, I beg you also, at the same time to mention the three compositions of mine, which, by His Majesty's command, are ready now for similar performances, namely the "Oedipus Colonus" of Sophocles, the Racine "Athalie", and the "Oedipus Rex" of Sophocles. The entire full scorces of the two former are completed, so that nothing further is required for their performance, but the distribution of the parts to the actors and singers. Also the sketch of the last "Oedipus Rex" is completed. I mention these works, hoping they may prove that I will always consider the fulfilment of His Majesty's commands a duty and a pleasure, so long as I can entertain any hope of performing the task worthily; and to show, that when I allow even one to remain unfulfilled, it arises solely from want of ability, and never from want of good will . . .

FROM A LETTER TO SENATOR BERNUS

Leipzig, October 10, 1845.

. . . I cannot tell you how often, indeed daily, I think of the last winter and spring, which I passed so pleasantly with you in Frankfort. I could hardly have believed, myself, that this visit there would have made such a lasting and happy impression on me. In fact, it goes so far that I have considered in all seriousness giving you a commission (according to your promise) to buy me a house with a garden, or have one built, and then I would return permanently to that glorious country with its gay, easy life. But for the time being, of course, such good fortune cannot be mine. A few years will have to pass and the work I have begun here must have produced concrete results and be considerably further advanced (at least I must have tried to accomplish this), before I can think of such a thing.

But I have the same feeling as formerly, that I shall only remain in this place so long as I feel pleasure and interest in the outward occupations which here seem the most agreeable to me. But as soon as I have won the right to live solely for my inward work and for composing—conducting and playing in public only occasionally, depending on how much I would enjoy it—then I shall assuredly return to the Rhine, and certainly—the way I think now—go to Frankfort. The sooner that occurs, the happier I shall be. I have always followed all my external musical pursuits, such as conducting, etc., purely from a sense of duty, never from inclination, so I hope, before many years are over, to turn up as a house builder.

Let us hope that by then either a solid, genuine nucleus in German-Catholic, enlightened, and otherwise new-German beings, will have developed, and a definite clear field won for it; or that the whole business will have vanished without leaving a trace —like other murder affairs—and be completely forgotten. Should neither the one nor the other occur, I fear we run the risk of losing our finest national characteristics, thoroughness, constancy, honest perseverance and the like, without getting any substitute for them. A collection of French phrases and facility would be too dearly bought at such a price. Let us hope for something better!

TO JOSEPH MOORE[1]

Leipzig, January 17, 1846.

My dear Sir,

Yesterday I received your letter of the seventh and answer it as early as I can. My oratorio is in full progress and becomes every day more developed; but whether I shall be able to finish it in time for your preparation, is another question which I shall not be able to answer positively before two months have elapsed. It will then be the middle of March, more than five months before the performance of your Festival, and if I should fail in my efforts of ending my work in time, (which I fully hope and trust to do), there will be ample time for you to make it up by something else.

Your question about Jenny Lind is very important to the success of the Festival, as I consider her without hesitation as the absolutely first singer of the day and perhaps of many days to come. But I am not able to undertake the negotiations which your chairman would entrust me with, as I know how much she is

1. *Joseph Moore was manager of the Birmingham Music Festivals.*

surrounded with engagements of all sorts, and how little likely it is that I could get anything like a positive answer from her. It is by no means certain that such an appeal would be successful, unless a formal application of the committee had previously been made to her; at any rate I think this is the only way, if there is one. When you formally wrote to me about the same subject, I was in Berlin and spoke to her about it, but then she said she should not go to England; she had declined it already twice, it was quite impossible, etc., etc., so that I did not make any direct inquiries about Birmingham and the Festival at that time.

When you have determined what you will do, and if you have written, or if another (perhaps at Birmingham) has negotiated for you, pray, let me know it, and I could then perhaps be of some use in removing some difficulties and in persuading her to accept the Festival, which I should be most happy to do. But at present I am afraid, by beginning to talk or corresponding with Jenny Lind about this subject, I would do your cause no good and therefore beg to be excused.

I remain, my dear Sir, very truly yours

F. M. B.

TO IGNAZ MOSCHELES

Leipzig, January 17, 1846.

My dear Friend,

Your last letter, and that of your wife, gave me the greatest pleasure, for they seem to hold out a promise that our wish to have you here will be fulfilled. On the day that brings your consent I will drain my best bottle of wine and cap it with a cup of champagne.

I hasten to answer your questions,[1] having duly consulted my wife and her account-books with the following results: The price of a flat—consisting of seven or eight rooms, with kitchen and appurtenances—varies from three hundred to three hundred and fifty thalers.[2] For that sum it should be handsome and cheerful, and as regards the situation, should leave nothing to be desired. Servants would cost about one hundred to one hundred and ten thalers per annum, all depending, of course, on what you require. Male servants are not much in demand here, their wages varying from three to twelve thalers a month. A good cook gets forty thalers a year, a housemaid thirty-two. If you add to these a lady's maid, who could sew and make dresses, you would reach about the above mentioned figure. Should you require a man servant in addition to these, that, to be sure, would increase the expense; but living as others do here, I think you would scarcely need one. Wood—that is, fuel for kitchen, stoves, etc.—is expensive and may amount to one hundred and fifty or two hundred thalers for a family of five, with servants. Rates and taxes are next to nothing: eight or ten thalers a year would cover it all. In a word, I think, you would live very well and comfortably on from eighteen hundred to two thousand thalers. It is difficult to fix the terms for your lessons, even approximately, for there is no precedent in Leipzig to go by. Madame Schumann-Wieck asked two thalers, but at that price found but few pupils, and those mostly among foreigners spending a short time here. I think it would be different with you, and I am confident that if you chose to say one and a half thalers you would be overrun with applicants. The same would probably be the case with two thalers. And so I return to what I said in my last letter: I believe that putting together the salary from the conservatory and what you would make by private lessons and

1. *This letter is in answer to Moscheles' inquiry with reference to the cost of living in Leipzig.*
2. *The thaler equalled at that time seventy-five cents.*

the publication of compositions (even if you published ever so little, but I trust it would be ever so much), your income would be sufficient for your expenditure, and it would still be open to you to draw on your capital or to leave it to bear interest. I do not think that I have in any way been over optimistic in giving you these estimates. I certainly made them after due consideration, and in accordance with my experience in this place.

Now I have but to add that I have no doubt your furniture will be allowed to pass free of duty; further, that I certainly have composed a "Lauda Sion" for a church festival at Liége; and finally that we are all well and looking forward with the greatest impatience to your next letter, which is to bring us the welcome news that you are coming.

Ever yours,

Felix.

TO EDWARD BUXTON[1]

Leipzig, February 13, 1846.

My dear Sir,

I send you herewith the English Te Deum of which I told you. As you wished to have something in my handwriting I copied it out for you and beg you will send me by some opportunity a printed copy in return when you have published it. By a curious coincidence I had a letter from Novello[2] yesterday while I was in the middle of my copy, asking me when he should get the English

1. *Proprietor of the English publishing house of Ewers & Comp.*
2. *English publisher.*

Te Deum of which we had spoken so many years ago. I beg you will send him my answer which I enclose. There must not be a German translation made of this piece for I do not wish to have it published in this country, as it is written for yours and for your Service; if they want to do it here on their own account I cannot help it; but I will not authorise a publication to Bote & Bock or any other German publisher, but keep it for yourself and England. If there are faults in the English words and their musical accent, I wish you to correct them, but you must tell me first. I wish to fix the price for this and the Trio (in C minor) at thirty Pounds. Can I say "English Service" on the title? or must it be "Service for the English Church"?

I was much surprised to hear of Moscheles being elected as Conductor of the Birmingham Festival while he is going to leave England so soon and to live here in future. Do you know how this came about? as you used to see "wheels within wheels" of which otherwise I would not have dreamt.

Always yours very truly

F. M. B.

TO WILLIAM BARTHOLOMEW[1]

Leipzig, May 11, 1846.

My dear Sir,

Many thanks for your kind letter of the 4th to which I hasten to reply and to tell you that the oratorio for the Birmingham Festival is not the "Athalie", (nor the "Oedipus", of course) but a much

1. *The well-known translator of Mendelssohn's important vocal works.*

greater, and (to me) more important work than both together;[1] that it is not yet quite finished but that I write continually to finish it in time; and that I intend sending over the first part (the longer of the two it will have) in the course of the next ten or twelve days. I asked Mr. Moore from Birmingham to have it translated by you and I have no doubt he will communicate with you about it as soon as he gets my letter, which I wrote four or five days ago; and I beg you will be good enough, if you can undertake it, to try to find some leisure time towards the end of this month that the chorus parts with English words may, as soon as possible, be in the hands of the chorus singers. And pray, give it your best English words, for till now I feel so much more interest in this work than for my others—and I only wish it may last so with me.—

Always very truly yours

F. M. B.

TO IGNAZ MOSCHELES

Leipzig, May 11, 1846.

My dear Friend,

I see from Mr. Moore's[2] letter, which you enclosed, that he would rather have the parts printed. I have no objection; but the question arises as to whether an English firm would be ready to publish them under the condition that Simrock agreed to; namely that any alterations I might think necessary would be made in the plates, even if that necessitated new ones being engraved. Will you be so

1. *The work referred to is the oratorio, "Elijah".*
2. *The British editor Joseph Moore wished to print the oratorio "Elijah".*

kind as to talk this point over with Mr. Buxton, of Ewers & Co., to whom I should best like to give the manuscript for publication. As there are so many copies required for Birmingham (42 sopranos, 20 violins, etc.), I have no doubt of his assent.

Then, there is another point on which I want your help, or at least your advice. I mean the question of terms for the work[1] (choral edition, etc.). What do you think I ought to ask for it in England? I wished Mr. Buxton to make me an offer, as I had some applications for the copyright from other quarters; and whilst giving him the preference, I should not like him to be the loser, or to lose, myself, by the transaction. He, however, leaves the matter entirely in my hands, and says he will be agreeable to whatever I propose. What do you think, in justice to him and to myself, I ought to ask? Please give me your advice; this matter ought to be settled before the parts are printed. But now let me have definite instructions by return of post whether I am to send the score only, or a copy of the parts also. If, as Mr. Moore desires, I am to send the latter, that will not prevent my forwarding the score of the first part of the oratorio to you in ten or twelve days; so that the translation can be made from that, whilst the parts can be copied from my manuscript.

Good-by. Do not forget instructions about house hunting in Leipzig. Please, copy the enclosed; it, too, concerns the Birmingham Festival. Excuse trouble and haste.

As ever yours

F. M. B.

---

1. Later the firm Novello in London bought the copyright of "Elijah" for 250 guineas. The same firm had paid for the "Walpurgisnacht" £24, for the "Midsummer Night's Dream" incidental music £47/5, the Violinconcerto £10/10, the first Trio £10/10, the second Trio £20.

(From the answer of Moscheles to the question: "I quite feel the responsibility of advising you in the matter; for if fifty years hence it is said, 'Mendelssohn received only so many pounds sterling for this grandest of works, this inexhaustible mine of wealth to the publisher, and that at the suggestion of Moscheles'—my ashes will be disturbed in their rest . . .")

FROM A LETTER TO PASTOR BAUER

Leipzig, May 23, 1846.

. . . Your friendly lines and the book gave me great pleasure. I only received the parcel a few weeks ago, and as little time is left me for reading, and as a work like yours cannot be read quickly by a layman like me, you will understand my delay in expressing my thanks. I have learned much from your book, for it is actually the first summary of church history that I have ever read. But for this very reason you are mistaken in my standpoint if you think I could oppose, either verbally or in writing, a valid difference of opinion to yours on such a matter, and that I might see it in a different light as a musician, etc. The only point of view I could have in such questions is that of a student; and I confess to you that the older I grow, the more clearly I see how important it is to learn first and then form an opinion; not the other way around nor both simultaneously. In this I certainly differ from very many of our contemporary leaders of thought, both in music and theology. They declare that he alone can judge correctly who has learned nothing, and needs to learn nothing; and my rejoinder is, that there is no man living who does not need to learn. I think, therefore, that it is more than ever the duty of everyone to be very industrious in his own sphere and to concentrate all his powers on accomplishing the very best of which he is capable. And that is why I am more ignorant of the recent church movements than you probably believe (perhaps more than you would approve), and that is also why I am glad that the reverse is true of you. In fact, I cannot understand a theologian who at this moment does not express his opinions, or who takes no part in these matters; but just as little do I understand some of those non-theologians whom I observe and

who talk of reformation and of improvement, but who are incapable of acquiring a thorough knowledge and perspective of either the present or the past, and who, in short, wish to introduce dilettantism into these highest questions.

I believe it is this very dilettantism which plays us many a trick, because of its twofold nature; necessary, useful, and beneficial, when coupled with sincere interest and modest reserve, for then it furthers and promotes all interests; but culpable and contemptible when fed on vanity, and when obtrusive, arrogant, and self-sufficient. For instance, there are few artists for whom I feel so much respect as for a genuine dilettante of the former class, and for no single artist have I so little respect as for a dilettante of the latter class . . .

TO HIS BROTHER

Birmingham, August 26, 1846.

My dear Brother,

From the very first you have taken such a friendly interest in my "Elijah", and thereby so stimulated my desire and courage to complete it, that I must write and tell you of its first performance yesterday. No work of mine ever went so admirably at its first performance, nor was received with such enthusiasm by both the musicians and the audience, as this oratorio. It was quite evident at the very first rehearsal in London that they liked it, and liked to sing and play it; but I confess, I was far from anticipating that it would have such vigour and attraction at the first performance. Had you only been there! During the whole hour and a half that it lasted, the big hall with its two thousand people and the large orchestra were all so concentrated on the subject in question, that not the slightest sound could be heard from the audience, and I was able to sway at will the enormous mass of orchestra and choir and organ. How often during the performance I thought of you! But especially when the rain clouds came, and when they sang and played the final chorus like furies and when, after the close of the first part, we were obliged to repeat the whole part. No less than four choruses and four arias were encored, and in the whole first movement there was not a single mistake. Later there were several in the second half, but even these were unimportant. A young English tenor sang the last aria so beautifully that I was obliged to exercise great self-control in order not to be affected, and to beat time steadily. As I said before, had you only been there!

Tomorrow I start on my return trip. We can no longer say, as Goethe did, that the horses' heads are turned homewards, but I always have the same feeling on the first day of my journey home. I hope to see you in Berlin in October, when I shall bring my score with me, either to have it performed, or, in any case, to play it over to you and Fanny and Rebecca, but I think probably the former (or rather both). Farewell, my dear brother, if this be dull, forgive me. I have been repeatedly interrupted, and in fact, it should only contain my thanks for your having taken such interest in my "Elijah" and assisted me with it.

Your

Felix.

FROM A LETTER TO HIS SISTER FANNY

Leipzig, September 29, 1846.

. . . So far I cannot make up my mind to a journey or anything else, but am vegetating like a bunch of flowers after the exertions of the summer and all the travelling back and forth. Ever since my arrival, when a single glance told me that all were well and happy, I have done nothing the whole day long but eat, take walks, and sleep, and yet I never seem to get enough of the three. I ought to be preparing the "Elijah" for publication, ought to be sending the parts to Bonn to have the German words added, so that it may be ready for an early performance in this country, but, as I said before, I must first be lazy for a little longer. In fact I have been idling since the moment the last note was played and sung at the Town Hall. I was asked to go to Manchester for two concerts, but declined and went to London instead, where my one and only really important piece of business was a "fish-dinner" at Lovegrove's at Blackwall, then I stayed another four days at Ramsgate to drink in sea air and eat shrimps, and I enjoyed myself with the Beneckes as I had done with the Klingemanns in London. Then I stayed a day at Ostend because I felt sleepy, and another at Cologne with the Seydlitzes, because I was too tired. Then four more at Horchheim, where my uncle walked me around in the broiling sun through the vineyards for one hour and a half, and took me such a pace that I was constantly on the point of telling him I could not keep up, but felt ashamed, and stopped my mouth by stuffing it with blue, warm grapes. Then I stayed a day at Frankfort because I was so weary, and ever since I have been back in Leipzig I have been resting . . .

FROM A LETTER TO KARL KLINGEMANN

Leipzig, December 6, 1846.

. . . Fortunately I was able to work the whole time, (though not at composing, I admit). I had sent to Dresden for the parts of Bach's B minor Mass (do you remember it from Zelter's Friday nights?), and from them—written mostly in his own hand and dedicated to the Prince Elector ("To His Royal Highness and Serene Highness of Saxony this Mass is dedicated in the most humble devotion by the author Johann Sebastian Bach" is written on the title-page), I have tried to weed out the innumerable errors contained in my score. I have often noticed them but never had the opportunity to correct them properly. This mechanical but occasionally interesting work was very welcome; but now, for some days, I have been back at work on "Elijah" with full vigour, and I hope to eliminate successfully many things that disturbed me at the first performance . . . One of the most difficult parts (the widow) is completed, and I am sure you will be satisfied with the alterations—I can really say the improvements. "Elijah" has become much more important and mystical in this part; it was the lack of these qualities that irritated me before. Unfortunately I only discover these things post festum, after having improved them. But also in other places we have talked about I hope to be able to express what I wish more precisely, and I intend to review everything that does not suit me perfectly, with the greatest care. I am hoping to get through with the work in a few weeks, and be ready to start something new. The parts which I have rewritten prove how right I was not to rest until the whole work is as good as I am able to make it; even though the fewest people hear it or wish to hear it, and even though a very great deal of time is spent on it. Because in return, you get a completely different impression, for the betterment of the single parts improves the quality of the whole. (You see, I am still highly gratified with the widow—completed today), and therefore I believe one ought never to be too easily satisfied—and conscience has its word to say, too . . .

Playing and conducting—in fact, any and every official appearance in public—has grown intensely distasteful to me, so that each time I only make up my mind to do it with the greatest reluctance and unwillingness. I believe the time is approaching—or perhaps is already here—when I shall put all this kind of regular, public performance of music on the shelf, in order to make my own music at home, to compose and let this existence continue, as best it may, without me. I do not believe there is much to be learned from it, and as for its usefulness, I have become convinced that a piece of paper covered with notes—even if it is worthless in itself—is of more use to me, and certainly gives me more pleasure, than 250 rehearsals and performances with excellent success. I have done this work for fourteen years now, and it seems to me that the time has come to do something else. I believe I am not mistaken, and I believe it will come soon. We will talk it over in Chester Square [1] and on some long evening stroll in Chelsea—for, God willing, we shall have those evening strolls again next spring. I firmly hope to be in London for a few weeks in April (this time not without Cécile) and I shall bring some new piece of music, only I am not yet sure what it will be . . .

1. *Klingemann's London quarters.*

TO SEBASTIAN HENSEL

Leipzig, February 22, 1847.

Dear Sebastian,

Thank you very much for the drawing which, as your own composition, and in regard to the technique (in which you have made good progress) I like very much. If, however, you intend to adopt painting as a profession, you cannot become accustomed soon enough to regarding the substance of a work of art as more serious and important than its form—in other words, that means (since a painter is so fortunate as to be able to select visible nature, herself, for his substance) to contemplate nature lovingly, closely, intimately and inwardly, and to study all your life long. Study thoroughly how the outer contours and the inward structure of a tree, or a mountain, or a house always must look, and how it can look, if it is to be beautiful—and then reproduce the impression with sepia, or oil, or on a smoked plate; it will be good in any medium if only it testifies to your love of substance. You will not mind this little sermon from a screech-owl, as I often am, and above all, do not forget the substance—as for the form (of the sermon) may the devil take it for it has very little value.

Your uncle

F. M. B.

TO GENERAL VON WEBERN

Frankfort, May 24, 1847.

Dear Friend,

Your letter did me good, even in the depths of the sorrow [1] in which I received it. Above all, your handwriting, and that you were so near to me just then, as well as each single word. I thank you for it my dear, kind, faithful friend. It is indeed true that no one who has ever known my sister can forget her all his life; but what we, her brothers and sister, have lost! And I in particular, to whom she was present every moment with her kindness and love; I, who could never experience any happiness without thinking how she would share it; I, who was spoiled, and made so proud, by all the riches of her sisterly love, and whom I thought nothing could ever harm because in everything hers was always the best and leading part. All this, I believe, we cannot yet estimate, just as I still instinctively believe that the mournful intelligence will be suddenly denied. And then again I know that it is all true, but never in all the world will I become inured to it. It is lovely to think of such a glorious, harmonious existence, and that she has been spared all the infirmities of advanced age and declining life; but it is hard for us to bear such a blow with proper submission and fortitude.

Forgive me for not being able to say or write much, but I wished to thank you!

My family are all well; the happy, unalterably cheerful faces of my children have done me good in these days. I have not yet been

1. *After Fanny Hensel's death.*

able to think of music; when I try to do so, everything seems empty and desolate within me. But when the children come in I feel better and I can watch them and listen to them for hours.

Thanks for your letter; may heaven preserve you and yours.

Your

F. M. B.

TO HIS SISTER REBECCA

Thun, July 7, 1847.

Dear Sister,

In your letter of yesterday to Paul you said you wished I would write to you again; I do so today, but what to write I cannot tell. You have often laughed at me and teased me because my letters always assume the tone around me or within me at the moment, and such is the case now, for it is as impossible for me to write a proper letter as to recover a proper state of mind. I hope that as the days pass they will bring more fortitude and so I let them flow past me, and in the society of Paul and in this lovely country, they flow equably and fast. Moreover, we are all in good health and sometimes quite gay. But if I become introspective, which I am always inclined to do when we chat together, I find that a basic colour is still lacking—there is not even black, not to speak of a brighter one.

A great chapter has now come to an end, and neither the title nor even the first word of the next is yet written. But God will make it right one day; that belongs at the beginning and the end of all chapters.

We think of going to Interlaken in a few days and establish ourselves there for another month; I will and must soon attempt, once more, to begin some regular work and would so much like to have a composition well begun before I start home. I hope to find you and yours in good health in September. Until we meet again, my dear good sister! Do not forget me.

Your

F. M. B.

TO HIS SISTER REBECCA

Interlaken, July 29, 1847.

Dear Sister,

When your dear letter arrived I was writing music; I force myself now to be very industrious, in the hope that later on I may once more become so from inclination, and that I shall take pleasure in it. This is "weather expressly calculated for writing, but not for gipsying". Since Paul left us, the sky has been so dismal and rainy that I have been able to take only one walk. Since the day before yesterday we have also had cold weather, a fire indoors, and teeming rain outdoors. But I cannot deny that I sometimes rather like such grim, rainy days, that compel you to remain in the house. This time they give me an opportunity of passing the whole day with my three elder children; they do writing, arithmetic and Latin with me, daub landscapes during their free hours, or play draughts, and ask a hundred wise questions which no fool can answer (people generally say this in reverse, but this is so!). The regular reply is, and always will be, "You do not understand such things yet", which still vibrates in my ears from my own mother, and which will soon be vibrating in my children's ears from me when they give their children the same answer; and so on.

As for Sebastian's profession, I think he is now at the age, and has days, when he feels that one must either be animated by conviction and enthusiasm for something that cannot be grasped by the hand, calculated in figures or expressed in words, or else one must eschew anything (as a livelihood) which presupposes such enthusiasm. He knows that as well as I do, and therefore I have confidence in him that he will not choose a profession which he might later wish to reject, or which might eventually become indifferent or boring to him. But as soon as I feel secure on this point, it is all the same to me whatever in the wide world he may choose and how high or low his path may lead. If only he pursue it happily! And as all agree that it is his decision and his alone which will be valid and as he is able now—or never will be—to understand the seriousness of life, and as this seriousness is a matter for his own heart, in which no one can assist or advise him—although it affects each of us deeply—I believe he will not be found wanting in this respect, and will do well whatever he decides to do. That advice I would wish to give him, but, otherwise, not the slightest suggestion of advice. It is the old story of Hercules choosing his path, which for several thousand years has always been re-enacted at some time in the life of every man, and whether the young maidens be called Virtue or Vice, and the young man Hercules or not, the sense remains the same.

In September, God willing, I intend to come to Berlin, and Paul has probably told you how seriously I am considering the idea of spending my life with you, my dear ones, and living with you, abandoning all other considerations. I wish to be with you, and I felt this strongly when the steamboat left for Thun with Paul and his family, and Hensel. And strangely enough (either for this reason, or in spite of it), it is almost impossible for me at this time to be with strangers. There is no lack of visitors here, both musical and otherwise; scarcely a day has passed lately without one, or several; but they all seem to me so empty and indifferent, that I, no doubt, must appear at least the same to them. So I heartily wish that we may soon part, and remain apart; and in the midst of all the phrases and inquiries and reports, I have only one thought: how short life is. In a word, I hope we shall soon be together, and for a long time.

Farewell, dear sister, till we meet!

Felix.

TO HIS BROTHER

Leipzig, October 25, 1847.

Dearest Brother,

I thank you a thousand times for your letter today, and for your suggestion about coming here, which I certainly accept with the utmost eagerness of heart. I still do not know to this day what to say about my plans. God be praised, my health improves daily and my strength is returning more and more; but the idea of travelling a week from today to Vienna (and this is the very latest moment which would get me there to a rehearsal for their music festival), this idea is quite unthinkable.[1] It is most unfortunate that they have made so many preparations, and that my coming should be put off a second time; also it is true that my improvement in health is greater and more assured from day to day. I have already written to ask whether they could postpone it for a week;

1. *Mendelssohn was to conduct the "Elijah" in Vienna.*

Interlaken, Switzerland.
Watercolour by Mendelssohn, 1847.

"AND AFTER THE FIRE THERE CAME A STILL SMALL VOICE
AND IN THAT STILL SMALL VOICE ONWARDS CAME THE LORD."
ELIJAH

Mendelssohn on his deathbed.
Drawing by Sebastian Hensel, 1847.

but, as I said, I do not believe it will prove possible and it looks to me as if I shall remain here. In no case can I attempt to travel before eight days from now; and as to my trip to Berlin, has not Herr von Arnim reported to you fully about it? If I cannot go to Vienna, the same reasons which prevent me going there must keep me here for a fortnight or three weeks, and cause the performance in Berlin to be postponed to the end of November at the latest; and even if I do go to Vienna, this must of course still be the case.

But it is definitely settled that after these concerts, which having once promised must now be fulfilled, I make no more engagements—even if I were not obliged to keep them! But one is! and now the only question is whether I shall see you again on Saturday? Say Yes to this; I believe you would do me more good than all my bitter medicine. Write me a couple of lines soon again, and be sure you agree to come. My love to you all! and continue your love for your

Felix.

This is Mendelssohn's last known letter.
He died on the 4th of November.

SOURCES

This volume includes letters and illustrations published in:

Benedict, Sir Julius, *A Sketch of the Life and Works of the late Felix Mendelssohn-Bartholdy*. London, 1853.

Chorley, Henry Fothergill, *Autobiography*. London, 1873.

Devrient, Philipp Eduard, *My Recollections of Felix Mendelssohn-Bartholdy and his Letters to me*. Translated by Natalia Macfarren. London, 1869.

Eckardt, Julius, *Ferdinand David und die Familie Mendelssohn*. Leipzig, 1888.

Edwards, F. G., *The History of Elijah*. London, 1896.

Hake, Bruno, *Mendelssohn als Lehrer, unveroeffentlichte Briefe*. "Deutsche Rundschau." Berlin, 1909.

Hensel, Sebastian, *The Mendelssohn Family*. Translated by Carl Klingemann and an American collaborator. New York, 1882.

Hiller, Ferdinand, *Mendelssohn, Letters and Recollections*. Translated by M. E. von Glehn. London, 1872.

Hogarth, George, *The Philharmonic Society in London 1812-1862*. London, 1862.

Mendelssohn-Bartholdy, Carl, *Goethe and Mendelssohn*. Translated by M. E. von Glehn. London, 1872.

Mendelssohn-Bartholdy, Felix, *Briefe aus den Jahren 1830 bis 1847*. Herausgegeben von Paul Mendelssohn-Bartholdy und Carl Mendelssohn-Bartholdy. Leipzig, 1863.

Mendelssohn-Bartholdy, Felix, *Letters from Italy and Switzerland*. Translated by Lady Grace Wallace. London, 1862.

Mendelssohn-Bartholdy, Felix, *Letters 1833-1847*. Translated by Lady Grace Wallace. London, 1863.

Mendelssohn-Bartholdy, Felix, *Letters to Ignaz and Charlotte Moscheles*. Edited and translated by Felix Moscheles. Boston, 1888.

SOURCES

Mendelssohn-Bartholdy, Felix, *Briefwechsel mit Legationsrat Karl Klingemann*. Essen, 1909.

Moscheles, Felix, *Fragments of an Autobiography*. New York, 1899.

"Musikalisches Magazin." Langensalza, 1909.

Petitpierre, Jacques, *Le mariage de Mendelssohn*. Lausanne, 1937.

Polko, Elise, *Reminiscences*. London, 1896.

"The Musical Times." London, 1905.

Wolff, Ernst, *Meisterbriefe von Felix Mendelssohn-Bartholdy*. Berlin, 1907.

INDEX

Albert, Prince Consort of England (1819–1861), 306 ff.
Alighieri, Dante (1265–1321), 219
Allegri, Gregorio, Italian composer, wrote a famous Miserere (1584–1652), 92, 98, 124 f., 140 f., 216
Auber, Daniel François Esprit, French composer of operas (1782–1871), 31, 245, 259

Bach, Johann Sebastian (1685–1750), 32, 35, 81 f., 96, 98, 177, 189, 199, 201, 211, 235, 240 f., 243, 259, 277, 286, 294, 336 ff., 357
Baerman, Heinrich Joseph, German clarinet virtuoso (1784–1847), 174
Bai, Tommaso, Italian composer and conductor at the Pontifical Chapel in Rome, wrote a famous Miserere (1650–1714), 140, 141
Baillot, Pierre-Marie, French violinist (1771–1842), 191, 330
Baini, Giuseppe, Abbate, singer in the Pontifical Chapel in Rome, wrote a famous Miserere (1775–1844), 97 f., 122, 125, 139, 148, 216
Bartholomew, William, English translator of Mendelssohn's vocal music (1793–1867), 350
Bauer, Pastor, Protestant minister, friend of the Mendelssohn family, 210, 235, 253, 353
Beethoven, Ludwig van (1770–1827), 32, 75, 81, 174, 202, 274, 277
Begas, Karl, German painter (1794–1854), 22
Bellini, Vincenzo, Italian composer of operas (1801–1835), 259
Bendemann, Eduard, German painter, Director of the Academy of Arts in Duesseldorf (1811–1889), 126
Bennett, William Sterndale, English composer and pianist (1816–1875), 332 ff.
Berlioz, Hector, French composer (1803–1869), 230, 244 f., 286
Bernus, Senator in Frankfort-on-the-Main
Boerne, Ludwig, German essayist (1786–1837), 187
Boguslavski, Wilhelm von, lawyer and amateur composer (1803–1874), 29
Boieldieu, François, French composer (1775–1834), 110
Bramante, Lazzari, Italian architect and painter (1444–1514), 219
Buelow, Baron, German diplomat in London, 47, 54
Bunsen, Baron Christian Carl, Minister to the Papal Court in Rome, later Ambassador in England (1791–1860), 100, 101, 113
Buxton, Edward, owner of the publishing firm Enver & Comp. in London, 331, 349, 352
Byron, George Gordon, Lord (1788–1824), 224

Catel, Charles Simon, French composer (1773–1830), 31
Cervantes de Saavedra, Miguel (1564–1616), 31
Cherubini, Luigi, Italian composer and theorist (1760–1842), 32, 194, 227, 245, 284, 286
Chopin, Frédéric (1809–1849), 232, 237, 246 f., 271, 286
Chorley, Henry Fothergill, English author and critic (1810–1873), 251
Clementi, Muzio, Italian composer, pianist, piano maker and publisher (1752–1832), 45, 47, 50
Collard, Frederic William, London piano maker (1772–1860), 53, 60
Cornelius, Peter, German painter (1783–1867), 113
Coventry, English music publisher, 336

INDEX

INDEX

INDEX

INDEX

Sontag, Henriette, German singer (1806–1854), 46
Sophocles (c. 496–405 B.C.), 344
Spagnoletti, P., Italian violinist (1768–1834), 46
Spontini, Gasparo, Italian composer of operas, General Musical Director at Berlin 1820–1841 (1774–1851), 70, 109, 171, 207, 276
Spohr, Louis, German violinist, composer, conductor and teacher (1784–1859), 180, 237, 300
Stieler, Heinrich, German painter, 78

Taglioni, Maria, Italian dancer (1804–1884), 183, 187
Tasso, Torquato, Italian poet (1544–1595), 90
Taubert, Wilhelm, German composer and conductor (1811–1891), 163
Taylor family, hosts to Mendelssohn in England, 58
Thalberg, Sigismund, Swiss piano virtuoso and composer (1812–1871), 289
Thorwaldsen, Albert B., Danish sculptor (1770–1844), 100, 128
Titian (Tiziano Vecellio) (1477–1576), 88 f., 101, 113

Veit, Philipp, German painter (1793–1877), 190
Vernet, Horace, French painter (1789–1863), 111
Victoria, Queen of England (1819–1901), 303, 306 ff.
Vittoria, Tommaso Ludovico, Spanish composer of church music (1540–1611), 125, 145
Voltaire, François Marie Arouet de (1694–1778), 29

Wagner, Richard (1813–1883), 324
Weber, Carl Maria von (1786–1826), 71, 82, 111, 180, 217
Webern, General von, 360
Wranitzky, Anton, Austrian violinist and composer (1761–1819), 22

Zelter, Carl Friedrich, German composer, director and conductor of the Singakademie in Berlin, teacher of Felix and Fanny Mendelssohn, friend of Goethe (1758–1832), 19 f., 22 f., 25, 41, 68 ff., 77, 80, 87, 93 f., 104, 117, 121, 125 ff., 133, 148, 150, 162, 166, 187, 224, 231, 243, 355
Zuccalmaglio, Anton Wilhelm, German author and critic (1803–1869), 297

DATE DUE

JAN 16 '75			
OCT 1 3 1988			
Ill: 5866634		4-26-02	
GAYLORD			PRINTED IN U.S.A.